The Amazing Dr. Strousberg

The "European Railway King"

Richard Hunt

First Published 2009
All rights reserved.

Published by: Richard Hunt,
　　　　　　　23 Garnet Lane,
　　　　　　　Tadcaster,
　　　　　　　LS24 9LD.

ISBN:　　　978-0-9561604-0-9

Contents

Foreword 1
Prologue 2
1. Strousberg's Origins 3
   Strousberg's family background 3
   Abraham Baruch Strausberg 3
   Bartel Hirsch 4
   Strousberg's education 5
2. Strousberg in London 7
   From East Prussia to London 7
   The Gottheimer brothers 7
   Building Society Agent 9
   On trial for embezzlement 10
   Interval: America 11
   Strousberg, the journalist and publisher 11
   In the insurance business 14
   Outward respectability 16
   The past revealed 17
3. Return to Prussia 21
   Berlin 21
   False starts 22
   A growing family 23
   Strousberg's doctorate 23
4. Railway construction in East Prussia and Russia 25
   The Tilsit-Insterburg Railway 25
   Map of railway lines in East Prussia (1899) 26
   Strousberg's system of financing railway construction 29
   Risk for the general contractor 30
   Strousberg's concept is adopted 31
   The second project: the East Prussian Südbahn 32
   The connection to the Russian railway network 34
   Conclusions 36
5. The Berlin-Görlitz railway 37
   Origins 37
   Finance and construction 37
   Strousberg takes over construction 37
   Changes and extra expense 38
   The Görlitzer Bahnhof 39
   Strousberg loses control of the Company 40
6. Other lines in Prussia 41
   The Rechte Oder-Ufer-Bahn 41
   Märkisch-Posener Bahn 42
   Halle-Sorau-Guben 42
   Hanover-Altenbeken 43
7. Vertical integration 47
   Strousberg's big idea 47
   Strousberg's purchasing policy 47
   Vertical integration 48
8. The idea becomes reality 51
   The 1868 acquisitions 51
   The Dortmunder Hütte Iron Works 51
   The "Glückauf" Colliery 52

The Hannover Machine Factory..52
The Neustadt Ironworks (Neustädter Hütte)..........................55
The Othfresen Blast Furnaces..56
Ore mines in the Siegerland...57
The Altwasser colliery in the Waldenburger Bergland..........58
Strousberg's contribution to the industrial revolution..........58

9. Property, Estates and a Palace..................................61
Strousberg's Country Estates...61
The Palace in the Wilhelmstrasse..62
Austrian Castle and Palace..64
5 Grosvenor Place in Westminster..64
Neidenburg...65

10. Strousberg - the Berliner..67
Strousberg's properties in Berlin...67
Commercial assets in Berlin..67
The Berlin Livestock Market..68
The Berlin Market Hall..70
The Geestemünde fisheries...71

11. Politics, Publicity and Social Engagement...............73
Strousberg's daily newspaper, "Die Post".............................73
Strousberg the politician...74
The German parliaments...74
Strousberg and the workers...75
Charity..77

12. Railway Construction in Hungary............................79
The situation in Hungary...79
The Hungarian Nord-Ost-Bahn...80
Concession, construction contract and raising the capital..80
Construction of the Hungarian Nord-Ost-Bahn...................81
Uncompleted railway projects in Hungary...........................83

13. Railways in Romania Part I.....................................85
The contractual basis of the 1868 concession......................87
The bond issue...88
Arrangements about construction and operation of the railways..........89
Use of the proceeds from the bond.......................................90
Construction..92

14. The peak of success and the turning point..............95
A successful businessman...95
Orders and honours...95
Personal events..96
The turning point...98

15. Railways in Romania part II..................................101
Strousberg's railway projects and the Franco-Prussian War of 1870/71..101
The state of progress in Autumn 1870................................102
Financial trouble..102
Strousberg acquires himself liquidity.................................104
The reaction of Romania..105
Unrest...106
Romania grabs for the railways..107
Diplomacy?..108
The bond holders become active..109
The new Romanian Railway Company Limited.................109
The 1872 agreement..110
The consequence: Strousberg has to get more liquidity....111

The completion of the Romanian railways	112
Romania: from ox cart to railway	112
Bond holders situation	113
Strousberg pays the tab	113

16. Antwerp..........115
Background..........115
The Convention of the 14th of October 1869..........116
Conflicting interests..........117
Strousberg leaves the project..........118

17. The Attack by Lasker..........120
Lasker's speech in Parliament..........120
What did Lasker achieve?..........121
The Commission of Enquiry..........122
Consequences from the Report..........123
Concluding observation..........123

18. The Fiefdom of Zbirow..........125
The Fiefdom of Zbirow..........125
Strousberg buys the Zbirow estates..........125
The renovation and extension of Schloss Zbirow..........126
Agriculture and forestry..........127
Industrial activities and dreams of a "Bohemian Manchester"..........127
Organisation of the management..........128
The work of the administration in Zbirow..........129
The liquidity problem gets worse..........129

19. Dealings with the Commercial Loan Bank..........132
Strousberg finds a new bank..........132
The Commercial Loan Bank in Moscow..........132
Strousberg's dealings with the Commercial Loan Bank begin..........134
Details of the loans..........135
Strousberg returns to railway construction..........138
The situation in Zbirow..........140
Purchase of the Schatzlar collieries..........141
The Commercial Loan Bank – the last resort?..........142
The Deutsch-Böhmische Actien-Gesellschaft..........143
The last days in Zbirow..........144

20. Arrest and Trial in Moscow..........145
Crisis at the Commercial Loan Bank..........145
Strousberg is lured to Moscow..........146
Strousberg in custody..........149
The charges and the first session..........149
Strousberg's memoirs..........150
The trial and the court..........151
The trial proceedings..........152
The verdict on the board members..........152
The verdict on the Directors and on Strousberg..........153
Bitter ending..........155

21. Bankruptcy proceedings in Berlin and in Prague..........157
The opening of the bankruptcy proceedings..........157
The situation in Berlin and in Bohemia..........157
The bankrupt assets..........158
The debts..........159
Measures taken in the Prague proceedings..........160
Disposal of the properties..........161
Other disposals..........163
Discharge from bankruptcy..........164

22. Back in Berlin and in London..165
    Family and friends..165
    "Das Kleine Journal" and Emma Vely......................................167
    Strousberg's final entrepreneurial ventures..........................168
    Further difficulties in Berlin..169
    Return to London – Mary Ann dies..170
    Back in Berlin at last..171
    Sudden death...173

Bibliography..175
About the author...176

FOREWORD

Many people have heard of "The Railway King", George Hudson, but how many have heard of "The *European* Railway King", Bethel Henry Strousberg? I'd come across the name of Strousberg several times whilst reading about railway development in Europe, but when I looked it up I found that there was not very much specifically about Strousberg available at all and none of of what was available was in English. This, I decided, was a real shame because it's a story worth telling.

Strousberg's story is pretty amazing. When he left rural East Prussia for London in 1839 he was a poor but ambitious and intelligent 16 year old Jewish economic migrant. When he died in Berlin in 1884 he was virtually penniless. Yet he'd been a successful publisher and insurance specialist in London in the late 1840s and early 1850s. Between 1864 and 1875 he had built up a huge private fortune: he'd constructed railways in Prussia, Russia, Austria, Hungary and Romania; owned iron-ore mines, collieries, steelworks, locomotive and railway wagon and carriage works; lived in a grand mansion in Berlin and a castle in Bohemia; owned over 75,000 hectares of agricultural land and forests.

This book might seem a bit dry, but I think Strousberg's story has some very obvious parallels and perhaps some lessons for the present day.

Richard Hunt,
Tadcaster, August 2009

PROLOGUE

MOSCOW DISTRICT COURT, SUNDAY OCTOBER 24TH 1876.
The foreman of the jury is asked two questions about one of the accused in the trial following the collapse of the Commercial Loan Bank, 53 year old Prussian citizen Dr. Bethel Henry Strousberg.
"Is the accused guilty or not guilty or not guilty of obtaining a 7 million rouble loan from the Commercial Loan Bank without sufficient security, and of not paying it back? Is the accused guilty or not guilty of obtaining those loans by bribery?"
"Yes," answers the foreman, *"guilty."*
Strousberg was only one of 21 directors and board members on trial charged with a total of 127 offences, but he was the main centre of public interest. This was the man who had built thousands of kilometres of railways, owned huge estates and an industrial empire, lived in castles and had a palace in Berlin; how could it have come to this?
As the guilty verdict was read out, Strousberg blanched and gripped the arms of his chair.
The public had got what it wanted. The jury had grappled as best as it could with banking technicalities and delivered its verdict. The bank's directors had also been found guilty, but in the public's mind it was Strousberg who was the villain: he had brought the bank to the verge of collapse, robbing thousands of ordinary people of their hard-earned savings. He deserved to be punished. The members of the bank's supervisory board, the men who were meant to keep an eye on the directors, were however found not guilty. They embraced each other in happiness and relief that the nightmare of the trial was over.
The state prosecutor demanded that Strousberg be banished to Siberia for life, and the court retired for a whole week to consider the sentence. There was relief when it was pronounced. He would be deported to Prussia and be forbidden from ever again setting foot in Russia, but not—like two of the directors—be sent to Siberia.
The mood in the court changed. Even people who had appeared against him during the trial came up to Strousberg to congratulate him. In popular and press opinion, this was as good as a pardon. The court had not fully backed up the jury's guilty verdict. It had to pass judgement on Strousberg but it had handed down a sentence which the accused might have dictated himself.
Strousberg could not leave Russia yet though: he would be kept in Moscow for another ten months as creditors pursued civil claims against him. The efforts of the Prussian and Austrian governments and his wife to secure his release came to nothing. Strousberg had to look on from afar as his assets and land were sold off in bankruptcy proceedings in Berlin and in Prague. He knew that he would be a poor man when he returned to Germany.

1. STROUSBERG'S ORIGINS

Strousberg's family background

Strousberg was born into, by the standards of the time, a prosperous and respectable Jewish family in the small East Prussian town of Neidenburg (now Ndzica in Poland). The family had been living in Neidenburg for a long time. At the end of the 18th century Strousberg's grandfather, Baruch Chemiak (who changed his name to Nehemias Baruch in 1813) became a legally resident *"Schutzjude"* ["protected Jew"]. At that time, Jews were not yet able to be full Prussian citizens. He ran a slaughterhouse and was a fairly large-scale agricultural merchant, as shown by the fact that in 1807 he was the only person in the district who was able to provide the occupying French army with all the supplies which it requisitioned.

His business interests were evidently profitable and made it possible for him to buy agricultural land in the Neidenburg area as well as building plots in the town; he built a Jewish prayer and bath house and a tavern. When he died in Königsberg in 1822 he didn't leave much to Strousberg's father, Abraham Baruch, one of nine children.

Abraham Baruch Strausberg

Abraham inherited a house in Neidenburg, Markt 43/44, which he had occupied since 1813 under the name Strausberg. He had married Caroline Gottheimer from nearby Inowrazlaw (now Inowroclaw) in 1816 and they lived there with their growing family.

Abraham Strausberg was a different sort of person to his father. According to his son, languages and music were more to his taste. Although he was Jewish, he was a Prussian patriot, serving as a young man in the wars of 1806/07.[1]

In 1813/14 he joined one of the Prussian *Landwehr* Uhlan regiments, a cavalry militia unit, and received a commission as a *Premier-Leutnant* (roughly equivalent to a Captain in the British army) and Adjutant. He was prevented from carrying out active service in the Befreiungskrieg (War of Liberation) against Napoleon[2] as a result of horse-riding injuries, but he won praise

---

[1] Prussia and France had gone to war in 1806 when negotiations about spheres of influence in Germany broke down. Prussia was heavily defeated by Napoleon Bonaparte's troops at the Battle of Jena-Auerstedt. As a result, Frederick William III and his family fled, temporarily, eastwards to Memel (now Klaipeda). As a result of the Treaties of Tilsit in 1807, Prussia lost about half of its area, including the areas gained from the second and third Partitions of Poland, which became part of the nominally independent Duchy of Warsaw. Prussia was also forced to make an alliance with France and join the Continental System.

[2] After the defeat of Napoleon in Russia, Prussia ended its alliance with France and joined the Sixth Coalition during the "Wars of Liberation" (Befreiungskriege) against the French occupation.

from many officers for his excellent leadership and patriotism. The Divisional General of East Prussia and Lithuania, General von Wuthenow, was particularly impressed by his attitude and recorded it formally. Strausberg's army service must have been really outstanding to get so noticed, especially considering that he was Jewish.

Once the war was over, Abraham Strausberg should have had every reason to try and improve his economic status but it seems he did not succeed. An export business, funded by his wife Caroline's father, was only profitable until she died in 1831, and the family then scraped by on Abraham's fees as a legal consultant.

Bartel Hirsch

Baruch Hirsch Strausberg, the fifth of eight children, was born on November 20th 1823. Baruch Hirsch is the name recorded in the Neidenburg synagogue's birth records, but Strousberg disputes this in his autobiography, saying that he was known by his family and friends and at school as Bartel Heinrich. This may have been true but whether he was Baruch Hirsch or Bartel Heinrich soon ceased to be important, as when he moved to England in 1839, aged 16, he anglicised it: Bartel Heinrich became Bethel Henry, and Strausberg became Strousberg so that the new name sounded as much like the old one as possible.

In Neidenburg, young Bartel Heinrich grew up with his siblings: four older and two younger sisters and the youngest, his brother Philipp Ferdinand, born in 1830. Whilst the sisters stayed in Neidenburg, Philipp Ferdinand also emigrated to London where he remained.

The family grew up very much as Germans but they were nonetheless heavily influenced by their grandfather Gottheimer who, according to Strousberg's autobiography, "...lived a life dedicated to God alone; each Friday evening his children, grandchildren and great grandchildren visited him to receive his blessing and partake of a glass of wine with him." Overall then, a family which had enjoyed modest prosperity under the grandfather, was not as successful due to his father's lack of business acumen, but was by no means living in poverty.

The later stories that he had risen from poverty obviously weren't true, but for a long time Strousberg did nothing to counter them. He only broke his silence in 1876 when his autobiographical memoir, "Dr. Strausberg and his Works" (*Dr. Strausberg und sein Wirken*) was published. This contained a whole series of facts and details which were supposed to show that the rumours about him were not true and to justify his actions, but some of the 'facts' were a bit dubious. He described his grandfather as "one of the most respected and wealthiest men in the Province of East Prussia", which is perhaps understandable in comparison to other Jews at the time. Strousberg stated that his great-grandfather had been resident in Neidenburg since 1726 and been ennobled in Poland.

He traced this back to documents showing that a merchant and landowner called Nehemias Strausberg (a man with the same name as Bethel Henry's great-grandfather) had been awarded the honorary title of *"Generosum Patricium de Nidborg Nehemiam Strausberg"* by King August II of Poland for services to the Polish army.

However, this Nehemias Strausberg can not have been Bethel Henry Strausberg's great grandfather. Bethel Henry's predecessors were first living in Neidenburg in 1776 without resident status, so one of them could hardly have been the man referred to. Furthermore, the dates of birth and death of the Polish Strausberg and his family do not correspond to those of Bethel Henry Strausberg's family.

If Strousberg had really believed what he claimed in his book, then he would almost certainly have attempted to have it officially recognised in Prussia. However, some kind of link between Bethel Henry's family and the Polish family can't be ruled out. Bethel Henry's father chose Strausberg as the family's surname in 1813, when the Polish family had already been using it for at least a century.

Strousberg's education

Strousberg's formal education took place, despite the strain it must have been on the family finances, at a *Gymnasium* (roughly equivalent to an English Grammar School of the time) in Königsberg (now Kaliningrad in the Russian Baltic Kaliningrad Oblast), then the provincial capital of East Prussia.

Königsberg must have been a bit of a shock for a boy from a small town. At the time Königsberg had become the leading economic and cultural city of the Prussian east. Once a leading member of the Hanseatic League, it had been the home of the philosopher Immanuel Kant, and was the city where the first King of Prussia had been crowned in 1701. The cityscape was dominated by the watchtower of the medieval castle and other great buildings such as the castle church, the city hall and the cathedral. The streets were busy and the banks of the river Pregel were lined with docks, warehouses and merchants' buildings.

Strousberg detailed some of his achievements at school—in Latin—in a curriculum vita which he submitted to the University of Jena in 1855 to support his application for a doctorate. According to this, he obtained the *maturitatem secundi ordinis* when he was in his 13th year. An incredible feat considering that Königsberg only allowed boys to enter a Gymnasium at the age of nine. When Bartel's father died on March 10th 1839, he was still at the Gymnasium, aged 16. As his father's death and the end of his school

5

career more or less coincide, it is more likely that he obtained his certificate them. This is just one example of a tendency to be economical with the truth, something which was rather characteristic.

The *maturitatem secundi ordinis* was a respectable school leaving qualification. The *Abitur* (matriculation for university entrance) was only taken by those who really wanted to be allowed to study at a university. Teaching at a *Gymnasium* emphasised Latin, usage of which had to be fluent in both written and spoken forms: owning a German-Latin dictionary was regarded as a disgrace. Whether or not Bartel Heinrich reached these heights is not certain, but his fondness for Latin quotes suggests that he felt at home in the language. At any rate his schooling gave him a solid foundation for his later occupation as a journalist.

In 1839 Strousberg's parents were both now dead. That meant he would have to make his own way as his seven siblings, dependent on a small inheritance, could not support him. Returning to Neidenburg was out of the question anyway; he dreamed of seeing the world. His mother's brothers, the Gottheimers, had gone to London and were in business there. Why shouldn't he go to London too?

2. STROUSBERG IN LONDON

From East Prussia to London

With the death of his father, there was now nothing to keep him in Königsberg. Until the end of April the *Frisches Haff* (the fresh water Vistula Lagoon) was still frozen preventing access to Königsberg from the Baltic Sea via the port of Pillau (now Baltisk, in the Kaliningrad Oblast of Russia).

Strousberg worked his passage to London on board the *Sirene*, arriving in London on September 27th 1839. The ship's captain had only one foreigner to report to the authorities: "Bartel Strausberg, Occupation warehouseman, Country Holland, coming from Königsberg, without papers".

The new arrival did not mention his officially attested Prussian citizenship, but instead described himself as Dutch, possibly to avoid awkward enquiries in East Prussia or, worse, deportation back to Prussia. Consequently, he kept quiet about his education. His declared occupation fitted with the Gottheimer's business. It looks as if he had thought it all out and done what economic migrants do when crossing borders today, that is give the details most likely to get in without arousing suspicion.

The Gottheimer brothers

The Gottheimer brothers had been in business in London since the 1830s. Their "fancy goods" business imported items from France and Germany for resale in England. Peter and Lesser Gottheimer jointly owned a company in Newgate Street, and the third brother, Berton, operated from Fleet Street. Bethel Henry went to live with Peter and his family at 72 Newgate Street.

In 1839, Queen Victoria's reign was two years old. The 1832 Reform Act had led to a massive change in the nation's political scene and much of the growing middle class (but not women) was now able to vote. The newly-enfranchised voters embraced the existing two-party system with Conservatives and Liberals being dominant. Social issues were to the fore in domestic politics. The Slavery Abolition Act came into effect in 1833 and in 1835 women's and child labour were regulated and there was a new Poor Law, although the consequences of the industrial revolution meant that the situation for many remained grim. 1839 saw the brutal repression of the radical Chartist movement. The situation was calmed somewhat by a transition to free trade, especially the repeal of the Corn Laws in 1846 which led to a reduction in the price of bread; in 1847 the 10-hour working day was introduced.

All these events will not have had an immediate effect on the new arrival but just being in London, then the largest city in the world, must have been a shock after Neidenburg or even Königsberg.

London and its suburbs had a population of about four and a half million. Strousberg's relatives, the Gottheimers, lived in the City. By day, there was constant activity and a stream of people engaged in business thronged the streets. Horse-drawn cabs, carriages and wagons filled the mostly unpaved carriageways; but at night, it was relatively quiet, as most people went home to the residential districts, leaving only about 120,000 people actually living there.

London was expanding and developing rapidly. Gas street lights had been introduced in 1823, roads were being paved and traffic was exploding. By the 1840s, railways were pushing the edge of London further outwards. Alongside all the economic activity people lived out their everyday existence, as chronicled in fiction by Charles Dickens.

We do not know about the Gottheimers' exact status, but it is a fair bet that they, and their nephew, enjoyed a respectable lifestyle in keeping with their status as proprietors of a successful "fancy goods" (toy and novelty) business. Strousberg was able to gain experience of all aspects of the business, but according to his autobiography did not seek to make use of his family connections choosing instead to distance himself from the business as soon as an opportunity arose.

This is surprising, as it would have been a good opportunity to gain commercial experience. Were there, perhaps, other reasons?

Possibly the explanation lies in this sentence from Strousberg's memoirs:

> "Straight after my arrival in England at the behest of my uncles and for linguistic reasons I began to write my name as Bethel Henry Strousberg, this was confirmed at my baptism when I converted to Christianity."

To put it bluntly, they disowned him for abandoning the Jewish faith.

This clearly shows that while the Gottheimers encouraged and approved of anglicising his name—which would indeed be useful for anyone planning to stay in England—the conversion was another matter.

Being Jewish in Britain was not a problem, at least not on the scale it remained in Germany. Indeed one of the most famous Victorian Prime Ministers, Benjamen Disraeli, was Jewish. The Gottheimers had been brought up as observant Jews, and remained so. In 1871, Berton Gottheimer even left a legacy to the First London Synagogue of British Jews, but nothing to his sons Albert and Maurice who had married non-Jewish women. Peter Gottheimer, in whose home Bethel Henry lived, and his probable father-in-law L. Zachariah had described themselves in 1842 as members of the Great Synagogue.

Bethel Henry's motivation for converting was clearly emancipation but not a rejection of his Jewishness.

Strousberg did not say exactly when he split with the Gottheimers, but it must have been before 1845 as in that year he married an English girl. The Anglican marriage service was held on March 13th 1845 in St. Bride's parish church in the City of London. The groom, Bethel Henry – occupation: trader – declared that his father's name was Alfred Strousberg, (Gentleman). His bride, Mary Ann Swan, was only 16; her father, George Swan, was a linen draper. One of the bride's sisters was a witness, but nobody from the Gottheimer family was present.

As Strousberg recounted in his 1876 memoirs, much of his time during this period, and also whilst he was staying with the Gottheimer family, was taken up with a thorough and intensive self-motivated programme of study. He gained knowledge of law, insurance and actuarial maths, economics, finance, banking and the workings of the stock market. This was to form the basis for his later work as a journalist and author.

Strousberg's memoirs do not mention how the young couple made a living. He begins only with his occupations as a magazine publisher and as an insurance company manager which did not commence until 1851 and 1853 respectively. What he kept quiet about, and not by some oversight either, is the period when he was working for the building societies.

Building Society Agent

The early Building Societies were nothing like today's sophisticated financial institutions are. They were self help organisations in the form of clubs or mutual societies. Members paid in their contributions to a shared fund. When there was enough money in the pool, one member – chosen by drawing lots – would receive an interest free sum to purchase a house. Members had to remain in the society until everyone had received their loan. Obviously this could only work if all of the members trusted each other, and the building societies were also subject to legal regulation.

Strousberg was an agent for three building societies, two of which we know the names of: *The Times Building Society* and *The Fifty Pound Building Society*. His annual salary was just 2 shillings per member share. His job was not too onerous, but it was important: he had to collect the members' contributions and pay them in to the relevant Society's bank account on a fixed date each month.

At the beginning of July 1847, Strousberg did not turn up to bank the money which he had collected at the appointed time. One of the members became suspicious and went straight to Southampton by train [the London & Southampton Railway[1] had opened in 1840] just as the SS *Washington* which had left for America the previous day was returning; already at sea, the ship's crew discovered that the wrong grade of coal for her boilers had been loaded and she had to turn back.

This was Strousberg's misfortune as the ship was searched and he was found, travelling without his wife, under the assumed name of Bartholdi. He was arrested at the harbour and taken back to London.

---

[1] *Later the London & South Western Railway. When it first opened the London & Southampton Railway's London terminus was at Nine Elms Railway Station in the Battersea district, which was too far from central London. Waterloo (then called Waterloo Bridge Station) did not open until July 1848 when the L&SWR opened its "metropolitan extension" from Nine Elms*

On trial for embezzlement

The turn of events might almost be comic, but for Strousberg they were serious indeed. On July 17th 1847 he appeared before Alderman Hughes, the magistrate at the Guildhall Police Court in London, charged with the felony of embezzlement.

The court sat for three days. It found that Strousberg had collected about £100 from members of the Times and Fifty Pound building societies but not paid it in to the designated bank accounts, intending to use it to pay for a passage to America.

When arrested, he still had £19 in his possession. He had paid £30 for the passage, which the magistrate felt sure the shipping line would refund, leaving £50 unaccounted for. It appears that during the proceedings Strousberg had managed to pay back most of this amount, leaving £7 and 17 shillings outstanding.

Under the relevant pieces of legislation (the *Act for the Regulation of Benefit Building Societies 1836* and the *Friendly Society Act 1829*) an employee of a Building Society who embezzled or dishonestly obtained money had to pay back *twice* the amount immediately, or face up to three months imprisonment with hard labour. Strousberg explained that he could not raise the required £15 and 14 shillings and his lawyer stated that there was nobody in England who could pay on his behalf (Strousberg obviously did not expect or want any help from the Gottheimer family, although they could easily have afforded it) and there was not enough time to get money from Germany. Strousberg was duly found guilty and the magistrate sentenced him to the maximum term.

This might seem harsh, but the courts took a dim view of breach of trust, and the magistrate had obviously not been impressed by the defence's first argument that the Friendly Society Act was not applicable because, when it was taken, the money was not yet the societies' property as it had not been banked. His lawyer's second argument, that the societies had not suffered financial loss because they were insured, was thrown out straight away.

What can Strousberg have been thinking of to embark on such a risky venture? He must have known that he would be found out almost immediately, but he was not put off and was ready to leave his young wife without any income for an indeterminate period in London. Was he making an attempt to do a runner from some failed scheme? Unlikely, as this would have emerged during the legal proceedings. It must have been pre-planned, perhaps with the idea of leaving England for good and settling in America. Or was it perhaps a sign of his almost unlimited optimism, thinking that he would quickly make his fortune, then return and pay back the stolen money and all would be forgiven?

Bethel Henry was released late in 1847 and returned to his wife. A year later their first son, also named Bethel Henry, was born. According to the birth certificate, Strousberg was at that time an accountant. Life went on, but thoughts of America remained.

Interval: America

In fact the Strousbergs did actually go, even if only briefly, to America. On January 31st 1849 the barque *Thames* arrived in New York from Liverpool with over 300 passengers, amongst them the Strousberg family. That is the only part of the visit which is documented; there isn't any mention of the visit in Strousberg's autobiography. The reader is obviously meant to get the impression that Strousberg and his family were in England throughout this period. Later newspaper reports gave some speculative reports about Strousberg's time in America. He was reported to have worked as a language teacher, or a salesman, yet another report says he ran a boarding house in New Orleans with his wife. Whatever the truth was, all of the reports agree that while he was in America, Strousberg came into money, by selling off a salvaged cargo of textiles, bought cheaply, at a large profit.

He now had money, and in 1850 the family returned to England. The exact date is not certain, but on April 8th the passenger lists for ships arriving in London from New York included one entry for a "B. Stauberg & wife, Prussia".

Their second son, Arthur, was born on the 15th of October or November, and the family lived (as recorded in the 1851 Census) at 39 Bartholomew Close in the City. Strousberg listed two occupations in the census: those of actuary and of magazine publisher.

Strousberg, the journalist and publisher

In the curriculum vita which he presented to the University of Jena in September 1857 to support his application for a doctorate, Strousberg outlined how his writing career began. He prepared himself for it with a programme of independent study and attending lectures at the Universities of London, Oxford and Cambridge. He had started by writing newspaper articles, more than a hundred in all, many of which were reprinted and sold as pamphlets. When he had success with these, he began to publish magazines under his own editorship.

The first of these magazines to appear, in February 1851, was *The Assurance Record*. In a message to the readership in the first issue Strousberg promised to faithfully analyse subjects and reassured readers that he would be critical but not polemic. The editorial section contained amongst other things a comparison of premiums from 120 life insurance societies, reports on the insurance markets, banks and building societies, legal topics, opinion on monetary policy, American economic data, book reviews, and a report on the Great Exhibition in London.

The remarkable thing is that Strousberg was not just the publisher, but also editor and copywriter for a magazine in his second language. The name Strousberg did not appear as the author or publisher at all. He was however named as the printer of issue 1; the following five had "P. Fischeil" as the printer. This was none other than his younger brother Ferdinand, who was also now in London.

There were only six issues of *The Assurance Record*, in February and March 1851, probably because Strousberg was also involved with producing and publishing *The Tradesman's Journal*, and *The Chess Player*, a weekly journal with chess problems and commentaries, of which he was both printer and publisher.

At the beginning of 1852 Strousberg began publishing *The British Journal* which was initially just an entertainment magazine with fiction serials, small articles and book reviews. From the middle of 1853 it also included political and economic coverage and an *Events of the Month* section.

This was followed by the monthly *Lawson's Merchant's Magazine*, the most significant of Strousberg's magazines. According to the front page he was the publisher between 1852 and 1854. Again, he wrote the articles himself.

Strousberg had set himself an ambitious target for this publication, namely bringing the readership (businessmen, politicians and interested laymen) a summary of up-to-date economic and political news and statistical material. Without a doubt it was also Strousberg's intention to expound on economic and legal questions, mainly in the form of series of articles.

For example, in the seven-part series *Our Commercial System* Strousberg examined Britain's economic situation in relationship to other countries as well as expressing his opinion on the prospects for future development. He called for increased social mobility both for the middle class and the working class, but rejected socialism and communism as espoused by Karl Marx as a solution to the problem: in this series of essays he expressed the same opinions here that he held later as an industrialist and continued to represent until his death. As Strousberg himself put it:

> "the wealthy few... look only to the Privileges of wealth, forgetting the Privileges of humanity."

These few words give us an insight into Strousberg's views at that time. It is hardly surprising that he champions free trade, libertarianism and enterprise. On the other hand, it is obvious that he thought "Manchester capitalism" as described by Friedrich Engels, driven only by selfish individualism was not really tolerable, and further distances himself from unfettered capitalism by using the word "humanity", which can not have been many industrialists' favourite word.

Strousberg also criticised, in an essay entitled *Our Monetary System*, the dual role of the Bank of England as a central bank and a player on the free market as well as the lack of a fiscal policy for controlling the economy.

Other economic themes covered in *Lawson's Merchant's Magazine* included free trade and protectionist customs policy, the recent gold finds in California and Australia and their effects, the general economic outlook, public finance, foreign trade, shipping, harbours and railways, mining, fishing, emigration, labour questions and strikes. As well as all this the *Money Market Review* covered up-to-date financial news and there was a report on parliament and politics in general. There can be no doubt that these articles, whether not one agrees with their contents, are the products of an author with a profound knowledge of economics and finance, as well as a wish to communicate this knowledge to the readership in plain English – not his first language.

Strousberg penned two articles about the "Railway King", George Hudson[1]. Ironically, Strousberg was himself nicknamed *der europäische Eisenbahnkönig [the European Railway King]* some 25 years later, although the two had very different careers. Strousberg's empire was based primarily on railway infrastructure construction whereas Hudson's empire was built largely on managing and merging lines which had already been built. However there were undeniably some common themes: both came from relatively modest backgrounds, both used some dubious financial schemes, rose to prominence very quickly and both crashed spectacularly.

Strousberg's articles depicted Hudson at the height of his career, lauded from all sides and in demand as a manager. Fabulous rewards and power were offered and Hudson could not resist the temptation to take them. Hudson himself had not created the circumstances under which he failed; they had been created for him. The parallels with what would later be said about Strousberg can not be overlooked.

He was also the author of most of the non-fiction articles in *Sharpe's London Magazine*, an illustrated monthly. Although the authors of the individual articles are not named, a series of essays entitled *A Talk about Newspapers*, about news-

---

[1] George Hudson was born in Howsham, in the parish of Scrayingham north of Stamford Bridge, east of York in 1800. In 1815 he left his home village in disgrace having fathered a child. After an apprenticeship as a linen-draper in York, he became a successful merchant. In 1827 he inherited £30,000 which he invested it in North Midland Railway shares, and was shortly afterwards appointed a director. In 1833 he founded and managed the York Banking Company, and in 1837 was elected lord mayor of York. He had long believed in creating a successful railway to York and he played an active role in securing the passing of the York and North Midland Railway Bill, and was elected chairman of the new company when the line opened in 1839. He initiated the Newcastle and Darlington line in 1841. Along with George Stephenson he planned and carried out the extension of the North Midland to Newcastle, and by 1844 had control of over a thousand miles of railway. The mania for railway speculation was at its height, and he was dubbed "the railway king" by the economic commentator Sydney Smith. Although already wealthy, he was presented with a tribute of £20,000. Deputy-Lieutenant for Durham, and thrice Lord Mayor of York, he was elected the Conservative MP for Sunderland between 1849 and 1851. The news was conveyed to London by a special train, which travelled part of the way at the rate of 75 miles an hour. Hudson was ruined by the disclosure of fraud in the Eastern Railway, along with the discovery of his bribery of MPs. Despite this he remained MP for Sunderland until 1859, but when the financial and political bubble burst he had lost influence and fortune. His later life was chiefly spent on the continent. Some friends gave him a small annuity a short time before his death in 1871.

papers and magazines in their socio-political role, was almost certainly Strousberg's work as this was his area of special interest.

We can see that Strousberg's publishing activities were virtually a calling. His articles may have been anonymous but they had a face and were obviously written with the same kind of passion he hoped to inspire in his readers.

In the insurance business

Strousberg was now 29 years old. He had become a public figure through his publishing activities, but he wanted to put his acquired knowledge of the insurance world to practical use, for which he would need a suitable position. He looked for a chance to draw attention to himself and found it in a fiercely conducted public controversy which had just broken out in this branch.

The cause of the dispute was a new development in life insurance. The insurance business had been well-established in England and Scotland since the beginning of the 18th century, with about 180 firms ('offices') specialising in life assurance and pensions alone. It was a well-run branch; however, at the beginning of the 1840s there had been a massive case of fraud at one company. The government had reacted swiftly, bringing in the Joint Stock Companies Act in 1844 which required that all joint stock insurance companies be officially registered and submit annual accounts. Between 40 and 50 new insurance companies were then started, and they complied with the regulations.

The new companies pursued their business aggressively. They appealed particularly to the middle and lower classes by offering cheaper premiums than the old offices. The older firms wrinkled their noses at the upstart competition and went on the attack.

The opening shots were fired by Robert Christie, a member of the Edinburgh-based Institute of Actuaries. On the 19th of July 1852 he sent an open letter to the minister of trade, Joseph W. Henley.

He alleged that the new companies were not solvent and were not in a position to pay out the amounts promised by their policies and that instead of proper balance sheets they had only submitted summaries of income and expenditure to the Registrar, which made it impossible to judge their true financial position.

Christie appended the figures for 44 London-based companies founded after 1844, which he said showed that the majority of their capital and premium income had been used to build up new business instead of being retained in the companies to cover liabilities arising from policies written. Christie demanded the formation of a parliamentary committee to investigate the matter and decide on measures to resolve the situation.

This was a solid, well prepared attack. Its weak point was that the old societies did not have to publish their balance sheets or annual accounts and that Christie was himself associated with these old offices. Indeed, some of them barred the press from their shareholders' meetings so that nothing got out. Several articles in the influential *Morning Chronicle* newspaper supported Christie's viewpoint.

The new companies felt threatened and fought back. It turned into a public discussion, into which Strousberg plunged on the side of the new companies. He too chose the form of an open letter, published as a pamphlet, to the minister of trade. Provocatively entitled *Conspiracy Detected* it appeared in September 1852.

Strousberg's very thorough argumentation and reasoning in this letter show that he was well versed and competent in insurance matters. His conclusion was that both the old offices and the new companies should be subject to the same conditions, and that the insurance companies founded after 1844 should not have to publish information which the old offices did not have to.

Such an even-handed approach was not a foregone conclusion. On the 8th of March 1853 Mr. Wilson, the Secretary to the Treasury persuaded the House to form a select committee to investigate the alleged wrongdoings of the new societies.

The Secretary had based his submission on a specific case of large scale breach of trust which had occurred at a life insurance society. What he did not mention was that this case happened in 1841, years before any of the societies under investigation were even registered, let alone trading. This was enough to motivate Strousberg to publish a second open letter, *Judgement before Trial*, in which he accused the Secretary of making subjective mistakes, followed by an extraordinary personal attack including an accusation that "he flagrantly misled the House" which is virtually saying that he had lied to parliament. "This Gentleman", Strousberg wrote "is not master of his subject". He had further used "fallacies and mere schoolboy sciolisms" to make his case and his behaviour had been unfair and unsatisfactory. Wilson was later forced to admit to the House that the fraud case he had referred to did indeed take place before 1844.

This was strong stuff. Strousberg was just 30 and although he was well known because of his magazines, he was not a name in insurance circles. He was a foreigner too, and yet he felt confident enough to attack a member of Her Majesty's Government in such terms. However this could have been precisely his motivation. He wanted to build up his profile in the industry. If you remember that his troubles at the Building Societies and subsequent imprisonment were only six years in the past, it is all the more extraordinary.

One of the points Strousberg made is worth mentioning in more detail. Strousberg criticised the old societies for their generous supply of capital and the fact that it was invested in highly liquid assets. Yes, the shareholders were paid a dividend (too high a dividend in Strousberg's view) from the interest on the investment, but in his opinion it would be better to put more resources into developing new business, as the new societies did.

This critique was to do with the question of liquidity, something which would later play such an important role in Strousberg's business life. He thought that the old societies' high liquidity provision was not required and they did not need to keep most of the premium income as an instantly available reserve; the obligation to pay out promptly on life policies did not require that. The statistical life expectancy of those insured meant that the vast majority of policies would only become due years hence. In the meantime, the revenue could and indeed should work for the ongoing business, for growing the business and acquiring new policies. Keeping liquid assets on hand to pay liabilities which, according to statistics, would only become due years later were a false policy.

This point of view is something which came up again later, in Strousberg's behaviour as an entrepreneur. He would do exactly as he suggested the insurers should do and disregard the security provided by the holding of liquidity.

Back to Strousberg's participation in this public debate. He'd got what he wanted and established himself as an expert in the field of insurance, and it paid off with his appointment as manager and actuary of the *Oak Mutual Life Assurance and Loan Company* in London.

This company was very new, having been registered in 1852. It had a capital of £50,000 and its shareholders included an Earl, a Baronet and professional people like lawyers and doctors. Strousberg joined the company in April 1853, and also became a shareholder with 280 £5 shares. £1400 was a considerable sum, but it is possible that as a manager he received the shares free or at a discount -- normal practice at that time. His brother Ferdinand also became a small shareholder, with £25 of shares.

Outward respectability

By May 1854 Strousberg had achieved a certain respectable status in the City as a magazine publisher and as actuary of a small, but active, life insurance company. He was now living in Mornington Road on the Camden side of Regent's Park, with his wife and two sons (a third son, Thomas, had died shortly after birth in 1853). Mornington Road, divided from the smart villas in Regents Park itself by the cutting for the London & Birmingham Railway's line to Euston station which had opened in 1837, was a definite improvement on the rather cramped apartment in Bartholomew Close. It is now known as Mornington Terrace.

Bethel Henry and his wife kept their private life just that, but we do know the names of some of the people Strousberg socialised with and from them it seems that he was upwardly mobile socially as well as professionally

Strousberg obtained permission to use the Reading Room at the British Museum; he was recommended by the renowned amateur geologist Devonshire Saull and member of several prestigious societies, such as the Royal Geological Society, the Royal Society of Arts and the Royal Astronomical Society. In January 1853 Strousberg was admitted as a Fellow of the Royal Geographical Society. This entitled him to put the letters F.R.G.S. after his name and make his social standing obvious.

He was supported in his application by John Matthews, an insurance director, Colonel William Henry Sykes, director of the East Indies Company and naturalist, and Thomas Hodgkin, doctor, researcher and philanthropist.

These, and other, important people had obviously accepted the young Strousberg into their circles. He was no longer just another immigrant Jew but a valued member of Society. He "belonged".

The family soon moved again, to a town house in Sydney Place, Brompton, a well-to-do neighbourhood, and they now employed a housekeeper. However, even before they were settled in properly, something awful happened. Strousberg had thought that his problems of 1847 were long forgotten, but suddenly they were aired in a court case. Worse still, the case was reported in *The Times*.

The past revealed

The background to the case lay with a possible attempted fraud on several insurance companies. Policies with a total value of £14,000 had been taken out on the life of one man, with different insurers and discussions were under way on a further £15,000 worth of cover. Not surprisingly, word of this got around and the insurers became suspicious. Shortly thereafter the insured man died. He had been terminally ill before the policies were signed, a fact which had not been disclosed to the insurers, and not unnaturally they refused to pay out. One of the companies was Strousberg's Oak which stood to lose £1000.

A brother of the insured man, a Mr. Bryson, demanded payment from, amongst others, the Oak. On behalf of the company, Strousberg refused. Bryson reacted by sending a letter to the Oak demanding that he examine their books and bank accounts as, contrary to the regulations, they had not made their balance sheet available for public inspection at the Registry Office. When he got no reply, Bryson went in person to the Oak's offices where Strousberg told Bryson that he had no right to see the books as he had no connection with the company. There was then a loud argument which almost came to blows. The police were summoned, Bryson was taken away, and on the 27th of March he was fined £10 for breach of the peace by the Guildhall magistrates.

Bryson wouldn't give up. He brought a case against the Oak because they had not lodged their balance sheet and accounts at the Registry Office on time.

The Oak, Bryson claimed, did its business with the poorest of the poor and therefore its accounts required particularly close supervision. He called Strousberg, the Oak's manager, into the witness box. Strousberg explained that the apparent delay in submitting the balance sheets was caused by a perfectly legal change (approved by the shareholders) of six months in the company's financial year end and that therefore the rules had not been broken.

That should have been the end of the matter, but there was further debate about the legitimacy of Bryson's action and about some of the Oak's business practices although this was not really relevant to the case. Eventually they got round to the supposed fraud involving Bryson's brother. Strousberg said that Bryson should be careful about admitting in public what his contribution had been. Bryson replied that if he was recommending caution, then Mr. Strousberg ought to remember that this very court had sentenced him to three months hard labour for embezzlement.

This was about as bad as it could get for Strousberg. The deed which he had carried out seven years ago, and thought forgotten, was being dragged out in an open court hearing and it would be all over the press tomorrow; the court reporter from *The Times* was in the room. Then, he'd been a nobody and noone was particularly interested, but now he was the well-known City figure Bethel Henry Strousberg.

It did not really matter that the Oak had won the case. His explanation that there had been a lot of confusion over that case which could be easily explained and one of the Oak's representatives statement that Bryson had not really brought the case because of the balance sheets but just to make accusations against respectable people and use the Court and the press to stir up bad feeling did not help. The only thing which mattered was that this ugly episode had been dug up. A year previously he had written his open letter *Judgement before Trial* which contained allegations about irregularities in the Building Societies. A can of worms indeed, and one which would have been better left unopened.

At a stroke, all that he had achieved in England was in doubt. His successful work as a magazine publisher, his respected position in the insurance field, his elevated social standing culminating in Fellowship of a Royal Society — how much of that would survive? He would be stigmatised all over the world when it was reported in *The Times* and morally disqualified from keeping his position in London. Any thoughts of further advancement seemed to be gone.

Things must have looked black to Strousberg at that point. The first thing he did was to offer his resignation as manager and actuary at the Oak. The Oak tried to hold on to him, offering him a testimonial signed by all nine directors in conjunction with a unanimous vote of confidence by the board. The directors promised to protect Strousberg from any similar attacks in the future and gave him permission to publish the testimonial in the press, signed by them all.

Their desire not to let Strousberg go was genuine. In his favour was that—so it said in the testimonial—he had fully informed the directors of the Oak about the affair reported in *The Times* before his appointment and the Board had investigated thoroughly, with the result that even the Building Societies concerned agreed there was nothing in Strousberg's past to stand in the way of his employment as manager of the Oak.

Strousberg did not publish the testimonial, despite having permission to do so. However convincing its content were, it would only draw more attention to the affair, and so it was not really much use to him; his reputation was already ruined. He could no longer expect to have a career in England fitting for a man of his ambitions and talents. His dream of making England his permanent home was over.

So he came to the decision to return to Prussia but not to Königsberg or Neidenburg, but to Berlin, a city he had never even been to. He had no idea what awaited him there, personally or professionally.

In England, Bethel Henry had followed various professions quite successfully, a considerable achievement for a fairly young man of 33. But there was not yet any sign that this was a man who would later have such an astonishing career characterised by overflowing dynamism or even extravagances.

One thing was clear: he wanted to be the boss and if possible the owner, not a mere manager as he had been for the Oak. He had already had a taste of this with his magazines where he soon became the self-sufficient businessman.

From a personal point of view as well, Strousberg must have found the decision to leave London incredibly difficult. He had only recently managed to become reasonably well-off. No less importantly, he had built up close acquaintances and probably personal friendships with people from the upper echelons of society. Being a foreigner was either not a hurdle or one that he had managed to overcome. Now, in Berlin, he would be in his own country but he would not know anyone. It must have been even more painful for his wife, Mary Ann, to leave London: she had after all grown up here, had family here and had never lived in a non-English speaking country. "Prussia" was just a faraway place.

The Amazing Dr. Strousberg

3. RETURN TO PRUSSIA

Berlin

In his 1876 autobiography, Strousberg gave "an almost overwhelming desire to return to my homeland" as the reason for his move to Berlin. Furthermore he said that all of his efforts in England had been directed just earning a living and he did not have the time for writing. A bit of a feeble excuse for someone who had arrived in London virtually penniless some sixteen years previously and worked his way up to become a successful magazine publisher, manager of a life insurance society, Fellow of the Royal Geographical Society and member of other learned societies, living with his family in the respectable Brompton district.

He had scarcely thought about Prussia in all those years; in fact he had presented himself as being quite British in his magazines. In *Lawson's Merchant's Magazine* an article entitled "*How do we stand? Warning of increasing competition from abroad.*" which he had written stated bluntly that

> "the Continent, the Germans in particular, will out-strip and leave us behind" and "the Germans ... are driving us out of the American trade."

Shortly before the court case Strousberg had announced future plans for *Lawson's Merchant's Magazine* and for making *Sharpe's London Magazine* even more attractive for its readers. In reality, instead of implementing these ambitious plans Strousberg simply moved the production of both magazines to Berlin, delivering from there to his subscribers in London. In his memoires he said that his judgement was basically correct "as one could print more cheaply and at least as well as in England", although he had to admit that he had

> "overlooked the fact that the German printer, the German carrier and the German bookbinder had not yet learned to value time and punctuality."

In other words, it had not worked as well as he thought it would. For several months the magazines arrived late with their customers in England and he lost almost 2000 subscribers to *Sharpe's London Magazine* alone, although the problem of slow delivery was solved by 1857.

The result was that he had to sell both titles. This was really inevitable, given the production problem of German typesetters handling English text, and of course without being in London and meeting his contacts daily, Strousberg could not write the editorial material properly, especially for the *Merchants' Magazine*.

The fact that he had not thought the business consequences of relocating to Berlin through properly points to the report on the court case in *The Times* on May 10th 1854 as being the real reason why Strousberg left England.

Berlin and London at that time were hardly comparable. London was *the* world city: and with its population of 4.5 million was about five times larger than Berlin (even including adjoining towns such as Charlottenburg and Spandau which were later to become *Bezirke* (districts) of the German capital).

In 1839, when the young Bartel Heinrich left Prussia, the country was just beginning to revive, thanks to the reforms introduced by Stein and Hardenberg since 1806 after the defeat by Napoleon[1]. There had also been the failed revolution of 1848.

In the late 1850s Berlin was under the control of the ruthless police chief, Karl Ludwig Friedrich von Hinckeldey, who had become a notorious hate figure. He was not just Chief of Police in Berlin but was also head of the hated Prussian Secret Police. Use of informers, suppression of the press, arrest of suspicious persons up to senior level, house searches and the confiscation of private correspondence were common, and not limited by a constitution or by law.

Strousberg must have felt restricted by this atmosphere; he had been born in Prussia but had lived all his adult life in England, where people could express their opinions openly and he had come to take that for granted.

False starts

Strousberg was faced with needing to make a living, although he still had some income from his magazines in London. His first steps were not very impressive and showed that he needed time to get used to his new surroundings.

He first tried his hand in the art market, putting on an exhibition of German paintings in London, because "German art is scarcely represented in England." This venture made a substantial loss, as only a few German artists took part and Strousberg had to fill the exhibition rooms by purchasing a number of "second and third-rate pictures." It nonetheless appears that Strousberg could obviously afford to fund a loss-making venture like this.

Selling his magazines had evidently brought in a tidy sum. In a statement to the Berlin police in 1863 Strousberg, when asked about his income mentioned an annuity of 2000 Thaler — possibly financed by the sale of the

---

[1] Stein and Hardenberg both introduced sweeping reforms in Prussia which included the liberation of peasants from serfdom, the emancipation of Jews and making full citizens of them, changes to the education system and the institution of conscription for military service as part of military reform in 1813. Municipalities became self-administering in 1808 and crucially in 1818 free trade was introduced.

London magazines. In addition he claimed to have earned "the not insignificant sum of £10,000" for his work as an expert in the field of life insurance (this was perhaps payment and royalties for *Conspiracy Detected* and *Judgment before Trial*).

This had obviously put Strousberg in a good position, financially. However he still needed a regular income and it was easiest to turn to the areas in which he had experience, insurance and writing.

He used his connections in London to acquire the Prussian representation for the Waterloo Life Insurance Society. It is doubtful that he made much money from it as the society did not have official permission to operate in Prussia, which obviously did not stop Strousberg from touting for business on its behalf.

Strousberg's venture to launch a literary magazine, the *Literarisches Leseblatt (Literary Paper)*, didn't have much luck. It contained short stories by young German and foreign writers, and the nominal publisher was a Berlin bookseller, Abelsdorff. Abelsdorff cancelled the arrangement after two issues and when Strousberg ignored the cancellation and continued to produce further issues with Abelsdorff named as the publisher, Abdelsdorff reported the matter to the police. As a result, in September 1857 Strousberg was prosecuted and fined 100 Thaler for breach of the press regulations by the Berlin *Stadtgericht* (City Court).

A growing family

Strousberg's family was growing in the meantime. In 1856 and 1860 Agnes and Alice were born making four children including Bethel Henry and Arthur, born in England. Four *surviving* children that is: two sons and a daughter born in the 1850s had died in infancy.

Since their arrival in Berlin in 1855, the family had lived at various addresses Dorotheenstrasse 55 (1856-7), Lenneéstrasse 8 (1860-61) and then from 1863 at Bellevuestrasse 9. The latter two were very 'good' areas near the Tiergarten park. They could obviously afford the same standard of living as they had enjoyed in London.

Strousberg soon made several contacts at the British diplomatic representation and became friendly with the Reverend Robert Bellson, Vicar of the Berlin Anglican Church (later on he would christen the children, and remained in contact until the 1880s).

Strousberg's doctorate

Strousberg was granted the title of Doctor of Philosophy from the University of Jena in 1857 and henceforth he was always Dr. Strousberg or simply "the Doctor" to all but family and close friends.

In the 19th century, certain faculties of some reputable universities would confer doctorates based on experience and non-academic study, supported by documentary evidence and scrutiny by the members of the faculty.

Strousberg made his formal application on the 1st of September 1857 after an initial enquiry, in which he referred to his Fellowship of the Royal Geographical Society, on the 10th of August, with a curriculum vitae in Latin and printed excerpts from his London magazines in support. The application was processed remarkably quickly as it was approved by the Dean on the 17th of September and ratified by the members of the faculty on the following day.

Karl Marx had obtained his doctorate like this, also from Jena, in 1841.

4. RAILWAY CONSTRUCTION IN EAST PRUSSIA AND RUSSIA

On the 22nd of June 1865 *The Times* printed a report from its Berlin correspondent about the ceremonial opening of the Tilsit (now Sovestk, in the Russian Kaliningrad Region) to Insterburg (now Chernyakhovsk, in the Russian Kaliningrad Region) railway.

The report stressed that this was the first railway project in Germany to be financed with British capital. During the ceremony the Prussian trade minister, Count Itzenplitz, paid tribute to "Mr. Strousberg and his role as a middleman between the money markets in the two countries."

Until then the state-owned Preussische Ostbahn [Prussian Eastern Railway], from Berlin via Königsberg to Eydtkuhnen (now Chernyshevskoye in Russia) on the Russian border, had been the only railway in East Prussia. Transport in Prussia's eastern outpost meant horse and cart at best and the leading circles in the region demanded the building of modern local railways. But, as ever, the State had nothing in its budget for such projects: the parliament had been refusing to authorise the taking out of loans since a dispute arose about a planned army reform. Railway construction would therefore only be possible if private capital could be found.

The chambers of commerce in Tilsit, Insterburg, Memel (now Klaipėda in Lithuania) and particularly in Königsberg had been pleading for years with increasing urgency: East Prussia needed railway lines to open up the country and provide links to harbours. Königsberg was only 45 kilometres from the ice-free port of Pillau on the Baltic. Apart from this it was important to have a line running southwards within Russia to link up with the main Russian routes, making direct connection with St. Petersburg, Moscow and Odessa possible.

Eventually, the Prussian government agreed. The comparatively short and minor route from Tilsit to Insterburg—just 54 kilometres—was to be a pilot project for privately financed railway construction. Other proposals for longer routes followed: the East Prussian Südbahn would be 243 kilometres long, with a route from Pillau via Königsberg and Rastenburg (now Kętrzyn in Poland) to Lyck (now Ełk in Poland) and from there to the nearby Russian border. A connecting line would be built in Russia via Bialystock (now Białystok in Poland) to Brest-Litovsk (now Brest in Belarus) and the Russian network. The Südbahn ought to be built by 1868 and the connecting line on Russian territory by 1873. These huge projects could not be financed without someone to push them through and convince the Prussian trade minister, Count Heinrich Friedrich von Itzenplitz, that they were feasible. The ingenious man who did this was Bethel Henry Strousberg.

Map of railway lines in East Prussia (1899)

This is an excerpt from an 1899 map of railways in Germany showing the lines in East Prussia.

Strousberg was directly involved in the line from Insterburg to Tilsit and the East Prussian Südbahn from Pillau to Königsberg, then via Rastenburg and Lyck to the Russian border at Prostken. From Prostken to Grajewo there were two parallel tracks, one in standard 1435mm gauge and one in Russian 1524 mm gauge.

The Tilsit-Insterburg Railway

Strousberg's initial efforts to start a new business career in Berlin had been short lived and did not indicate that he was about to set off on the path to being a great industrialist. Now fortune was to smile on him.

While he was trying to establish himself in Berlin, Strousberg had made a conscious effort to make and maintain contacts. Some of these contacts were with the British Embassy. Here he had had the opportunity "quite by chance" to assist the Ambassador, Lord Bloomfield, with an expert legal opinion on a case, with the result that he was "was frequently consulted on legal matters."

One day a group of British businessmen, with a recommendation from the Embassy sought Strousberg out in order to seek his "Advice on obtaining the concession for the Tilsit-Insterburg Railway". They had already been negotiating, fruitlessly, together with a group of Prussian interested parties, for three years with the section of the Prussian Trade Ministry responsible for granting the concession. The spokesman for this group was a respected lawyer called Geppert. He knew Strousberg through his work for the Embassy and that he was a bright man. He advised the British group to follow Strousberg's suggestion to "regard all the previous negotiations as not having taken place, and to start the negotiations afresh on the basis of proposals to be made by me". This was the point at which his new career as an industrialist in Germany began.

What was the problem which the would-be investors from Britain faced? Germany's first locomotive operated railway, the *Ludwigbahn* from Nuremburg to Fürth in Bavaria had opened in 1835, and lines in northern Germany soon followed. In contrast to Britain where railways were promoted entirely privately and often speculatively and the government only intervened reluctantly, the various German state governments became involved at an early stage.

In Prussia, the government passed the *Gesetz über die Eisenbahn-Unterhnehmungen* (Law on Railway Enterprises) to regulate the construction of railways by private enterprise. The government felt duty-bound to regulate this new means of transport with its potentially dangerously high speed of 30 kilometres per hour (four to five times faster than walking pace), and therefore an office to deal with railway matters was set up at the Ministry of Trade.

Apart from wanting to ensure operational safety, the government also had a fiscal interest in private railway construction and operation. Contradictory as it might sound, the law was conceived for building state railways with private finance: the government had the right to purchase a privately-financed line 30 years after it opened to traffic. For this reason privately-built railways were subject to the same standards as government-owned railways.

A company wishing to construct a railway required a government concession which detailed 1) the route of the line, 2) the amount allowed for construction costs including 3) approval of the cost calculation method for every item: the permanent way, the rails, bridges, crossings, stations, signalling equipment, sidings, carriages, goods wagons, locomotives and even administrative expenses.

The Prussian Railway Authority (*Eisenbahnamt*) checked that all these details had been followed before giving the go-ahead to open. The Railway Authority also examined the company's articles of association, its financing and how much of the share capital had actually been paid; the construction costs could not exceed this sum without permission.

The sticking point which the British investors had so far been unable to overcome was that the authorities wanted to be sure that the share capital was not just a nominal figure printed on the certificates but was actually available in full and could be used for construction in order to ensure the railway's operational safety.

This was clearly laid down in the Prussian Law on Railway Enterprises: Section 2 Paragraph 1 stated that the Railway Company could only issue its shares "after payment of the whole nominal value", the amount printed on the share certificate. So a 1000 Thaler[1] share could only be issued against a cash payment of 1000 Thaler; issuing shares at less than face value was expressly forbidden. The purpose of this rule is clear. If 10 million Thaler were required for the construction of a railway line, but the shares were offered for sale at, say, 80% of face value, the company would have only 8 million Thaler available and so it was likely that corners would be cut compromising standard of construction and safety.

In theory, this sounds fine, but obtaining the full amount of capital is only possible if there are investors who will buy the shares at face value. From an investor's point of view, it looks risky. On offer is a share at 100% of face value in a newly established company whose only asset is a concession for a railway which hasn't been built yet and won't be finished for several years: no property, not a single metre of track, no rolling stock. The prospective investor is bound to ask himself whether or not the line will in fact be fin-

---

[1] The Thaler was the unit of currency and account in Prussia. From 1857 it was replaced by the Vereinsthaler divided into 30 Silbergroschen, each of 12 Pfennig. Thaler continued to be the usual term. The Vereinsthaler was also used and issued in Austria, to a lesser extent, alongside the Austro-Hungarian Guilder, at a rate of 1.5 Guilders to 1 Thaler. The Thaler was itself replaced after German unification in 1870 by the Mark at a rate of 3 Marks to 1 Thaler.

ished and if so, whether or not it will be profitable. Can asking 100% of face value be justified at this stage?

Obviously, it can take years for a railway to be completed and return a profit from which to pay a dividend. The authorities knew this and therefore shareholders were to receive an annual 5% interest payment until the line was completed. 5% was clearly not very exciting, considering that government bonds, a safe and easily convertible investment, paid 4½%. Putting money into a railway that is still under construction is risky and your investment is tied up.

Too risky for investors in fact and they stayed away. The edict that shares could only be issued at face value had the effect of making private capital for railways inaccessible although the requirement for railways was more than urgent. All over rural Prussia, railway committees had been formed, plans drawn up and preparatory work done, often with ministerial approval. All of this was in vain, because capital couldn't be obtained.

This was the situation in which the British investors found themselves. Although they were happy to invest, they were not prepared to tie their money up until the line was finished as if they wanted to get out early this would mean a loss, as it would only be possible to dispose of their shares at 80% or less of face value.

Strousberg's system of financing railway construction

Strousberg came up with a possible solution which had several components. His basic idea was not to pay for the shares with cash but by performing services. These services would be performed by a general contractor, who was obliged by contract with the railway company to deliver the complete railway. This is how it would work:

The general contractor would commence work, say by constructing the first ten kilometres of permanent way. When this was ready, he would transfers its ownership to the railway company as the first step towards fulfilment of the whole contract. The railway company would then make payment for that stage by issuing the contractor with the number of share whose nominal value matched the value of ten kilometres of permanent way. This amount was fixed, laid down in the construction plan authorised by the Railway Authority.

The same method would be used for each following stage. Step by step the contractor would hand over everything needed by a railway: the track bed, rails, bridges, stations, signalling equipment, locomotives and rolling stock stock, and each stage would be paid for, in shares to the value of the authorised amount for each item. When the line was finished, with everything handed over, the company would own assets whose officially confirmed value matched the issued share capitals.

Strousberg suggested that just one person should be the railway company's general contractor. He was familiar with this idea from his time in England where it was the usual method of railway construction. The general contractor employed subcontractors to actually build the railway, sourced the railway equipment from various suppliers and then handed over the completed line and rolling stock. Using this method made sense: that way, shares would only have to be issued to one person. Paying all the subcontractors in shares, even if they agreed, would have been an administrative nightmare.

Importantly, each stage would be checked as it was handed over, not just for compliance with the agreed figures but also for quality: the Law on Railway Enterprises required a strict inspection of construction. Officials from the Railway Office examined every step of the work as it was completed. They checked everything and inspected every technical detail — and if they weren't satisfied then they wouldn't give permission for the line to be opened. In addition, the Police checked the line's operational safety by "walking the line".

The overall result was that the railway company had become the owners of the line (as contractually agreed); the line was certified as to quality and safety by the Railway Authority and the Police.

The total price would be the same as the amount of share capital which the general contractor had received in payment. Because the company would have exchanged its shares for the completed line, it would have issued them at face value. As far as the company – and the law – were concerned the result would be the same as if all of the shares had been sold at face value and the contractor had been paid in cash.

Risk for the general contractor

Obviously the general contractor would have to convert the shares received in payment into cash so that he could pay his suppliers and subcontractors. He could not expect to find a buyer for the shares at 100% of face value; if that had been possible the railway company would have done so to start with. So, the contractor now sold on the shares at less than face value. If, for example, he sold shares with a nominal value of 1 million Thaler at 80% of face value then he'd get 800,000 Thaler. The whole process depended on the general contractor being able to even out these losses. The line would still have to be built even though the amount specified for construction in the authorised plan would definitely not be available.

The idea of building the line to a lower standard to reduce costs could be discounted as this would be prevented by the checks and inspections carried out by the Railway Authority and the Police.

Curiously, the fixed prices authorised by the Railway Authority gave the contractor some breathing room. These costs were based on those which the officials had experience of before the state had built any railways itself. The officials were used to paying higher prices than those prevalent in the current downturn. In view of the long period needed to construct a railway they were not prepared to revise them downwards. Just as today, public sector projects tended to be more expensive than private ones, as Strousberg noted in "Dr. Strausberg and his works" (1867):

"Whatever the state does, will always end up more expensive, than it costs a private person to do... Civil servants are experts in their subject. Punctual, honest, dedicated, economical and something else: they have got no real understanding of business, they are penny wise and pound foolish; there's no stimulus."

There was an urgent requirement to reduce the line's construction costs and the bill for the general contractor. As all the orders to suppliers and subcontractors were issued by one person, the general contractor, this obviously put him in a strong negotiating position and allowed him to drive a hard bargain. However if he did not manage to deliver, to the right quality, a line costed at 3 million Thaler (such as the Tilsit-Insterburg line) for 2.4 million or less then a loss would be incurred, as no top-up payment could be expected from the railway company. The contractual agreements suggested by Strousberg laid down that the general contractor had to

"do everything, without demands for extra payment and without challenge, that the company's or the Government's technical experts may advise."

Strousberg's concept is adopted

Strausberg succeeded in getting his concept approved by the trade minister, Graf Itzenplitz, and this proved to be the breakthrough. On the 22nd of December 1862 the king approved the Tilsit-Insterburg railway and a one-off state subsidy (at the suggestion of the cabinet, signed by Bismarck) of 140,000 Thaler. The subsidy showed how important the cabinet felt railways were.

The position of general contractor was filled by experienced British engineer, Joseph Bray, and George Barclay Bruce (who was responsible for large parts of the Indian railways[1]). was appointed as engineering consultant. Everyone involved was relieved that the project could get under way at last. The British investors signed up for the capital of 3,089,000 Thaler (£463,350), half in ordinary and half in preference shares. As the shares would be issued at face value in payment to the general contractor, the investors did not have to invest any actual cash. Bray accordingly released the investors from their financial obligations, knowing that he bore all of the risk.

In accordance with the company's articles, two committees of the board were formed: the audit committee (German stakeholders) and the finance committee (British investors). As the British investors had no intention of remaining in East Prussia, they appointed Strousberg as their representative. This meant that for all practical purposes, Strousberg was the finance committee and had a central position while the line was being built.

Construction of the Tilsit-Insterburg Railway began in 1863 and the line was completed in 1865.

The second project: the East Prussian *Südbahn*

As early as 1860, there had been proposals for railways from Königsberg to the ice-free harbour at Pillau and from Königsberg to the province's southern border, but they had come to nothing. Now, after completion of the Tilsit-Insterburg line the Prussian government recommended that they be built. Like the Tilsit-Insterburg line, the Südbahn received a one-off state subsidy payment, in this case 360,000 Thaler.

It took quite a lot of effort to get all the parties for this project together, but it did earn Strousberg a considerable commission. He travelled all over the area through which the line was to run, and met the influential landowners

---

[1] From 1836-41 Bruce was apprenticed to railway pioneer Robert Stephenson. From 1841-43 he worked on the construction of the Newcastle and Darlington Railway, and from 1843-45 he was resident engineer on the Northampton and Peterborough line. After working for Robert Stephenson on the building of Royal Border Bridge, in 1850 Bruce gave an account of his time there to the Institution of Civil Engineers, earning him a Telford Medal. He then worked mainly on the construction and maintenance of railways in India, principally the East Indian Railway and the Madras Railway, returning to England due to ill health in 1856. After returning from India, Bruce became a consulting engineer and worked on many projects at home and abroad. Bruce acted as a consultant to the South Indian Railway, Great Indian Peninsular Railway and the Indian Midland Railway. He worked with Strousberg on several lines including Tilsit-Insterburg and Berlin-Görlitz. He also worked in Spain, Argentina (the East Argentine Railway and the Buenos Aires Grand National Tramway in Argentina) and Portuguese West Africa (the Beira Railway). Bruce worked with many British railway companies including works on the Stonehouse and Nailsworth; Peterborough, Wisbech and Sutton; Kettering, Thrapston and Huntingdon; and the Whitehaven, Cleator and Egremont railway lines. He favoured the 5 ft 6 in rail gauge which was popular amongst the British colonies at the time.

in the region. They formed a land committee which agreed to give Strousberg all the land needed to construct the line and in return he would "arrange" the British financiers and the main contractor. The contract laid down that Strousberg had to pass the building land on to the yet-to-be-formed railway company for 300,000 Thaler in ordinary shares: he would also represent and head the finance committee.

There were a few changes to the committee membership, especially regarding the audit committee whose new members mostly came from the central part of East Prussia. They included Karl Graf Lehndorff-Steinort, the older brother of the King's adjutant-general, Freiherr von Romberg-Gerdauen (the trade minister's son-in-law) and the banker Moritz Simon from Königsberg. These three connections would be important in Strousberg's later activities too.

The organisation was almost the same as it had been for the Tilsit-Insterburg line. Once again Strousberg had the central role as authorised representative for the British members of the finance committee and as the deputy chairman of the administrative board. Joseph Bray was the general contractor with George Barclay Bruce as engineering consultant.

As first planned the line was to run from Pillau to Königsberg and then via Rastenburg to Lyck. The share capital was set at 13,000,000 Thaler; in 1867 the share capital was reduced to 9,000,000 Thaler with the 'lost' 4,000,000 Thaler being replaced by a 5% bond.

This was done because Bray resigned as general contractor at the beginning of 1866. He had received a payment of 5,790,000 Thaler in shares but had been unable to resell most of them. Financial market conditions at that time were difficult and Prussian stocks were generally an unknown and therefore risky investment. The brief Prussian-Danish war played a role too, because the small Prussian navy could not prevent the superior Danish fleet from blockading the Baltic ports (and trade with east Prussia).

Bray had had to find millions of Thaler, either from his own resources or from loans to cover the line's construction. It was too much. Bray lost almost all his money, some three million Thaler, and Strousberg had to get the finance committee to relieve Bray of responsibility for the construction. Strousberg had identified a financial risk for the general contractor in his original concept and it had turned out to be very real.

After Bray's departure the East Prussian Südbahn company itself dealt directly with the subcontractors and suppliers, which would previously have been Bray's job.

Until his departure Bray had been diligent and energetic with the line's construction commencing in April 1864. Work on the section from Königsberg to Pillau was finished the same year and it was officially opened in 1865. The line southwards from Königsberg reached Bartenstein (now Bartoszyce in Poland) (57 kilometres) in 1866 and Rastenburg (150 kilometres) in 1867. The final section as far as Lyck, crossing the Masurian lakes, was difficult technically but was finished on December 8th 1868. The total length of the line, from Pillau to Lyck, was 226 kilometres.

The connection to the Russian railway network

The East Prussian *Südbahn* extension from Lyck to the Russian border at Prostken had always been part of the plan; in fact it had even been a condition of the original concession that it would be built but it required Russian approval to lay the line on their territory.[1]

Russia's permission did not come easily. At the end of 1869 the main route from the Black Sea to Brest-Litovsk was partially finished, but some sections were still under construction, and the Russian government's railway committee had no plans to extend the line from Brest-Litovsk to the Prussian border. For years this had been a political hot potato in Russia: the ultra-nationalists opposed the line on the grounds that it would give Prussia a strategic advantage, but on the other side European-minded politicians pointed to its commercial importance for Russia. Eventually a decision in favour of the railway was made, along a route from Brest-Litovsk via Bialystok to Grajewo on the Prussian border.

Count Lehndorff-Steinort and Baron Romberg-Gerdauen lead the negotiations with the Russian government and on the 12th/26th of December 1869 received the concession to construct a line connecting with the East Prussian *Südbahn* on the route described above, with a length of 203 Werst[2] (216.6 kilometres).

The concession would run for 81 years (until 1950) after which ownership would pass to the Russian state. The concession also set the share capital of the company to be formed for the project, the Brest-Litovsk and Grajewo Railway Company, at 1.5 million silver roubles (12.5 million Thaler).

Strousberg was to be the general contractor. It must be noted that in 1870, when Strousberg received this job, he had become the "European Railway King" rather than just a man who had come up with a clever trick for financ-

---

[1] RAILWAYS IN Russia use a broader gauge than those in the rest of Europe. At the time the Brest-Grajewo and East Prussian Südbahn lines were built, the Russian standard was 1524 mm (rounded down to 1520 mm in the 1960s). The European standard is 1435 mm. Obviously this prevented through trains: passengers had to change trains and freight had to be transferred. A single Russian gauge line ran to the station at Protken on the German side of the border and a single standard gauge line ran in parallel to Grajewo on the Russian side in order to make this easier.

[2] The Werst (Верста) was a measure of length in the Russian Empire, equivalent to 1.066.8 metres.

ing the construction of railway lines in East Prussia. He had already partially built five further lines in Prussia, was constructing major railways in Romania and Hungary, was involved in a harbour project at Antwerp and operated industrial undertakings in (amongst other places) Hanover and Dortmund.

This meant that the 216 kilometre Brest-Grajewo railway was a relatively small job for Strousberg. The line had long been his pet project, but he only applied himself half-heartedly. He later wrote:

> "One can not avoid one's fate. An inner voice warned me to keep my distance from Russia as I had already made several attempts to do business there and had been frustrated every time."

Nonetheless, he took on the task. In payment he received all of the shares in the Brest-Grajewo Railway Company, which he intended to place with the public himself.

Strousberg did not intend to supervise the construction himself as he already had commitments in other countries which would prevent him from being in Russia often enough. He did expect to "make my position quite comfortable" from the share placement, despite the fact that this would be made difficult because (unlike other Russian railway company shares) the shares did not have a state-backed dividend.

The offering and placement of the shares went badly wrong. One banker told Strousberg that 70% [of face value] was the right price and Strousberg let him buy a block of shares at that price. At the same time a broker thought that he could place the shares at face value. In all of this uncertainty, Strousberg appointed a consortium of banks to place all of the share capital. When the consortium invited tenders for the shares at a rate of 87%, the first banker offered shares for much less. As result, only 13% of the tender was taken up. The banks in the consortium concluded, correctly, that the shares which had been offered more cheaply could only have originated in Strousberg's portfolio. They blamed him for the failure of the offering and refused to pay for the shares they had not been able to place with the public. Strousberg, to his extreme annoyance, was left holding all the capital.

Meanwhile, the Prussian government had decided to allow the connecting line. King Wilhelm authorised the section to the Russian border on the 25th of July 1870 and agreed to finance it by issuing a 5% bond for 1.4 million Thaler. Progress was rapid and the new section was taken into service in November 1871.

On the Russian side, work on the Brest-Grajewoline proceeded. However, money was short because of the failed share placement and construction almost halted. In addition Strousberg was faced with problems relating to his activities in Romania, and had to remain in Berlin. He needed to raise money quickly, and borrowed 540,000 roubles from a consortium of Berlin banks against 2.7 million roubles in Brest-Grajewo Railway Company shares (which he had not been able to get rid of in the failed placement) as security. This was only 20% of the shares face value, and it did not cover the rest of the construction costs by a long way. Because of this, the consortium of lending banks was extended to include the Russian St. Petersburg Private Trade Bank. This bank then arranged the issue of a bond for 6.3 million paper roubles on the 17th/29th of December 1871, which enabled the line to be finished.

This was not the end of Strousberg's problems with this project: the quality of the rails was queried: during trial runs when the line was almost complete a large number fractured. Strousberg had made use of a general contractor, to construct the line but he had procured the rails himself (probably so that he could pocket a commission from the Belgian manufacturer) and so he was liable. The government insisted that the rails be replaced, which Strousberg later complained had cost him a fortune. The line finally opened on the 23rd of July 1873, but the final accounts for construction were not settled until 1874; Strousberg did actually make some money from the venture.

Conclusions

Strousberg's activities were without any doubt important in the Prussian context as they marked the first successful use of private capital for railway construction after a seven year period of stagnation.

The new lines were of great importance for the areas which they served. This was particularly true for rural East Prussia which had been, economically, quite underdeveloped. At the same time, the new railways were not the financial success which had been hoped for.

The Tilsit-Insterburg Railway would remain a purely local railway as long as it ended at Tilsit and did not extend to the port city of Memel. This meant building an expensive bridge over the Memel river, and as no private investors could be found, the line did not reach Memel until 1875, financed by the Prussian state.

The East Prussian Südbahn was in a better situation, but it needed its extension to Russia. In turn this required the line from Brest to Grajewo to be finished, and this was to take until 1873.

The ordinary share holders of both lines did not get a dividend for years, but at least from 1873 on the East Prussian Südbahn's priority shareholders got the 5% forecast in the company articles while the average rate of return for the Tilsit-Insterburg line was just 2.5%.

5. THE BERLIN-GÖRLITZ RAILWAY

Origins

To start with this was planned to be part of a direct railway route between Berlin and Vienna, which would run via Görlitz to the Austrian border at Reichenberg (now Liberec in the Czech Republic) avoiding the small Kingdom of Saxony. However a state treaty between Austria and Saxony expressly prohibited a railway between Austria and Prussia which did not go through Saxony and so it was initially only possible to think of a railway from Berlin to Görlitz, with a possible extension to the coalfields in the Waldenburger Bergland. There was interest in this shorter line partly because it was 45 kilometres shorter than the existing route from Berlin to Görlitz via the state-owned *Niederschlesisch-Märkische Bahn*. Two attempts to build the line, in 1856 and 1858, had already failed.

Finance and construction

The project was only revived when Strousberg and his British financial backers were persuaded to become involved. On the 18th of May 1864 the government granted a concession to the new *Berlin-Görlitzer Eisenbahn-Gesellschaft* [Berlin and Görlitz Railway Company] for the construction of a line from Berlin via Cottbus to Görlitz, with an authorised capital of 5 million Thaler.

The project used the same model as the lines in East Prussia: a general contractor who had to 'deliver' a complete railway and was paid in shares, with the British investors guaranteeing (but not actually paying) the share capital. The management team was the same too: Joseph Bray as the general contractor, George Barclay Bruce as engineering consultant, a finance committee made up of the British investors with Strousberg as their authorised representative and an audit committee with regional interested parties such as the mayors of Görlitz and Cottbus, landowners, as well as Strousberg.

Amongst the principal investors were Prince Frederick of the Netherlands (400,000 Thaler), the Prussian Royal Household (100,000 Thaler), the towns of Görlitz and Cottbus (400,000 and 200,000 Thaler respectively) and the Cottbus district council. Prince Frederick was a major landowner in the area.

Strousberg takes over construction

Bray began work on the line in 1865, but at the end of the year he had to resign his position as general contractor. Strousberg took over his duties. According to Strousberg the audit committee had pressurised Bray to resign as the share were only being taken up in dribs and drabs and the committee was worried that money to complete construction quickly would not be forthcoming. According to Westphal, the technical inspector, it was *Strousberg* who had pressurised Bray: but however it came about, Strousberg took over Bray's role as general contractor. There was a difference of opinion about the costs which had been incurred, but according to Strousberg, he agreed to forego between 600,000 and 800,000 Thaler which he had given to Bray and even promised Bray some compensation. Bray had "earned the amount advanced to him" in his role as general contractor. For Bray having to give up work on both lines was certainly a disappointment, but it must also have been a relief, if Strousberg's estimate of Bray's losses at three million Thaler is anything like accurate. Any strain which this caused to their relationship was only short term. A few years later, Bray's daughter Jossie and Strousberg's younger son Arthur were to marry, and when Strousberg returned near penniless from his arrest in Moscow Bray and Bruce were more than generous in their support.

According to his autobiography, Strousberg had serious doubts about becoming the general contractor, foreseeing "Trouble, danger and probable loss," but nonetheless "gave way to the general wish [of the shareholders]," and added as an acknowledgement that he had become used to giving the orders:

> "With my character, it was not easy to take orders instead of giving them, as I had to hand my power of attorney for the finance committee to Assessor Philippi, the technical experts became my bosses and I went pale at the problems that I foresaw."

Changes and extra expense

Alterations to the project, which the contractor was bound to deliver at a fixed price, must have caused headaches. And there were plenty of expensive changes. The line had to be diverted which made it longer, the authorities in Berlin required the station to be three metres higher, underpasses had to provided for the embankments, the bridge over the *Landwehr* canal in Berlin had to give more than three metres clearance for shipping and so on: all things which had not been allowed for during planning and therefore were not included in the original budget. It was later worked out that these 'extras' came to 946,000 Thaler.

In addition to this, German share prices were depressed in 1866 because of the war with Austria, and Strousberg had to bear the risk. One share depot had incurred a loss of 420,000 Thaler which, Strousberg said, could have been avoided if they had sold – at a profit – when he advised.

However Strousberg did not have to bear these losses as they were assumed by the Berlin-Görlitz Railway Company which had to issue a bond for 850,000 Thaler in 1867 in order to cover them.

Then there was another thing, which Strousberg simply had to accept: Count Roon, the war minister, called Strousberg to his office and remarked that in view of the military tension with and probable war with Austria the line's early completion as far as Cottbus was desirable. This would of course mean extra costs, but (unsurprisingly) the minister did not have any funds on hand to cover them; he would leave it up to Strousberg's patriotism to do the best he could. Strousberg did his best and in June 1866 the line was available for military use — which was never in fact neccessary as the war only lasted a few weeks. The minister never even thanked Strousberg for his efforts.

Strousberg later spoke of an overall loss of around 1 million Thaler for the construction of the Berlin-Görlitz railway, a sum disputed by Inspector Westphal as Strousberg and Bray had made 700,000 Thaler each from the line's construction.

The Görlitzer Bahnhof

At the end of 1867 the whole line to Görlitz, 208 km, was finished. One of the line's major works was the *Görlitzer Bahnhof* in Berlin, built between 1866 and the beginning of 1868. Designed by the well-known Berlin architect August Orth, it was meant to be the terminus for the planned route to Vienna and was accordingly grand. The station hall was, at 148 × 37 metres, unusually large for the time and set a standard for later railway stations in Berlin.

The reception building of the Görlitzer Bahnhof in Berlin, 1872

The station building was badly damaged during the Second World War. It was located in the Kreuzberg district, part of the American sector of Berlin. This isolated it from the rest of the line which now lay in the communist East Germany. It saw its last passenger train in 1951, being completely torn down in 1962.

Strousberg loses control of the Company

When Strousberg gave up his position as general manager, he rejoined the administrative committee. Together with its chairman, the Mayor of Görlitz, Richtsteig, he remained the most influential figure in the company. During this period the company gained concessions for, and built, several branch lines: Weisswasser-Muskau, Lübbenau to Camenz and Dresden, and finally Görlitz to Zittau (in Saxony) and via Prussian territory towards Reichenberg on the Austrian border.

On October the 1st 1871, Richtsteig was due to move to the main board and Strousberg was due to succeed him as chairman of the administrative committee. However, this was actively opposed by the Disconto-Gesellschaft, a powerful Berlin bank. It bought up Berlin and Görlitz Railway shares with the declared aim of removing "Dr. Strousbeg and his lackeys." The Disconto-Gesellschaft forced their representatives on to the administrative committee and one of them (Wilkens), not Strousberg became chairman. Strousberg remained a member and was reelected the following year, but the Disconto-Gesellschaft was now in control.

Strousberg was bitter about the bank's behaviour. At the same time Strousberg lost his chairmanship of the neighbouring Halle-Sorau-Guben Railway's administrative committee when five members loyal to the Disconto-Gesellschaft joined it. He could not see a way of fighting back because at the time "I had become unpopular due to the situation in Romania." The Disconto-Gesellschaft's interest in Strousberg's railways was obvious, as was their wish to get rid of him. The question remains of whether this could be justified by Strousberg's somewhat dubious business practices and lack of administrative capability or whether this was just a normal business power struggle.

Even if Strousberg had lost his powerful position of influence with the company he was still regarded positively, especially by those who had profited from his railways.

6. OTHER LINES IN PRUSSIA

A glance at a map of Prussia shows that the four lines examined here run roughly from east to west. This was not part of a grand plan. Each line had been thought of independently from the others. The inter-regional importance of the lines was obvious though, not least to the trade ministry. The ministry thought that extending the Märkisch-Posener and Halle-Sorau-Guben lines would logically lead to their routes converging at Guben station. In an easterly direction from Guben[1] there was the possibility of a connection from Posen (now Poznan in Poland) to East Prussia and further to St. Petersburg and Russia.

From Sorau (now Żary in Poland) a connection to Breslau (now Wrocław in Poland) existed (using an existing route) which could in turn link up with the line on the right bank of the Oder [the *Rechte Oder-Ufer-Bahn*] which in turn reached the Upper Silesia industrial region and made a connection with the Austrian *Kaiser-Ferdinands-Nordbahn* possible.

From Halle there was a connection westward to Kassel, the Rhineland and, eventually, France. Also from Halle there was the possibility of a route to the Ruhr, via Magdeburg, Braunschweig and Hanover (incorporating the Hanover and Altenbeken Railway).

The Rechte Oder-Ufer-Bahn

Since the 1840s, the Upper Silesian Railway [*Oberschlesische Bahn*] had connected Breslau to the Upper Silesian industrial area. It had been built with private finance but had been under under state control since 1856. Since 1858 there had been a privately owned and operated line from Oppeln to Tarnowitz. Just 76 km long, this was an oddity as it neither reached westwards to Breslau nor eastwards to the industrial area. The idea was for the new *Rechte Oder-Ufer-Bahn* to fix this shortcoming.

The new line, constructed between 1865 and 1870 and which—as its name implies—largely followed the right bank of the Oder river, drove a new transport route into the heart of the Upper Silesian mining region, its branches reaching straight to the pits and mines. Unsurprisingly the railway's main backers were the region's coal and iron ore magnates including the Dukes of Ujest and of Ratibor.

The new line brought new prosperity to many of the towns on its route. For example the small town of Kreuzberg (now Kluczbork in Poland) enjoyed a mini-boom in 1868. Grammar school teacher Jacob Oeri wrote to his uncle Jacob Burckhardt in Basel that the town

---

[1] Since 1945 the former municipality of Guben has been divided. The area east of the river Neisse including the old town is now Polish territory and known as Gubin.

"... thanks to the initiative of a Jewish entrepreneur has been connected to the railway network and has been developed to an important junction where several main lines cross ... The place where I'm living has intentions of becoming a big town ... In three weeks the *Rechte Oder-Ufer-Bahn* should be open at last ... There should be some major celebrations here then."

Strousberg was the general contractor for the line's construction, although he did not think he had earned much from it. But the railway was profitable as soon as it opened for traffic in 1870. With an average dividend to shareholders of between 6.5% and 7% it was the most profitable railway with which Strousberg was involved. In 1882, when the Prussian government took it over, along with other privately owned railways, they paid 185% of the shares' face value in compensation; a nice profit for those who had bought shares at less than face value.

Märkisch-Posener Bahn

The initial idea of building this line came from Duke Karl-Anton von Hohenzollern-Sigmaringen, who owned large areas of land east of Frankfurt/Oder and Guben. His estates were managed by a man called Ambronn, who was also a government financial advisor. Ambronn represented the Duke in the initial committee which founded the Märkisch-Posener Railway Company and later its management board.

Again, Strousberg constructed the line (with a length of 272 km) and, again, he said that he had lost a fortune because he could only place the shares at a very low price. The construction, between the end of 1867 and the middle of 1870, went smoothly, although arguments with the authorities about the building of bridges, stations and earthworks in Posen and Frankfurt/Oder caused delays.

Halle-Sorau-Guben

The line from Halle via Sorau to Guben had a difficult background. The older Magdeburg and Leipzig Railway had already obtained provisional clearance to construct this line in the early 1860s, but did not proceed because they feared it would bankrupt them. After years of argument, the concession passed to a committee lead by the Duke of Ujest. Among its members were seven Belgian financiers who wanted to provide the finance; initially Strousberg was not involved.

The concession granted in April 1868 was for a 271 km line from Halle to Cottbus, with a fork to Sorau and another to Guben; in 1872 a branch from Eilenburg to Leipzig was added. The concession was there, but work could not start as the Belgians could not raise enough money, not even the customary 400 000 Thaler deposit.

An urgent plea for help was telegraphed to Strousberg, who took over the construction. The attempt to replace Strousberg as general contractor and financier had not worked. There seemed to be no viable alternative to his "system". When the Belgians pulled out even the banks were not prepared to finance the project.

The Trade Ministry had forbidden the use of the previous model and so the contract was modified. Strousberg still had to deliver the completed railway and was still to be paid in shares, but not in one go for everything, rather in stages as work was completed, at contractually agreed rates.

Strousberg could only sell a fraction of the shares. He was left with most of them. Strousberg now did something extraordinary: he bought Halle-Sorau-Guben shares on the open market, some of them at levels way above that at which he had originally disposed of them. He placed some of these shares in a portfolio administered by the Bankhaus Jacques in Berlin, firstly in order to get at his money from the Romanian railway bonds which was lying there (an extremely problematic action which would play a very negative part in the story of the Romanian Railways). Secondly, by being a major shareholder he wanted to gain decisive influence on the Halle-Sorau-Guben Railway Company.

There had been efforts to merge the Halle-Sorau-Guben Railway with the Märkisch-Posen Railway and the Berlin-Görlitz Railway; corresponding resolutions had been passed at all three company annual general meetings in 1869 but the Trade Ministry refused to authorise the mergers.

Shortly after the planned merger came to nothing, Strousberg gave up his building contract so that he could join the management committee. As the largest shareholder he took over the chairmanship, but had to resign it in September 1871 due to the actions of the Disconto-Gesellschaft bank which was behaving here like it had with the Berlin and Görlitz Railway. As a mere committee member Strousberg did not have much influence on the company; so much for his large shareholding.

The line was never profitable and it was taken into State administration in 1877.

Hanover-Altenbeken

This line was planned to help integrate the state of Hanover (previously independent) into the Prussian "family": its main line from Hanover to Altenbeken was to provide a link to the Ruhr industrial region, a total length of 287 km.

The main instigators of this line included some of Hanover's most prominent figures: the Duke of Münster, the land-owning liberal nationalist politician Rudolf von Bennigsen and E. F. Adickes, another land owner.

They were granted the concession in 1868 and they would, with Adickes as chairman, dominate the management committee, of which Strousberg was never a member.

The construction contract was initially held by a Hanover businessman, Albert Cohen, however (as agreed beforehand) the contract was reassigned to Strousberg before work started. The terms were as for the Halle-Sorau-Guben line; that is deliver of the complete railway with payment in shares, but not just as a lump sum. Payment was to be per finished stage, at the rates laid down in the scheme approved by the *Eisenbahnamt*. The risk due to the share price again lay with the contractor, i.e. Strousberg, who complained about the poor rate at which he was able to dispose of the ordinary shares.

Construction began in 1869 but was soon delayed when, in the middle of 1870, the Franco-Prussian War broke out. Railway staff and building workers were called up, and the Army needed the railways for transporting troops and military supplies; they were hardly available for civilian users. The delays caused by the war and numerous changes to the route caused a major escalation in building costs. Especially around Hanover, land prices increased as well which affected the branch connecting with Strousberg's locomotive works in the Linden district (astonishingly, a locomotive works had become successful with no connection to a railway). These increases in cost had not been foreseen and there was a substantial shortfall in available caputal. During construction, costs more than tripled to nearly 3½ million Thaler.

The main line from Hanover to Altenbeken was ready by 1872, but Strousberg had to stop work on the branch from Löhne to Vienenburg in September 1873, before it was complete. He had run out of money, having sold all of the shares he had received in payment. The company refused to make him further cash payments and Strousberg did not have any resources of his own available to make up the difference, as his liquidity was stretched to the limit at that time due to his involvement with the Romanian railways.

So the contract was terminated "by mutual agreement" on September 15th 1873 and the line was finished by the company, using the money they had withheld from Strousberg.

There was another reason for Strousberg's withdrawal: the neighbouring Magdeburg-Halberstadt Railway owned the line from Halle to Vienenburg and wanted to expand, via Hanover, towards Westphalia; to do this it planned to merge with the Hanover-Altenbeken Railway. These plans were backed by the Disconto-Gesellschaft bank.

They came to an arrangement: the Disconto-Gesellschaft and the Magdeburg-Halberstadt Railway became participants in Strousberg's general construction contract and, as a sweetener, let Strousberg have access to funds. However, another unfortunate situation resulted. When his contract was terminated in September 1873 the Hanover-Altenbeken Railway refused to settle the final account saying that the incomplete section had to be finished by the new contractors before Strousberg would be paid. Worse, there were still unsettled accounts arising from the arrangement described above with the Magdeburg-Halberstadt Railway.

Strousberg took the Hanover-Altenbeken Railway to court, demanding payment of five million Marks, and the response was a counter claim for ten million. The case went on and on. It was still ongoing when Strousberg went bust at the end of 1875. In 1880 Strousberg's claim was turned down but the High Court reserved judgement and Strousberg's assets stayed frozen; the case went on. In 1885, a year after Strousberg's death, his daughters appealed to the king to at least release the deposit of 100,000 Thaler which Strousberg had been required to make before work on the Hanover-Altenbeken Railway began. On the advice of the Commissioner of Railways, Maybach, the appeal was declined as proceedings was still ongoing. In 1901, 17 years after Strousberg's death, the case was still unresolved.

Strousberg described his plans to use mergers and connecting lines to close the gaps in his network, but they never came to anything. However important the Prussian railway projects were in the context of Strousberg's entrepreneurial career, he was himself not satisfied. In his autobiography he wrote

> "That I left my work incomplete was caused by the accursed witch hunt pursued against me; things today would have been very different if they had not brought me down."

7. VERTICAL INTEGRATION

Strousberg's big idea

After Bray had resigned the position of general contractor to the Berlin-Görlitz Railway, Strousberg took on the task. He had seen how Bray had tried—and failed—to even out the losses arising from share price fluctuations. Bray was a very experienced civil engineering contractor and if he had not been able to make the necessary savings by economical construction then Strousberg would have to come up with something really good.

Conditions relating to the building of railways in Prussia had been altered fundamentally by the construction of the lines in East Prussia and from Berlin to Görlitz. Previously construction had been in dire straits, Strousberg had shown that it was quite possible to live with, even to profit from, the restrictive 1838 law[1]. In those areas where railway plans had previously come to nothing, he was the man of the moment.

Railway business came to him. Strousberg was in such demand that he could assume two, three or four more projects would be waiting once the Berlin to Görlitz line was finished. This gave him the advantage of being able to afford a permanent staff of experts who were experienced in all areas of railway construction. A newly-established railway company would have to find and recruit these people, whereas if Strousberg took on a new project they would be available immediately. In addition, Strousberg could make use of his skilled workforce more efficiently if he was managing several construction projects at once.

Strousberg's purchasing policy

"Purchasing's where the money's made" is an old business saying and one which Strousberg obviously subscribed to.

> "I got binding offers from the various works, for a sizeable quantity, with delivery over the course of three to four years in equal monthly stages. None of the works knew how big my requirements really were and so none of them asked much more than the going rate that day... as things were quiet at that time, the prices were low... I accepted all the offers".

Strousberg's purchasing policy covered his anticipated requirements for several years ahead. He negotiated – discreetly – with railway equipment suppliers, hauliers and shipping firms. If it had become known just how much Strousberg was ordering, the price would have gone up straight away and none of the suppliers would have agreed to long term fixed price contracts. Such was the secrecy that no one supplier knew of the others.

---

[1] *The Gesetz über die Eisenbahn-Unternehmungen.*

Just as Strousberg expected, conditions in the railway business heated up and the prices for material, transport and other services shot up year after year. He could now reap the rewards of his long-term planning. The higher price were now the current market prices, the ones used in the railway companies' plans which would be automatically approved by the trade ministry. The amount paid to Strousberg increased accordingly, and so did his profits, as his materiel had been bought at much lower prices fixed years beforehand.

Strousberg gives us one example: in 1871 he bought 500,000 hundredweight of rails for an average of 3 Thaler, but only used them later when the price was between 5 and 6 Thaler. The saving of nearly 1½ million Thaler went into his pocket.

Acquisition of land presented similar opportunities. When it came to building the *Görlitzer Bahnhof* in Berlin, Strousberg bought the likely site and (to hide what he was up to) a lot of other property before the official go-ahead; if he had waited, no doubt the price would have been very much higher. The result was that he'd got the land he needed more cheaply and he was able to sell the surplus property at a profit.

Because of his advance purchasing policy, Strousberg was able to buy materiel, transportation and other services as well as acquire land at lower cost, but that wasn't enough for him.

Vertical integration

Strousberg had found, again and again, how much he was dependent on his suppliers. He had to make part or sometimes even full payment before delivery and accept other irritating conditions. He particularly objected to the behaviour of August Borsig, the owner of the Borsig engineering and locomotive works in Berlin.

Strousberg had ordered thirty locomotives from Borsig for the Berlin-Görlitz line and agreed to make payment in stages: one third on placing the order, one third during manufacture and the final third on delivery. However, Borsig delivered the locomotives without their regulators (which meant that they could not be put into traffic). Borsig demanded that Strousberg pay the balance before they fitted the regulators. This was contrary to the agreement as Borsig had not delivered the locomotives complete and in working order. Strousberg wrote.

> "This abuse annoyed me to the extreme. It brought the idea that by purchasing or founding factories I could, to a certain extent, make myself independent of the market."

He also said

"At that time, one was obliged to use Borsig, and as I had decided to never order anything from them again, there was nothing left but to start a locomotive factory myself."

Strousberg then asked himself why stop at locomotives? Why not make the other items which he had to buy as general contractor? Why stop there? He could smelt the steel in his own blast furnaces, supplied with coal and iron ore from his own mines.

And he did just that. Just over three years later he owned and operated foundries, mines, steelworks and rolling mills, engineering factories and plants for making rails, wagons and locomotives: a complete, vertically integrated industrial chain, from raw material to finished product.

"... it was my intention to make the entirety so complete, that, although the individual branches would be administered separately, they would all be dependent on one another and make everything up to the finished product," he later wrote.

This was a completely new idea for Germany at the time of Strousberg. It brought him multiple advantages. Obviously, he didn't plan to meet all of his requirements – that would have been unrealistic – but it did allow him to use items of his own manufacture if there was a shortage of that item on the market. He also gained valuable insider knowledge to use in negotiations with other suppliers: no one could deceive him about the true manufacturing costs if he owned a works making the same item. As he said,

"In order to be able to decide whether or not the prices demanded are justified ... it is absolutely necessary to be close to that industry."

He also discovered that because of his reliability as a business partner his subcontractors would work for him between 20% and 24% more cheaply than for other companies or even governments.

Materiel or railway components from Strousberg's own works were obviously less expensive than if they had been bought in from other manufacturers. The quality was the same, but obviously the extra mark-up charged by the ore and coal suppliers, the steel maker and the engineering or locomotive works dropped out of the equation. These interim profits wound up in Strousberg's pocket, rather than the savings being passed on.

These savings, together with his long-term purchasing policy, made it possible for Strousberg to make large profits in the short term, despite huge losses on the sale of shares. Strousberg said that in many months the difference between income and expenditure was over a million Thaler in his favour, and even if that was not all profit he could sill use it to buy and construct profit-making objects.

Paying Strousberg in shares also had another, probably unforeseen, effect. As construction work progressed, he became the owner of more and more shares – with their associated voting rights – although this was usually if he could not place the shares on the market at a favourable rate. Bethel Henry Strousberg had come up with a revolutionary idea, but it was so revolutionary that his contemporaries did not grasp its importance and thought that he was "the man who buys everything".

8. THE IDEA BECOMES REALITY

The 1868 acquisitions

Central to Strousberg's concept were his acquisitions in 1868: "The first factories which I bought were the Dortmunder Hütte [Dortmund Iron Works] and the Egestorff Machine Factory; all of my later acquisitions were meant to compete these plants."

The Dortmunder Hütte Iron Works

The Dortmunder Hütte, established in the 1850s, belonged to Gustav Arndt & Co and had both puddle and rolling mills. It produced rails and heavy castings, so it was an ideal target for Strousberg. Selling up suited Arndt, who wanted to retire. By September 1868 Strousberg owned all of the shares and Arndt retired in October 1869 when the firm adopted the trading name of *Dr. Strousberg Dortmunder Hütte*."

Strousberg's purchase of the iron works caused considerable excitement in industrial circles. As the biggest customer for iron and steel at that time, it was expected that he would burst the bubble of complacency which surrounded the established iron and steel industry in Dortmund. It was obviously in his interest to produce iron and steel more cheaply than importing it from Britain. Capacity would be increased to make more rails in Dortmund, and at the same time he was buying Egestorff's Machine Factory in Hanover, an important locomotive works.

Under Strousberg's ownership, the ironworks expanded and brought more jobs to Dortmund. In 1868, before he took over, the firm had 812 workers. By the end of 1869 the figure was 1300 and in mid-1870 it was about 1500. He had also built housing for his workers on an area of roughly 40 acres, for which 20 million bricks were ordered.

Strousberg worked energetically at expanding the works, but the financial difficulties caused by his involvement with the construction of the Romanian railways meant that he was forced to sell the Dortmunder Hütte in 1872. The purchaser was the Dortmunder Union company (formally, the *Union, AG für Bergbau, Eisen- und Stahl-Industrie*) which paid 6 million Thaler for the iron and steel works, collieries and several iron-ore mines. They could be well satisfied with the improvements Strousbeg had made. Contemporary press reports spoke of the increased production made possible by the new puddling plant, of the important welding and rolling mill, the wagon and locomotive wheel factory which was renowned as a model for its type, the bridge construction works (overwhelmed with orders), the coking plant with 100 ovens and the work in progress on building the Bessemer converters. All were hailed as part of a grand plan, but Strousberg was not mentioned, leaving the casual reader with the impression that they were the Dortmunder Union's idea. This conveniently ignored the fact that the improvements were all in hand with some complete even *before* the sale.

The "Glückauf" Colliery

About three years after buying the Dortmunder Hütte iron works, Strousberg acquired the nearby Glückauf colliery, a deep mine which produced high grade coal. Strousberg bought the colliery, which had existed since 1769, in his wife's name for 1,750,000 Thaler.

The colliery could supply the coking plant at Dortmund, already enlarged to send coke to the new blast furnaces which Strousbeg had built at Othfresen.

As always happened when Strousberg became involved, the mine became a hive of activity. Annual production went up in the first year under his control from 750,000 tonnes to over a million tonnes, worth about 4 million Thaler, and the number of employees rose from about 800 to over 1000.

When Strousberg sold the Dortmunder Hütte, both the colliery and the blast furnaces in Othfresen were sold as well. The Glückauf colliery accounted for 2 million of the 6 million Thaler total.

The Hannover Machine Factory

The Hannover machine factory was Strousberg's second important acquisition, after the Dortmunder Hütte ironworks. The factory initially belonged to the Egestorff family; in 1835 Georg Egestorff started an iron foundry and engineering works which had built locomotives since 1846, 169 in total before Egestorff died in 1868. The family did not want to carry on the business and soon found a willing buyer in the form of Strousberg.

It fitted neatly into his grand scheme and, after a quick look round, he snapped it up for 700,000 Thaler in October 1868. Immediately afterwards he bought 12 acres of nearby land for a further 24,000 Thaler – a clear sign of plans for expansion.

Strousberg, as a railway construction contractor, was mainly interested in the work's locomotive building potential. He planned to expand the capacity from around 50 to 250 locomotives per year and to increase the workforce from 85 to 2500. In keeping with Strousberg's character and dynamism he threw all his energies into carrying it through. This included improving the machinery in the factory and hiring skilled workers.

The factory did not belong to Strousberg for long. Early in 1871, with the expansion in full progress, he decided to sell the plant. His involvement in Romania was already stretching his liquidity to the extreme. Even so, he had largely met his target. In the 2½ years in which he owned the plant, 280 locomotives were delivered. 55 of then were produced the first year, 1869, but a capacity of 200 locomotives per year was achieved from 1870 onwards. This was made possible by the new assembly shop which was opened in autumn 1869. It was an impressive 133 metres long and 73 metres wide and the shed roofs rested on 296 columns. Overhead cranes and transporters meant that 36 locomotives and 24 tenders could be assembled at the same time: a sort of assembly line, – nearly 40 years before Henry Ford.

The works now had 16 static steam engines, providing power for 800 lathes, milling machines, drills and other tools. The workforce had grown from 850 to 3200 blue collar workers and 250 office staff.

Further expansion continued according to Strousberg's plans after he sold the firm, being finished in 1874.

Borsig, the Berlin locomotive builder who had annoyed Strousberg so much, was in for a nasty shock. Previously Germany's largest locomotive manufacturers, they were rapidly overtaken by Strousberg. In 1862 the Borsig works turned out 162 locomotives reaching a peak of 181 in 1874. Between the middle of 1871 and the middle of 1874 the Hanover works delivered 613 locomotives whereas Borsig only managed 497.

This was a result of the two firms' different structures. Borsig was 'just' a locomotive manufacturer, but Strousberg was also the biggest single customer for railway locomotives in Germany at that time. Between 1865 and 1875, German railway companies ordered 793 locomotives of which more than half – 422 – were for lines built or controlled by Strousberg. His foreign projects were important too. At the beginning of 1870 the Hannover factory had 107 orders for German lines on its books, and another 158 from those countries in which Strousberg was then constructing railways.

Romania was the dominant source of foreign orders. So much so, that the works and its employees became identified with that country. Strousberg built a housing estate for his workers and it was soon nicknamed "*Klein-Rumänien*" ["Little Romania"], a name which stuck until the estate was demolished in 1937.

Provision of housing for his workers was part of Strousberg's business strategy. True, he looked after his directors tool, but the emphasis was on the houses which he built for the workers.

The rapid expansion of the works would have been impossible without an equally rapid expansion of the workforce. Skilled workers were, as ever, hard to find. Strousberg remarked that "they had to be brought together from all over the kingdom." It would obviously be easier to recruit people if he could offer them housing as well.

The model village which was built near the factory, on 31,500 sq m in the Linden area, consisted of 143 terraced houses for one or two families, each with a small yard or a garden. Streets were named "in honour of work"; there was a *Zirkelstrasse* (Compass Street), *Hammerstrasse* (Hammer Street), *Feilenstrasse* (File Street), and *Ambossstrasse* (Anvil Street), crossed by *Brunnenstrasse* (Well Street). The complex was ready for its first residents in mid-1869.

228 families and 700 to 800 single men, about 2000 people in all, could be accommodated. Full use of the living space was ensured by an ingenious system: the tenant of a house was obliged to sublet the attic space to between 2 and 7 single workers as lodgers, and their rents offset the tenant's rent. Admittedly, this meant that the houses were crowded, but they were by no means slums.

"The workers were happy," said Strousberg, and he had reason to pleased too. The housing guaranteed him the loyal workforce he needed. Occupancy of housing in the estate was limited to those who worked for the firm, or to put it another way anyone who quit had to move out. This obviously fitted into Strousberg's self-image of himself as a patriarchal figure for his workers. But it would not be fair to say that he only built the works housing to make the workers more dependent. Strousberg was no class warrior. For him, it was simply a way of recruiting and retaining staff.

One of Strousberg's decisions would have been genuinely popular with his workers: the reduction of the working hours from eleven to ten per day. This really was radical and even attracted the attention of Friedrich Engels. On September 5th 1869 he wrote to Karl Marx:

"Strousberg is undoubtedly the greatest man in Germany. The fellow will be the Kaiser next. Everywhere one goes to, everyone is talking only of Strousberg. Actually, the chap is not so awful. My brother, who has had negotiations with him, described him to me in lively terms. He has a lot of humour and some genial traits and is head and shoulders above the [British] "Railway King" Hudson. At the moment he is buying up all kinds of industrial establishments and immediately cutting the working day to ten hours, without reducing wages. He obviously is quite clear that he will end up as a pauper. His main principal is to only cheat shareholders and on the other hand to be quite fair with suppliers and others in industry."

When Strousberg decided to sell the works, they were taken over (in March 1871) by the newly-formed "*Hannoversche Maschinenbau-Aktien-Gesellschaft*" [Hanover Machine Building Company Ltd.], better known later as Hanomag. The new company was owned by a group of Hanover banks.

Strousberg received 3 million Thaler in payment for the fixed assets (the works, land, machinery and workers' housing) as well as an estimated 1 million Thaler for stock and work in progress. Strousberg had originally paid 700,000 Thaler to the Egestorff family but he had invested a huge amount in works in the interim. The new company was very profitable for the next two years, paying dividends of 8% and 10% respectively; much of this was due to orders from Strousberg's railways, but then came the difficult years of recession after 1873.

The Neustadt Ironworks (Neustädter Hütte)

Neustadt am Rübenberge was a small country town about 25 kilometres northwest of Hanover. In 1860 its population was about 2000 and its main 'resource' was a huge area of peat deposits. This peat, it was planned, would be the main source of energy for the ironworks. Iron ore would come from Haverlahwiese near Salzgitter. A company to operate the ironworks was set up in 1856, but peat turned out not to be a suitable fuel for iron production—it does not burn hot enough and generates too much ash—and in 1858/59 the works went bust. The creditors eventually sold it in the middle of 1869 to Strousberg for just 200,000 Thaler.

Strousberg awoke the dormant works without delay. He increased the workforce to over 400 and doubled output within two years. As shown by the amount of coal and coke consumed, peat was hardly used as fuel any more. The iron works owned several iron ore mines. The largest, at Haverlahwiese near Salzgitter, was described in an expert report as "inexhaustible", and it operated until 1982.

Just as in Hanover, skilled workers were needed. To attract them, Strousberg built works housing. In 1870 houses were built for 24 families and in 1871 for 32 families. In 1875, 100 houses were being built with 60 expected to be finished by the summer.

The Neustadt Ironworks, uniquely, had a Catholic chapel to serve the increasing number of skilled workers from the Catholic areas of the Rhine, Westphalia and Silesia who had moved to the strongly Protestant area.

The Neustadt Ironworks was never of great importance, which makes Strousberg's socially oriented efforts noteworthy. He never behaved like a cold-blooded capitalist to his workers.

The works had been able to increase its output by 40% in 1872, but the economic slump in 1873 and 1874 almost forced it to close. However in 1875 the new "Siemens Regenerative Peat-Gas Firing Process" became available which made it viable to use peat as a fuel source[10]. Strousberg embraced the new process enthusiastically. The whole plant was converted from coal and coke to peat-gas, and manufacture of pig-iron in a blast furnace ceased. The rebuilding amounted practically to building a new plant on the same site.

---

[1] Peat gas is produced by the dry distillation of peat. It contains less energy than coal gas, and is an environmentally unfriendly fuel, being highly acidic. One tonne of peat produces about 200-280 m^3 of gas 250-300 kg of charcoal, 30 50 kg of tar and 150 to 280 kg of ammonium hydroxide. It needs as much as 70 kg of chalk per 100 m^3 of gas to purify it.

Strousberg had scarcely been able to commence operations at the rebuilt works when, in October 1875 he became insolvent. In September 1876 the Neustadt Ironworks were put up for auction. Years later, Strousberg did become the Neustadt Ironworks' owner once more.

The Othfresen Blast Furnaces

The Othfresen Blast Furnaces were the only industrial works which Strousberg built from scratch on a green field site. The location was chosen so that the iron ore reserves in the nearby North Harz could be exploited. Othfresen is a tiny village, part of Liebenburg, which is about 12 kilometres north of Goslar. It was once the site of an inn – the Posthof – on the old coach route.

Iron ore had been mined in the northern Harz region since early times. The ores mined here were rich in phosphor but had a low iron content, thus requiring a lot of processing before high quality iron could be extracted from them. Strousberg later said that "the ironstone extracted from the surface had too high a sulphur content and not enough iron content."

Strousberg planned to build the blast furnace plant at Othfresen in order to exploit these deposits and produce pig iron for the growing industrial area around Dortmund in particular.

The works had four blast furnaces, arranged in two towers, each with a pair of furnaces. Each of the 24 metre towers were equipped with lifts, used to charge the furnace with iron ore and coke. They were built, unusually for this type of plant, in what was known as "Windsor style", the same style as was used for the administration building at Neustadt. The works also included an engine house, boiler plant and foundry.

A 2.33 kilometres double track narrow gauge railway linked the works to the ore mine and a 7.55 kilometres standard gauge line ran from the works to Ringelheim, connecting with the railway to Braunschweig.

In total, the works needed over 43 hectares of land. Strousberg was able to purchase the land for the works itself from the two previous owners but the rest belonged to many individual owners and it took until 1871 to buy it all. Strousberg also bought – for 30,000 Thaler – the old Posthof inn to use as the works offices.

Construction began at the end of 1879, needing 300 workers. It was a challenge to find enough labour in the area, and at the same time a real boost for the local economy. Some housing was built near the Posthof; there is still a Strousberg-Strasse there today.

Strousberg bought four ore mines near Gross Döhren (Fortuna, Rothe Rose, Dorothea, Glückauf) and the Glücksborn site from the Salzgitter Ironworks Company for 250,000 Thaler in July 1869. Production began in 1870 and due to the nature of the reserves in that area, Strousberg also acquired four mines at Altenau near Goslar to produce red ironstone and brown manganese ironstone.

The blast furnace works was complete and operational in 1872, by which time Strousberg no longer owned it. He had been forced to sell it because of the situation in Romania. The price was 1 million Thaler for the works at Othfresen and the ore mines, 650,000 Thaler in cash and the rest to pay off mortgages.

The works only remained open until 1874 when, after the blast furnaces and iron ore mines had operated well during 1872 and 1873, the generally weak economic situation and in particular a fall in pig iron prices led to its closure.

Ore mines in the Siegerland

In his 1867 memoir, Strousberg only makes brief mention of

"a number of iron-ore workings in the Siegerland, which were one of the most valuable complexes in any area, and were calculated to produce fourteen thousand truckloads of ironstone for Bessemer iron per year."

Strousberg intended to use the ironstone, along with coal from the *"Glückauf Tiefbau"* colliery, in the new Bessemer converters[1] at his Dortmund plant. The steel from these would be used to make railway rails more cheaply than buying them in. The ironstone in the Siegerland, in contrast to the ore from the workings near Othfresen were almost free of phosphor which made it ideal for use in Bessemer converters.

Once again, his plans were overtaken by events, in Romania and the consequences of the Franco-Prussian war. The Bessemer converters in Dortmund were not even finished by the time that Strousberg had to sell the Dortmunder Hütte ironworks.

This did not mean that the ore workings in the Siegerland had been lying idle. In 1870 and 1871 four of them produced a total of 3,500 tonnes of iron ore. Admittedly that is trivial compared to the Fortuna workings at Othfresen which produced 20,000 tonnes in the same period.

Strousberg did not sell the Siegerland ore workings in 1871 and 1872. In 1875 they became part of his *"Aktiengesellschaft für deutsche und böhmische Eisen- und Stahl-Fabrikate"* ["Company for German and Bohemian Iron and Steel Products Ltd."]. The company articles listed 63 excavations in the Siegerland.

---

[1]The Bessemer process, invented by Henry Bessemer who took out a patent on the process in 1855, was the first inexpensive industrial process for the mass-production of steel from molten pig iron. The main point is that impurities are removed from the pig iron by oxidation with. Air is blown through the molten iron to achieve this. When oxidation is complete, the molten steel is poured into slabs for rolling.

During Strousberg's bankruptcy proceedings, the ore workings were sold off and changed hands several times before, except for the *"Bergmannslust"* and the *"Schmiedeberg"*, ending up as part of the Thyssen conglomerate.

The Altwasser colliery in the Waldenburger Bergland

In February 1870 bought the "Seegen-Gottes-Grube" ["God's Blessing Mine"] in Altwasser from its owners, the von Mutius family. Coal had been mined in the Waldenburger Bergland for centuries and was some of the best quality coking coal in Germany. The "Segen Gottes-Grube" had extensive reserves.

Strousberg claimed that he did not acquire the mine as part of his grand plan, but to help the owners over a crisis. Very noble, but rather doubtful as the von Mutius family were not closely involved with Strousberg. In general things were anything but rosy for the coal mines in the Waldenburger Revier mining region at this time; the *Segen Gottes-Grube* was no exception.

After several years of declining production and of increasing labour costs but no increase in the sales price, there was a bitter miners strike in 1869 which further cut output from 400,000 to 208,000 tonnes per year. At the beginning of December the mines owned by the von Mutius family threatened to sack all the strikers who did not return to work within three days. After several prominent politicians intervened, the strike came to an end on January 28th 1870.

Strousberg became the owner of the Altwasser mine just a few days later, and began to turn it round. In 1870 production increased to 834,000 tonnes. In 1871 and 1872 the local chamber of trade reported production of 592,000 and 1,116,000 tonnes but did not list Strousberg as the owner. He had sold it straight after the Franco-Prussian war to the industrialist Paul von Kulmiz.

Strousberg's contribution to the industrial revolution

The industrial revolution was the epoch making phenomenon of the 19th century. Britain had about fifty years' head start on Germany. Wars. The Napoleonic occupation, lack of capital and the lack of a colonial expansion had allowed Germany to fall behind British technology and industry. However, once it got going, Germany caught up fast.

Industrialisation required men with entrepreneurial spirit to organise, make decisions innovate and take on risk. In Germany, arguably the driving force and leading sector for industrialisation was the railway industry and the revolution which it brought in transportation.

German industrialists were able to follow British examples and this worked best if they hired British consultants to pass on their know how at first hand. This is exactly what Strousberg did.

Strousberg already had business acumen. He had lived in England for nearly two decades, and although he had not himself been an industrialist there. He had been a publisher of financial and economic magazines, writing most of the articles himself. He'd met many leading industrialists and government figures.

In raising capital for building his railways, he had been able to work out a 'system' whereby the financial backers did not actually need to pay any cash in themselves. They simply had to say that they were prepared to pay up if need be. Crazy, risky, maybe even reckless. But it worked. Without it, no concessions would have been granted and the lines would not have been built.

Strousberg did not have any idea how to actually build a railway when he started. So he hired two men who did: George Barclay Bruce for the engineering side and Joseph Bray for the construction.

The results of Strousberg's work as a railway promoter were obviously visible: 1700 kilometres of railways in Prussia, mostly in areas which were economically underdeveloped and where they formed a foundation for further growth. They might have had one or two problems, but the main point is that they were transporting people and goods safely.

9. PROPERTY, ESTATES AND A PALACE

Building and buying palaces and acquiring country estates can be seen as a manifestation of Strousberg's efforts to emancipate himself. This did not just mean being a proper citizen and not just another Jew; his ambitions stretched much further than that: even if his status as a wealthy self-made man was not enough to get him into the upper echelons of society, he would do his best to make it possible for his offspring.

Strousberg had spent his youth in Britain. Obviously, the impressions and experiences of that period stayed with him for the rest of his life. As an inquisitive journalist, he had studied the British class system at work. The landed gentry was the highest rank to which someone from outside the nobility could ascend. Owning land in the country and an impressive town house were the first requirements for this.

This is probably what Strousberg had in mind when he began to acquire unusually large amounts of land in the country shortly after his career took off. Soon, he could use the title *Rittergutsbesitzer* [roughly equivalent to the British Lord of the Manor] after his name and thus show he was above the bourgeoisie. However, it was not to last. His wealth was too sudden and anything but established and consolidated; it would all be gone in a few years.

Strousberg's Country Estates

In the years from 1864 to 1870 Strousberg bought almost 47,300 hectares of land, not including the former fiefdom of Zbirow in Bohemia. This figure includes the associated mills, yards and so on. Over 10,000 hectares were in the provinces of East Prussia or West Prussia. In East Prussia, the Preussisch Eylau District (about 50 kilometres south of Königsberg) included six Rittergüter (Gross Peisten, Egdeln, Sienken, Worienen, Wiecherts and Schwadtken) totalling 17,000 Morgen[1]. In West Prussia Strousberg owned two estates totalling 9000 Morgen, Lniannek and Mszanno, in the Schwetz District about 50 kilometres north of Thorn and a property consisting of three Rittergüter (Hohenfier, Krumfliess and Strassforth) in the Flatow District, 30 kilometres north east of Schneidemühl, another 14,000 Morgen.

More of the agricultural estates which Strousberg owned were in the province of Posen. One of these, the Rittergut Tarnowo in Posen District was in Mary Ann Strousberg's name. It ran to over 4,100 Morgen. There were several further estates in the province of Posen. In the Fraustadt District the Lissa estate comprised 10,000 Morgen and the Rittergüter Alt-Laube, Prieb-

---

[1] MORGEN WAS derived from the area of land which could be ploughed by one man with an ox. Confusingly, its size varied from area to area. In Prussia it was 2553 square metres until metrication in 1870. This fixed the Morgen at a quarter hectare or 2500 square metres.

isch and Neu Garthe added 9,200 Morgen. Also in Posen province, Strousberg owned the Rittergüter Womwellno with Klein-Antonin, Miruczin and Jaszkowo in Wiritz District, between Bromberg and Schneidemühl, over 8500 Morgen.

In the Lausitz area of Silesia, Strousberg owned the Rittergut Moholz (3,400 Morgen) and the Rittergüter Diepensee (2000 Morgen) and Dahlewitz (3,000 Morgen) in the Mark Brandenburg, south of Berlin.

The largest single property, at 108,000 Morgen even larger than Zbirow, was the Krasnosielce estate in Poland, some 80 kilometres west of Warsaw.

Strousberg's stated aim was to be able to leave an estate to each of his seven children, but clearly he exceeded this total, and when he went bankrupt the family only managed to hold on to Diepensee (with help from George Barclay Bruce, Bethel Henry junior's father-in-law).

How much did these purchases cost? That is difficult to say. Purchase prices are only known for a few properties, and the amount financed by mortgage debt is not known at all. Extrapolating from the known figures we come to around 38 million Mark.

Taken together, the purchases seem to have been extraordinarily irresponsible behaviour for a man who was so skilful at arranging business finance.

The Palace in the Wilhelmstrasse

The Palais Strousberg was built in 1867/68, designed by Berlin architect August Orth[1]. The plot was small for such a grandiose building with a frontage of just 40 metres to the Wilhelmstrasse and a depth of 50 metres.

Strousberg insisted, instead of the more restrained design suggested by Orth, on a facade with four mighty Corinthian columns crowned by a richly sculpted portico. Obviously this was to impress any visitor as they climbed up the steps to the main entrance between the two middle pillars.

The visitor to the *Palais* first entered a two-storey atrium lit from above. The room was clad in white marble, and with a red carpet. The chairs and sofas were upholstered in red velvet.

Turning to the left, one entered the large reception room and then a music room complete with a small stage. Beyond this was a boudoir for the lady of the house. At the heart of this floor was a large dining hall with places for about fifty guests, with heavy renaissance furniture; adjacent to this was the

---

[1] AUGUST ORTH was born in 1828 at Osterode in the Harz mountains. He studied architecture in Braunschweig, Berlin and Munich. From 1856 to 1863, when he opened his own practice, he was employed by various railway companies. He enjoyed a close relationship with Strousberg; apart from the Palais Strousberg (1867-1868) he also designed the railway bridges over the Landwehr canal in Berlin (1864-1866) Görlitzer Bahnof in Berlin (1866-1868) and renovations for the Schloss Zbirow in Bohemia (1870-1871) for him.

billiards room, though which one gained access to the picture gallery. This gallery, with about 200 paintings by contemporary German and French artists, was regarded at the time as the best private collection in Berlin.

To the right of the atrium, leading to Strousberg's private office were a small reception room, decorated with trophies and weapons like a hunting lodge, and a library with over three thousand volumes on two floors and lit through a skylight. The private office itself was wallpapered in green and furnished with light wood furniture with leather inserts. There was a large bureau type writing desk, a cupboard full of technical books and opposite the window side was a brown-red marble fireplace whose mantelpiece was decorated with family photographs.

There was a small quiet room adjacent to the study, which incredibly contained a four-poster bed, behind which stood a huge safe. According to one report, this was "big enough to hold all of the shares for the railways in Strousberg's empire and a mass of other stocks and bonds."

The family's private rooms were on the upper floor. The press also reported about them and even details about the Strousberg's marital bedroom. The whole room was characterised by the deep green of the coverings, wallpaper and curtains, reports said. The beds were in a curtained-off niche which was connected from both sides to the dressing rooms. Their elegance and luxuriousness were described in great detail, especially a chaise longue whose cushions disguised a bath tub.

Strousberg's bathroom was a thing to be wondered at. It had "deep, fiery red walls" and was "decorated with Pompeiian friezes," and the floor was white marble. Half of the room was taken up by a huge sunken bath "which is big enough to swim a couple of strokes in." Adjacent to this were a sauna, bathtub and shower.

Apart from the five guest rooms, the upper floor had bedrooms, a playroom and a schoolroom for Strousberg's five daughters (then aged 6—14) and accommodation for their nanny and governess. His two sons, aged 19 and 21 when the Palais came into use, had already left home. The household staff were accommodated in the basement and the attics.

Technically speaking, the Palais was bang up-to-date with gas lighting and central heating throughout. Amenities included a large conservatory, two fountains (one in the atrium, one in the courtyard), a grotto, an aquarium and a bowling lane. Behind the house were mews for a carriage and stalls for for four horses, a gift from the Prince of Romania. A carriage entrance to the Wilhelmstrasse meant that Strousberg could leave the Palais in regal style, driven in a coach and four.

Construction costs for the Palais, including its fittings, were about 900,000 Marks, excluding buying the plot. Strousberg had made his wealth obvious for all to see by building and fitting out his palace. Flaunting his prosperity seems to have been extraordinarily important to him.

One must also consider the palace's location in the Wilhelmstrasse, the political centre of the Kingdom of Prussia and then the new German Empire. The offices of the Prussian Minister-President, and later the Reichskanzler, were at Wilhelmstrasse 74. The Foreign Ministry and Bismarck's residence were at Wilhelmstrasse 76 on the same side of the street as the Palais Strousberg. On the opposite side were the *Palais Radziwill* (later to become the Chancellery) and the residence of the Duke of Ratibor.

Austrian Castle and Palace

In 1868 Strousberg bought the lordship of Zbirow in Bohemia for ten million Austrian Gulden. He extended the castle considerably, work being completed in 1870, the design work again being carried out by August Orth. Unfortunately, the completion of work coincided with the beginning of his financial difficulties, and he could not attend the celebrations. The Schloss Zbirow was now available to the family as a summer residence.

In May 1869 he also acquired another prestigious building, the Palais Rohan in the Vienna suburb of Jägerzeile for 400,000 Gulden. This purchase had a story behind it. Strousberg was going to receive the Prussian Order of the Crown, 3rd class (he had been awarded the 4th class in 1864) when doubts we expressed in government circles about Strousberg. He had just bought the estate in Zbirow, did he intend to stay in Prussia, or shift the focus of his activities to Austria? The Austrian government was reported as being very accommodating and "has already put the Palais Rohan at his disposal on very advantageous terms." Strousberg then reassured the authorities by letter on the 19th of March 1869 that he had no plans to move his residence away from Berlin and that his feelings of patriotism towards Prussia were as strong as ever. The Prussian honour was duly awarded, less than a week later, on the 24th of March.

A few weeks later he did buy the palace in Vienna. It is not known what his reasons were for acquiring it, or whether he ever lived there. At any rate, he no longer owned it when he became insolvent in 1875.

5 Grosvenor Place in Westminster

At the beginning of 1872 Strousberg rented 5 Grosvenor Place, near Hyde Park, in Westminster from the Earl of Grosvenor at an annual rent of £3000. This seemed at the time to confirm rumours that following the failure of the Romanian ventures, he wanted to leave Berlin with his family. There was even talk that he had tried to sell the palace in the Wilhelmstrasse.

5 Grosvenor Place had been built for Earl Grosvenor by the architect Thomas Cundy III in 1869/70 on a newly-acquired site. Built in French style,

it only had a narrow frontage of 15 metres on to Grosvenor Place. It went back 44 metres giving an area of 660 square metres. The building had three stories and boasted a ballroom clad in black marble and featured central heating and electricity. A two-storey stable block to the rear covered 900 square metres.

The Earl had intended to live there himself, but in 1869 he became the Marquess of Grosvenor on the death of his father and inherited his residence. Later, in 1874 he became the first Duke of Westminster.

Strousberg had the house furnished in 1872, but did not move in with his family until the beginning of 1873 when he left Berlin after being denounced in the Prussian parliament by Lasker. Just six weeks later he moved back to Berlin to attend to urgent business there. Shortly thereafter the general upheaval following the massive Vienna stock exchange crash (the *Gründerkrach* or Founders' Crash) meant that he was not able to live there ever again.

Strousberg probably went back to Berlin in mid-March 1873, as on the 22nd of March his brother Ferdinand applied (unsuccessfully) to the Grosvenor Estate's managers for permission to convert the mansion into a high class hotel or club. This leads to the conclusion that by then Strousberg had already decided that he would not be living there again.

At the beginning of 1876, after Strousberg had gone bankrupt, the rent remained unpaid and Strousberg was asked to end the lease. Through his lawyer, Strousberg tried to claim £5,000 back from the Estate for decoration work and alterations that he had carried out, but the reply was clear: "His Grace will not approve to the German decorations," and on the 29th of November 1876 the keys were returned to the Estate.

The new tenants were meant to be the Austrian Embassy, on an 80-year lease at £2,000 per annum, but they did not take it up. The tenant from Autumn 1877 on a 42-year lease at an initial rent of £2000 was brewery magnate Edward Cecil Guinness, later Lord Iveagh. He lived at 5 Grosvenor Place until his death in 1927.

Neidenburg

Strousberg never said anything about his relationship with his sisters who had remained in Neidenburg. However it would be wrong to say that he had forgotten about them when his career took off. He had purchased, from the daughter of his father's eldest brother, a lot of property there

> "consisting of numerous dwelling houses, storehouses, barns, about 500 morgen of land, the old Jewish churchyards, and a disused building which had served as the synagogue in the last century and the first half of the current one."

He intended these properties to be "used as a refuge for poor relatives."

Before this, as early as 1864, he had bought the place where his parents were buried and erected proper memorial tablets.

10. STROUSBERG - THE BERLINER

Strousberg's properties in Berlin

Strousberg owned a considerable amount of property in Berlin.

The first property which Strousberg bought in Berlin, in 1864, was not a building but a fairly large piece of undeveloped land, about four hectares, near the zoo.

Jägerstrasse 22 was bought, jointly with Joseph Bray, to use as offices. It was also the management office for the Berlin-Görlitz Railway.

The enlargement of the staff which Strousberg needed for his railways and other industries meant that more office space was needed. In 1867 Strousberg bought the impressive building at Unter den Linden 17/18, into which he moved his central office. At the height of his empire, this office employed almost 400 staff. As a consequence of the problems in Romania, Strousberg had to sell this building and move his offices to a less prestigious one in the Behrenstrasse, which he also had to let go a year later.

Without a doubt, the most prominent bit of real estate which Strousbergs bought was Wilhelmstrasse 70 which he bought in 1868 to build the *Palais Strousberg* on. In the same year he bought the undeveloped land in front of the Kottbuser Tor [Cottbus Gate] and in front of the Schönhauser Tor [Schönhaus Gate] but it is not clear why he bought them. In 1869 and 1870 he bought the site at Akkerstrasse and Brunnenstrasse on which the large livestock market was built. Also in 1869, Strousberg acquired Jägerstrasse 61a and the "Moritzhof" at Heydtstrasse close to the zoological park.

For a long time Strousberg and his family lived quite happily in large rented houses in the respectable Tiergarten area, at Lenneéstrasse 8 and Bellevuestrasse 9, until they were able to move into the Palais Strousberg at Wilhelmstrasse 70 in 1870. Once again "Romania" meant that he was not able to enjoy a lengthy period of residence there; he had to move out and moved into a villa at Tiergartenstrasse 29 which he purchased from his old business friend Rushing, but he obviously did not pay for it fully. In 1875 when he went bankrupt, Frau Rushing claimed 373,000 Marks in settlement of the purchase as a debt. When Strousberg went bankrupt, this was the only property in Berlin which he still owned.

Commercial assets in Berlin

The Berlin livestock market and market hall projects and Strousberg's venture into the fishing industry at Geestemünde have to be looked at together. Strousberg wanted Berlin to enjoy the same kind of quality of food supply as London did. The livestock market would supply good meat in the same way that Smithfield did for London, the Geestemünde fisheries would supply fresh fish and the market hall would sell it to Berliners. Strousberg admitted that it was not really his area but justified it by saying "but doing good, not making profit, was my only motive here."

The Berlin Livestock Market

The rapidly-growing city of Berlin had a sensitive problem in the supply of foodstuff for its population. Unlike most other large European cities, it did not have a modern livestock market and slaughterhouse complex. The city fathers were aware of the problem but could not decide whether to build a public facility or let a private firm do it.

Eventually they decided to let a private firm do it. A company, the "*Berliner Viehmarkt-Kommandit-Gesellschaft auf Aktien Sponholz & Co*" was formed with a capital of 1.1 million Thaler, and on the 2nd of June 1867 the Prussian Trade Ministry and the Berlin Police granted the company a concession to build and operate a livestock market and slaughterhouse. It was to be built on a 9 hectare public park in the Wedding district.

The man behind the project to start with was a Dr. Ebers and Strousberg was only involved as general contractor responsible for building the complex according to the architect's (August Orth) designs. Strousberg's interest was aroused because some railway work would be involved. To avoid having to drive cattle through the Berlin streets, the new livestock market would be connected to the nearby Berlin-Stettin Railway and the Berliner Verbindungsbahn by a goods branch.

Strousberg soon engaged himself more intensively. He bought up all the shares in the company and soon the complex became much bigger than the original company had planned. Strousberg already owned adjacent plots of land and the complex expanded to roughly 30 hectares.

The Berlin Assembly did not want to hand over a strip of the Humboldthain for the line. Strousberg solved this problem by offering them a piece of land twice as big in exchange, which they accepted.

The livestock market complex was not a simple shed. At its centre was the trading hall, 56 metres long and 12 metres wide. At its sides were offices for the inspectors. The building also had administration offices, rooms for the vets, a restaurant and even overnight accommodation. Four market halls for cattle and two for sheep, each almost 180 metres long and 22 metres wide, provided space to sell 3700 cattle and 6000 sheep and a smaller hall for calves. There was also capacity for 7200 pigs as well as stalls for 2800 cattle and 6000 sheep, as well as open pens which could be used in summer for a further 17000 sheep. This trading area was strictly separated from the neighbouring slaughterhouses. There were three platforms for bringing in livestock; 150 wagons at a time could be unloaded.

The livestock market was opened on the 1st of June 1870 with a grand ceremony, including a fireworks display and an open-air concert. On the same day a horse show opened with patrons including three privy counsellors, two Generals and – who else – "the *Rittergutsbesitzer* Dr. Strousberg". The show was visited by the Crown Prince. Bethel Henry Strousberg must have delighted at being in such elevated circles.

The livestock market was a successful and flourishing business, not least because Strousberg had spent much more on its construction than originally planned. The same went for the slaughterhouse facility; it proved worthwhile in 1870 during an outbreak of Rinderpest when only Strousberg's slaughterhouses were allowed to continue operating. The direct unloading of cattle from the trains and the sanitary and veterinary arrangements really saved the day. Soon, a weekly livestock market was set up, and eventually the annual wool market moved from Alexanderplatz into Strousberg's complex.

Strousberg was not able to enjoy this success for long; once again, the cause was his financial problems due to involvement with the construction of railways in Romania. The livestock market was just one of the things he had to sell off.

In spring 1871 a limited company was registered in London with the purpose of buying up the Berlin livestock market, which was almost complete. The share capital was £400,000 of which £25,000 was earmarked for operating capital and £375,000 for the actual purchase.

Strousberg used a London company with an office in the City and with a board whose members included a Lord and a Viscount. Perhaps he wanted to show that despite the problems in Romania his international status was not compromised. At any rate it was not necessary to use a company based in London as the shares – although denominated in sterling – were offered for sale in Berlin and were fully subscribed within a week. The new company then constituted itself in Berlin as well, with a capital of just 2,000,000 Thaler, rather less than in London.

The livestock market continued to do well even after Strousberg's involvement came to an end. When the City of Berlin wanted to buy the complex for 8 million marks in 1877, the share holders rejected the offer as "totally inadequate." They should have taken the money. The City built its own municipal livestock market and slaughterhouse. It opened in March 1881 and it soon drove the complex originally owned by Strousberg out of business.

The Berlin Market Hall

The market hall was designed by Friedrich Hitzig, a well-known Berlin architect who also designed prominent buildings such as the old Berlin Stock Exchange and the Reichsbank headquarters as well as numerous residential properties. The market hall was built between 1865 and 1868 in the Friedrichstadt district, on a 5300 square metre plot between the Karlstrasse and the Schiffbauerdamm where the Panke flows into the Spree. The building was designed according to what was then the best practice.

The Markthalle was built for the *"Berliner Immobilien-Aktien-Gesellschaft"* [*"Berlin Property Company Limited"*] whose board included a number of prominent Berlin residents. It opened in September 1867. There were 545 stalls for meat, fish and all kinds of foodstuff, florists, furnishers and so on. However, the public did not come.

This was partly due to a dispute between the Police Authority (for) and the City of Berlin (against). The City was against the project because it would mean closure for the traditional weekly markets all over the city. The design of the market also had an obvious defect: meat, fish and vegetables were all sold on different levels and customers had to carry heavy baskets up and down endless flights of stairs. So people carried on using the old, unhygienic, weekly street markets in preference.

Six months after the market opened, the company informed the Police Authority that the market hall would be closed from mid-May because of poor patronage, which the company blamed on the City for allowing the open air markets to continue. Further attempts to reach an agreement with the City, in 1869 and 1873, met with no success.

Strousberg initially had nothing to do with this development. In May 1869 it was announced, to everyone's surprise, that he had taken a long-term lease on the Markthalle. Before he could restart operations the Franco-Prussian war broke out and Strousberg had to postpone the reopening. He eventually allowed the Markthalle to be used as storage by a war relief charity.

Strousberg had not been able to make a success of the market hall. The only good thing was that (unusually) he had only leased, not bought, the building. At one time it looked as if he had ambitious long term plans for the market hall: apparently he intended to build a horse drawn tramway to the market hall from his estate at Diepensee, 20 km south of Berlin, at a cost of 100,000 Thaler, and use it to transport vegetables grown at Diepensee to the market hall. Nothing ever came of this idea.

The market hall was taken over in 1874 by the Circus Renz, who were followed by the Circus Schumann. In 1919 the entrepreneur Hans Poelzig rebuilt it as a theatre. Between 1933 and 1945 it served as a meeting hall. It survived the war and became the *Friedrichstadtpalast* entertainment venue in East Berlin.

The Geestemünde fisheries

In his memoirs, Strousberg wrote:

> "During the years when I still had the means, I always had the desire to do something practical for the benefit of my fellow citizens, and I used a some twenty thousands of Thaler to start a fishery company in Geestemünde; I had started the market halls in Berlin in order to take measure to supply the population of Berlin with cheap, good quality fresh meat and fish. The whole set up was such that it was bound to succeed but unfortunately the war intervened, the ships could not go out to sea, and so the company had to be dissolved and I lost my money."

That is his version. But why did Strousberg really get involved with a project which was so obviously way outside his sphere?

Up until then only preserved and salted fish were available in inland Germany, because fresh fish could not survive the lengthy journeys. Fresh fish needed packing in ice; this was expensive and only possible on a small scale, making fresh fish a luxury item.

In Britain, the problem had been solved. Larger distant water trawlers landed fish which was already gutted and packed in ice, ready to be transported by train for sale in the cities. Indeed, between 300-400 British boats were operating off the German North Sea coast.

To survive this competition the German fishing industry would have to adopt the same methods as the British had. To obtain suitably equipped modern ships would take the sort of money which could only be raised by issuing shares in a company. The second point was that in order to transport the fish once it was landed, the port needed to have a railway connection and neither of the main German North Sea fishing ports (Bremerhaven and Geestemünde) were connected to the railway network until 1861/62.

In the second half of the 1860s, two attempts to do this were made. In 1866 the *"Erste deutsche Nordseefischereigesellschaft"* ["*First German North Sea Fishery Company*"] was founded, but it folded very soon as it was undercapitalised, had inexperienced crews and, critically, the railways would not allow the fish to be transported in fast trains.

The second company, the *"Fischereigesellschaft auf Aktien, Weser"* ["*Weser Fishery Share Company*"], founded in 1867, had even worse problems. Here too, the capital was insufficient and the company was only able to buy three of the planned six ships. However, when Strousberg got involved in November 1869 they increased their capital to 300,000 Thaler and elected Strousberg as chairman of the management board.

One of Strousberg's motives for getting involved was the plan to build a railway line from Geestemünde to Hamburg which would connect with the existing line from Hamburg to Berlin. This would make it possible to send fresh fish directly from Geestemünde to the capital.

The war with Denmark in 1870/71 made it impossible to carry out the plan. The blockade of the Weser in August/September 1870 and the call up of the crews for military service put a stop to the fishery industry. Resuming it after the war proved impossible due to a lack of trained crews. In the end, the railway was not built not was the extra capital raised and in December 1872 the shareholders' annual general meeting decided to dissolve the company.

Before we leave Strousberg's not very successful fishery ventures, we ought to mention something else which amused the public: the *Kreuzzeitung* newspaper reported on November 12th 1872 "Strousberg's End! – the German schooner Dr. Strousberg has recently sunk in the North Sea." There really was a ship of this name. On passage from Hartlepool in England to Itzehoe, she began to take water and sank near Helgoland. Luckily the four man crew escaped. The ship in fact did not belong to either the Geestemünde fisheries or to Strousberg himself but was just named after him.

11. POLITICS, PUBLICITY AND SOCIAL ENGAGEMENT

Strousberg's daily newspaper, "Die Post"

Die Post was founded by Strousberg in 1866 and remained in his hands until 1872. The first issue came out on the first of August 1866, and contained what would now be called a mission statement:

"The struggle against the absolute, the irresponsible night watchmen in all areas of political and social life—there you have our programme."

An anonymous pamphleteer remarked that it was not yet possible to work out the new paper's political line as it was liberal on some things and conservative on others. This possibly shows Strousberg's sympathy towards the new *Freikonservativen* [Free Conservatives] whose parliamentary faction he tried unsuccessfully to align himself with[1]. The other, probably the main, reason for starting the paper was to act as a publicity vehicle for his industrial enterprises. Of course, he never acknowledged this but in reality it was glaringly obvious: naturally everyone knew who was behind the editorials. The paper warned about the dangers war with France would bring; Strousberg had more to lose than most industrialists as his system for financing railway construction was vulnerable to even the slightest interruption or tremor on the finance market and he had several schemes on the go.

The *Post* was not always objective when reporting Strousberg's own projects. For example, in January 1870 and again in July it reported that that there was vast interest in Romanian railway bonds (issued by a consortium led by Strousberg) when there was no real demand for them.

The nominal publisher at first was Thomas Köhler's book shop, and from 1867 onwards the firm of Burmester & Strempell. The editor to start with was named as H. Wild, and from 1868 A. Flatow. From 1870 onwards, the paper was printed in Strousberg's own printing works.

"Die Post" had morning, evening and Sunday editions with sections on politics, economics, culture and lifestyle like all the other big Berlin papers. Starting up a new paper like this must have been an expensive job. Estimates are that it needed between 40,000 and 80,000 Thaler subsidy every year to keep going.

As was usual for one of Strousberg's projects, growth was rapid as shown by the number of copies printed which were already at 10,400 in December 1869 and by March 1871 stood at 15,000. The Sunday supplement *"Das Haus"* must have been a good selling point. It described itself as an illustrated

---

[1] The Free Conservatives had split from the main Prussian Conservatives in 1866. They backed Bismarck and his reforms but were not so reactionary as the 'old' Conservatives.

family paper and was aimed at women readers, including family and household tips and even sewing patterns. Strousberg was obviously able to draw here on his earlier experiences with *Sharpe's London Magazine* which had enjoyed a wide readership amongst family circles.

Die Post was taken over in 1872, when Strousberg was desperate for cash as a result of his problems in Romania, by a consortium (lead by the Disconto-Gesellschaft bank) which paid a price of 80,000 Thaler for the newspaper only. The illustrated supplement *"Das Haus"* had already been sold off separately and from April 1871 it appeared as a standalone tile published by the *Dr. Prager & Otto Neugebauer* publishing house.

Strousberg the politician

Bethel Henry Strousberg expressed his opinions on political questions frequently and very decisively in his autobiographical memoir of 1876 and in his writings some of which he published at the end of his career as an industrialist. His role in politics is sketchy, even though he was a member of both the *Zollparlament* (from 1868 until 1870) and the North German Confederation *Reichstag* (from 1867 until 1871).

The German parliaments

The German *Zollverein* [Customs Union] had been in existence since 1833. Most of the German States had joined together economically under the leadership of Prussia; Austria remained outside the Customs Union area, partly because it could not afford the lower Prussian customs tariffs due to its less developed industry. After the Austro-Prussian war in 1866, Bismarck began organising Germany as a nation state (under Prussian dominance) although he first concentrated on northern Germany, with the creation of the *Norddeutsche Bund* [North German Confederation].

In parallel, Bismarck concluded secret agreements with the southern German states which provided for their integration. The members of the *Zollverein* decided to create the *Zollparlament* which was to be the first parliament on German territory directly elected by free general elections. Its members, from northern and southern Germany, met for the opening session on the 27th of April 1868. The *Zollparlament* meant that the independence of the southern German states became even more limited.

"Dr. Strousberg, *Rittergutsbesitzer*" became a member of the *Zollparlament* as representative for the constituency of Allenstein-Rössel, in the Königsberg region although he listed his place of residence as Berlin, initially at Bellevuestrasse 9 and then – from 1869 – Wilhelmstrasse 70 (the *Palais Strousberg*). Strousberg's name does not appear a single time in the list of members who spoke during any of the three sessions during which he was a member.

In 1867 he twice stood for election to the North German Confederation Reichstag. He first stood, unsuccessfully, for the Rothenburg-Hoyerswerda constituency in the Liegnitz region, where he owned the Gut Moholz estate. He obviously spent a lot on propaganda; the constituency was reported as being "covered with forests of placards" which proclaimed that Strousberg was the only man to bring happiness to the Fatherland and bring about German unity. The message was reinforced by large newspaper advertisements in a similar tone. Despite this effort his opponent, Otto Theodor ovon Seydewitz[1], was returned. However Strousberg did obtain a mandate in the constituency of Allenstein-Rössel, representing it in the Reichstag session which began on the 19th of October 1867.

Strousberg does not appear in the Reichstag speakers' list at all and only rarely graced the attendance register. On the other hand, his name does crop up in connection with choosing a Speaker, with regard to both institutions. At the beginning of the Reichstag's 1869 session the Speaker was re-elected as were his first and second deputies, Count von Ujest and von Benningsen. In the election for first deputy speaker there were six votes for Strousberg, proposed as a candidate by members who felt that von Ujest was too close to Strousberg's business interests.

More or less the same thing happened the next year regarding the election of the speaker for the Zollparlament. Although this protest was directed against Ujest, its target was also Strousberg. The issue was not just the Duke's high profile participation in commercial enterprise but also his acceptance of Strousberg as a business partner.

Strousberg was directly affronted by the Free Conservative leadership when he tried to join their grouping in the Reichstag. He sent a message asking for admission to the leader, Wilhelm von Kardorff, who replied:

"Tell Dr. Strousberg, that as a racehorse stable owner, he ought to know that you should not allow a two year old to run with a heavy weight. We Free Conservatives are a young group and we can not carry such a heavy burden as him."

After this insult, Strousberg joined the Old Conservative grouping, but he later wrote that he "... never felt at one with my party and for this reason I never spoke."

Strousberg and the workers

Strousberg made several rather grandiose and not entirely objective statements about his relationship with his employees in his writings:

---

[1] A member of the nobility.

> "I can say with a clear conscience that I have earnestly attempted to create a practical model where capital, managers and workers work happily together"
>
> "I owed them large sums in the latter years, but they never complained... because the people know that I care about my workers, that I discuss things with them and that all of my plans are aimed at ensuring their happiness"
>
> "The worker is simply dismissed when he's no longer required, his wages are reduced as far as possible and only recently has anyone concerned themselves with where he lives and what will happen to him, and then are surprised if he succumbs to demagoguery."
>
> "It is true that the efforts of the workers, as currently directed, will lead to the ruin of their industries and, if they ever achieve their aim will cause the collapse of society. The remedy is in the hands of the state and the industrialists."
>
> "One would be mistaken if one believed that I gave my workers anything as a gift... in my factories, I was the Boss, and everything had to be as my directors and I wanted. The worker had to work for his wages and what I provided for him had to be paid for. The worker does not need alms."

He tolerated workers' organisations, as long as they confined themselves to practical aims and improving the lot of the workers, but he rejected anything with political overtones. In particular, Strousberg hated the socialist movement:

> "Socialism is a plague, an epidemic, with which society must battle; because this disease has to be seen as generally dangerous, one must be alert and suppress it ruthlessly whenever its tracks appear. It is not a political but a mad or criminal movement to which the normal respect for differences of political opinion is not applicable."

He regarded the Christian Socialists as the worst, because in his opinion they elevated socialist ideas to a religious level.

Strousberg was, as far as railway construction was concerned, the general contractor. He did not employ the workers; his sub-contractors and suppliers did. There was little potential for trouble in his Prussian factories either, as when he owned them he was still solvent and the problem of not being able to pay the wages in full or at all did not arise. Strousberg was in fact quite generous, employing more workers as he expanded as well as reducing the working day and providing housing.

However on the Zbirow estate, where Strousberg employed thousands of workers, his financial difficulties soon led to reduced or even missed wage payments, which were, according to the earlier quotes, what he wished to avoid. Strousberg had in fact dismissed those workers who led the complaints promptly.

Strousberg was a leader in the provision of workers' housing. Quite obviously, it was primarily a means of recruiting and retaining workers from the "newly proletarianised masses, who only yesterday or the day before were bonded to agricultural labour." In Hanover-Linden, in Dortmund and in Neustadt he built housing for about 4-5000 people, and at least the same number on his Zbirow and Am Borek estates. There was a social component too; the provision of a Catholic chapel and a school in Neustadt for workers from the Rhineland and Silesia is a sign of this.

Charity

The winter of 1869/70 was very severe in Berlin and when the temperature dropped to -15°C Strousberg decided to distribute free firewood to the poor and open kitchens to give out warm meals at no cost. He did this anonymously, but it soon became public knowledge that Strousberg was behind it, as the firewood and meals were distributed from the market hall, which he rented, and in the livestock market's grounds as well as in a former artillery depot. Between the 10th of February and the 8th of March about three thousand meals a day were served. Initially, meals were served three times a day, but the demand was such that the kitchens had to be open from nine in the morning until five in the evening, and the Police had to maintain order and control the queues.

Obviously it might appear as if this was a cynical attempt to lift his image. Knowing how skilled Strousberg was at media manipulation this can not be ruled out. A public relations exercise? Possibly, but something which was very much needed and certainly hugely expensive.

The amount reported in an anonymous pamphlet as Strousberg's annual private charitable budget, 30000 Thaler, is probably exaggerated. It is true that Strousberg himself regarded projects like the livestock market, market hall and north sea fishery as 'charitable' but they can really be counted as commercial projects, albeit the fishery and market hall were not profitable.

12. RAILWAY CONSTRUCTION IN HUNGARY

The situation in Hungary

Austria's defeat in the war of 1866 led to a real shift of power in the Austro-Hungarian empire with the Austrians losing complete control and increased ethnic autonomy. In 1867, the Austro-Hungarian *Ausgleich* (Compromise)[1] came into being: the ancient Kingdom of Hungary was re-established with the "dual monarchy" system whereby the Austrian Kaiser was also the King of Hungary.

The two parts of the Dual Monarchy had a joint military and common financial and foreign policy, but Hungary had its own legislative and executive, its own parliament and cabinet.

The Austrians and Hungarians had an agreement between them that no agreement similar to the compromise could be considered regarding the Slav dominated parts of the Empire. Attempts by the Czechs to bring this about were frustrated by the Austrians and Hungarians. This would become very important for Strousberg, whose interests would soon be concentrated in Bohemia.

The Hungarian Ministry of Public Works and Communication published plans for a Hungarian national railway network to be built partly by the state itself and partly by private companies operating under concession. Because of the weak financial position the lines were all to be built as cheaply as possible.

---

[1] Before the Compromise, the Habsburg Empire had attempted more limited reforms. Increasing nationalism during the first half of the 19th century and the revolutions of 1848, forced the government into a series of constitutional reforms which did not resolve the situation. When Austria lost the Austro-Prussian War in 1866 it lost the opportunity to have a continued influence in a unified Germany and any remaining claims in Italy. It had to redefine itself if it was to avoid splitting up due to nationalist pressures. Initially the idea of the dual monarchy came from the Habsburgs but Hungarian statesman Ferenc Deák was one of the main players. Formerly an advocate of the Hungarian Revolution of 1848 and an independent Magyar state, he broke with other nationalists to back a modified union under the Habsburg monarchy. Deák favoured full internal independence for Hungary but with defence and foreign affairs left common to both Austria and Hungary. He also felt that Hungary benefited through continued unity with a wealthier, more industrialised Austria.
Under the Compromise, Austria-Hungary had two capital cities, Vienna and Buda (later Budapest). The two regions had their own Prime Ministers and Parliaments that created and maintained different laws. Austria-Hungary was still unified with one head of state, Franz Joseph, who was both Emperor of Austria and-King of Hungary. The army and navy were managed by a common Ministry of Foreign Affairs. Trade regulation was also unified under the Ministry of Finance. Terms of the Compromise were renegotiated every ten years.

This seemed to be very necessary, as the plans included almost 4,800 kilometres of route. A crude estimate of 100,000 Hungarian Guilders per kilometre for construction gives a capital requirement of 480 million Hungarian Guilders, a staggering sum for a new country to raise on the international market.

The Hungarian Nord-Ost-Bahn

This line, 580 kilometres in length, had two main aims: to provide a rail link to Szigeth (an important city at the centre of a resource-rich area) and to provide connections with other lines. Two routes were to lead to Szigeth, each between 200 to 250 kilometres in length: one route from Zombor (later changed to Szerencs for a connection with Budapest) and the other from Debreczin (with a connection to the Theissbahn). All kind of factors were taken into account including not just economic but also military and strategic ones. Many members of the aristocracy also had an interest as their holdings would be direct or indirectly affected; quite a number of them were involved with obtaining a concession for construction of the line. They included Baron Paul von Sennyey, Koloman von Tisza (later, the long serving prime minister), Graf Erwin Schönborn-Buchheim, Severin Graf Dunin-Borkowski, Gabriel von Varády, Dr. Eduard Chornitzer to name just a few.

However, all the effort put in to planning would be wasted if the capital could not be raised. Under the 1867 compromise, Hungary had its own budget for certain things, and railway construction and the raising of capital for that purpose was one of those items. Unfortunately, previous Hungarian attempts to raise money on the international finance markets had not gone well. "As usual," Strousberg remarked "in this situation they turned to me." He was soon taking part in discussions with the government and applicants for the Nord-Ost-Bahn concession. Strousberg decided to buy in to the project. He took over the construction of the line without himself holding a concession, paying the concession holders the sum of 2,000,000 Hungarian Guilders.

The capital, 47 million Hungarian Guilders, had to be raised by the concession holders, not the government. However, the state provided assistance in the form of a guaranteed annual payment of 36,600 Hungarian Guilders plus 500 Hungarian Guilders depreciation for every completed Meile[1]. This revenue would then be used to pay the interest on the capital. Without an arrangement like this it would have been impossible to sell shares or bonds in a Hungarian railway company.

Concession, construction contract and raising the capital

The concession holders awarded Strousberg a contract to build the railway.

---

[1] Meile here means the Austro-Hungarian Postmeile of 7585.9 metres.

The concession stipulated that the line had to be built "in accordance with the State's standards," but this was a contentious point, When the concession was awarded, Hungary was still using the pre-1867 Austrian standards, but what would happen if (as expected) Hungary introduced its own, differing, regulations? If the plans had to be altered to comply with changed regulations, who would pay? In general, it seemed that the railway office had the right to insist on changes to the route or the method of construction at the discretion of either the local authorities or the military budget office.

Formally, the conditions of the concessions were a matter between the government and the concession holders but any changes affected Strousberg financially: he was contractually obliged to 'deliver' the railway in compliance with any changed rules but without extra payment. Which meant that increased costs in one are had to be paid for by economies in another or by a cut in profit.

This alarmed Strousberg. He saw that this meant fundamental changes could be made to the route creating a whole new set of costs. The Ministry remained inflexible, but declared that the concession holders "are happy with the situation".The technical data relating to the routes, according to the contract, had to be worked out in detail by the concession holders; in practice this was dealt with by Strousberg and his staff. They prepared four volumes of technical drawings which covered every detail right down to rail profiles an track fixing, over 320 pages in each volume. This was top quality preparation and it shows just how thorough Strousberg was as a railway contractor. It does not fit with the widely propagated view that Strousberg was nothing but a greedy speculator.

The capital for construction, 47 million Hungarian Guilders, was split 40:60 between shares and priority loan stock. The shares were issued, shortly after the concession was awarded, in two tranches of 10 million Hungarian Guilders.

Construction of the Hungarian Nord-Ost-Bahn

An office to take charge of construction was set up in Budapest and work began towards the end of 1868. Strousberg was contractually required to invest 2 million Hungarian Guilders in the first year of construction and had to lodge a deposit of ½ a million Hungarian Guilders with the finance ministry. Strousberg paid 464,000 Hungarian Guilders to the finance ministry and instructed then to buy bonds in the Hungarian railways with a face value of 500,00 Hungarian Guilders, at the market rate of 93% of face value; he then lodged the bonds as security for the full 500,000 Hungarian Guilders, but his trick had saved him 36,000 Hungarian Guilders.

It seemed as if construction would go according to plan, but then numerous alterations were made, which the contracts specified the railway administration was allowed to make:

The route to Munkács was to be ten kilometres shorter than was originally planned. Construction costs in that area were very low, and because of the method used to work out Strousberg's payment per mile – an average of high cost and low cost sections – if a cheap section was shorter than expected he received a lot less money overall;

The route of the line towards Szigeth was to be changed, with expensive alterations to the stations, bridges and level crossings;

The last 30 kilometres of the line to Szigeth was now to be on the right not the left bank of the river Tisza, in order to reach the government salt works. The Tisza is not a small river and is liable to flood extensively, so the extra costs included flood protection works and Strousberg demanded compensation of 360,000 Hungarian Guilders, of which the railway administration were only prepared to pay 100,000 although they would negotiate about the rest;

The western tip of the line which had been going to end at Zombor was now extended a few kilometres to Szerencs so that Nord-Ost-Bahn customers could make the connection to Budapest more easily;

S. A. Ujhely station was to be rebuilt as a junction station for the connecting lines to Kaschau-Oderberg, to Przemysl and to Munkács.

All of this added a great deal to Strousberg's costs, not that it bothered the Ministry who took the attitude that the contractor had to do what the government demanded, without passing on extra costs.

These alterations must obviously have had significant extra cost implication yet it was by no means clear how much of them the state would compensate for. It would of course affect Strousberg in his role as construction contractor. He later expressed his misgivings about Hungary quite robustly: "Every businessman has, until now, lost his money there," he wrote and continued "the problems which the officials there caused me extend beyond belief."

Strousberg reached the decision to withdraw from the Nord-Ost-Bahn project. This happened when, because of his problems due to involvement with the railways in Romania, the board of the Hungarian railway attached tougher conditions to their payments. Strousberg looked for a way out which would save face.

At that time, several Austrian banks were competing with each other for railway concessions. He approached one of the most active, the Vienna Union Bank. They were receptive and agreed to take on all of his obligations as general contractor. As well as this, Strousberg managed to take 1 million

Hungarian Guilders out and the Nord-Ost-Bahn company was pleased to have a major bank and not an individual as construction contractor.

Strousberg could afford to be satisfied with the outcome; not so the Union Bank, who were later forced to pay 22 million Hungarian Guilders in damages to the Hungarian government, losing over 16 million Hungarian Guilders on the deal overall.

How much railway route kilometres did Strousberg actually build in Hungary? When the Union-Bank took over the construction contracts in March 1871 it was hoped to open 310 kilometres that year; which would mean that that much was almost complete. However, those deadlines were not met, which means that it is not possible to stick a "Built by Strousberg" label on a particular stretch of line.

Uncompleted railway projects in Hungary

Strousberg did not take up two further railway construction concessions which he had been granted, giving then up at the same time as he transferred the Nord-Ost-Bahn to the Vienna Union-Bank.

Near the town of Komärom, about 100 kilometres upstream on the Danube from Budapest the rivers Váh (Waag in German) and Nitra (Neutra in German) join the Danube. Two competing railway lines were planned from there to Trentschin, one along the Waag valley (the Waagtalbahn) and one along the Neutra valley (the Neutratalbahn). Clearly, one of the lines seemed to be superfluous, but which one? Strousberg had made a bid to build the line along the Neutra valley, at better terms than the bidders for the Waag valley route; he was granted the concession.

The second project was for a number of lines in Gömör county about 150 kilometres northeast of Budapest. Here, Strousberg held the concession jointly with a group of local aristocrats.

As already mentioned, he did not carry out either project. The concession for the Neutra valley line was transferred to the Union-Bank and he lost the concession in Gömör because he did not comply with certain government requirements.

Strousberg believed that this would be the end of his involvement in Hungary. He stated: "I advise foreigners to avoid Hungary like the plague," but this appears not to have prevented him from further activities there a few years later.

13. RAILWAYS IN ROMANIA PART I

For centuries Romania had been in the hand of either Russia or Turkey. Two of the main Romanian-speaking regions were principalities owing allegiance to Turkey. Russia, in its push to the Balkans and the Dardanelles, was challenging Turkey for dominance. During the 19th century, Russo-Turkish wars between 1806 to 1812 and 1828 to 1829 brought both principalities temporarily under Russian control. The Crimean War, in which Britain and France fought with Turkey, ended in defeat for Russia. As a result of the Peace of Paris in 1856 the two principalities ceased to be Russian protectorates, Russia lost control over the Danube estuary and the Danube was opened to international shipping. Formally though, the principalities still belonged to Turkey. In fact from a practical point of view, Austria and Russia had more importance and influence.

The two principalities—Moldavia and Walachia—administered themselves, and gradually merged. In 1858 they formed an administrative union and in 1859 elected a joint prince, the Moldavian *Bojaren* Alexander Cuza, as head of state. However Cuza was removed by a military coup in 1866. His successor was a foreign prince, Karl, the second son of Prince Karl Anton of Hohenzollern-Sigmaringen. He became Prince Carol I.[1]

Romania had a parliamentary constitution, based upon that of Belgium, with a chamber of deputies and a senate with the monarch having a veto under certain circumstances. Despite this, it was still basically a peasant country where the feudal landowners were dominant, even if serfdom had been formally abolished under Cuza. Centuries of foreign domination had left their mark on the ruling classes: political morals were less important than than a talent to arrange things so that the regional powers were playing each other, and corruption was rife.

In August 1863 the Prussian Consul-General at the United Principalities of Romania, St. Pierre, reported to Bismarck of a "deeply corrupt administration." He complained about the Romanian tendency to gloss things over and a tendency to prefer the comfortable status quo. The administration neglected two very basic things, he said: firstly, they had failed to establish an elementary school system (although universities existed) and secondly they did not build any paved roads; he said that the existing roads became an impassable sea of mud after heavy rain. Ambitious railway projects were under way although they would be of little use with no decent roads to move people and goods to and from the railheads.

---

[1] In 1888 the United Principalities became the Kingdom of Romania and Carol became King.

By 1866, Prince Carol had ascended the throne and the railway plans were taking a more concrete form. Carol was an energetic personality. He had become ruler without knowing Romania and its people or speaking the language but he was determined to be successful, and he thought that railways would be very important to the country. Previous attempts had resulted only in one line, from Bucharest to Giurgiu on the Danube.

At this time the Austrian Ofenheim Group, which had already built the Lemberg (now Lviv in the Ukraine) to Czernowitz (now Chernvitsi, Ukraine) line, wanted to extend it through the northern tip of Moldavia (that is, through Romanian territory) via Jassy (Iaşi) and Kischinew (now Chişinău, capital of Moldova) to Odessa on the Black Sea. At the same time the Austrians applied for the ambitious railway project to build a line from Jassy and Roman in northern Moldavia to Galatz (now Galaţi) on the Danube and then to Bucharest and through Walachia to the Austrian border. Prince Carol took an interest in this scheme and made contact with Strousberg via his private secretary, Otto Ambronn. Strousberg already knew Ambronn well. In his role as a representative of the house of Hohenzollern-Sigmaringen, the two had often met during the construction of the Märkisch-Posener Eisenbahn.

In 1868 when he was approached about Romania, Strousberg had his hands full. Only the Tilsit-Insterburg line in Prussia was complete and the other six lines in Prussia were still under construction, his involvement in industry in Dortmund and in Hanover was just beginning, in Berlin he was busy with his Palais, the livestock market and market hall, in Hungary he had taken on the building of the Nord-Ost-Bahn and in Bohemia the massive project at the Zbirow estates was under way.

So, he now had Romania to deal with as well. The project was extremely problematic. Romania was not yet an established nation state and it would be impossible to finance a project of this size from its own means. Construction costs for nearly 900 kilometres of railway would be around 245 million Francs, four times the Romanian states' annual income. It was clear that whoever took on this project would also have to provide their own finance.

Both of the groups which were applying to build railways in Romania eventually got permission. The Ofenheim Group satisfied itself with the project to extend its Lemberg-Czernowitz railway in northern Moldavia to connect with a Russian line to Odessa. The concession for the main railway, from Roman to Galatz and Bucharest to the western border of Walachia went to Strousberg, or more accurately a group led by Strousberg. Strousberg was quite able to manage the construction side of things, but he could not take on a financial obligation for the huge sum required on his own; he needed partners, and he got them: Hugo, Duke of Ujest and Prince of Hohenlohe-

Öhringen, and Karl Count Lehndorff-Steinon (who Strousberg already knew from his projects in Prussia), and Victor Duke of Ratibor (a senior member of the Princely House of Hohenlohe-Schillingsfürst), who had been persuaded to join in by Ujest.

An impressive group, which included prominent members of the Prussian nobility with close ties to the ruling circle. The four partners formed a consortium to take up the loan jointly. The construction would be handled by Strousberg alone. To third parties it appeared as if all four were jointly liable for debts arising from the loan, but in reality it was Strousberg's sole responsibility; by secret agreement he had obtained powers of attorney and in return absolved the others from all debts resulting from the bond.

The Romanians were happy with this consortium but Prince Carol sought reassurance from Bismarck via the Prussian Consul-General in Bucharest, Count Heinrich Keyserling, about the participants. Bismarck wrote the answer with his own hand: he could vouch for Ratibor and Ujest, but his reply about Strousberg was couched in diplomatic terms:

> "Strousberg, successfully and skilfully involved in many railway enterprises, has done brilliant business in that field, but naturally I can not give a verdict on the current state of his assets and can not guarantee even indirectly the capabilities of a private person."

The four-strong consortium received the concession to build and operate the railway in Romania and on the prospectus inviting the public to subscribe to the Railway Bond, four names appeared as joint issuers: Ujest, Ratibor, Lehndorff, Strousberg[1].

The contractual basis of the 1868 concession

The idea as laid down in the concession granted by the convention of November 1868 for the consortium to issue a bond in its own name for the amount of the construction costs and then use the proceeds from the bond to finance construction of the railway. The line would then become the consortium's property and be operated by them with all profits accruing to the consortium. The interest on the bond would be paid by the consortium: during construction, from the construction budget and from operating revenue after completion (the bond would also be amortised from revenue).

If the line crossed land which was state property then it would be given to the consortium for nothing, but Romania would make no general financial contribution, either towards construction costs or towards servicing the bond; there was however a last resort guarantee to pay the bond interest if the consortium could not do so.

---

[1] Three of the four signatories were Prussian aristocrats, giving an impression of solid respectability.

The carrying out of the whole enterprise rested on two pillars: the take up of the bond to raise the construction capital and the contract between the Romanian states and the consortium members which gave them the concession to build and operate the line.

In theory, the concession ran for ninety years—until 1957— after which the railway would become the property of the state, without any further payment. The state could take the line over after thirty years but only if it also took on the servicing of any open loans.

The bond issue

Obtaining the capital using the bond issue was vital as if it did not succeed the construction of the line was unthinkable. The amount to be raised was based on the railway's construction costs, and as these were not exactly specified in the contract—the precise length of the line was not yet known—the sum of 270,000 Francs in Railway Bonds per kilometre was laid down.

The length of the planned railway was provisionally estimated at 908 kilometres. This gave a sum to be raised of 245 million Francs and a bond issue for that amount was raised. The bonds were offered for sale in several tranches on the Berlin, Vienna, London and Paris stock exchanges, denominated in the respective currencies.

The placing went smoothly and the promised conditions looked attractive. At a rate of 7½% on a 100 Thaler bond, the subscriber would get 7½ Thaler annually. The bonds were being issued at 71% of face value (in other words, a subscriber only had to pay 71 Thaler for a 100 Thaler bond) which made the effective interest rate 10.5%.

That was a very tempting rate; at the time a Prussian government bond was effectively paying only 4.8%. But in that case it was the Prussian state which owed the money, not four private individuals investing in a risky venture in an unknown country.

Security was in effect a charge on the railway, but at the moment when the subscribers handed over their money the railway did not exist as it was to be built with that money. So the security was way off in the future. Then there was the matter of the government guarantee. In effect, the government guaranteed to pay 7½% annually for the whole duration of the concession, if Strousberg and his partners had not paid it *for any reason*. Was this guarantee worth anything? Nobody could really say. True, the Romanian state had fulfilled its previous obligations, but the railway was yet to be built and it came down to whether or not the prospective purchaser trusted Strousberg and his aristocratic partners.

At the end of the day, the issue did succeed, and was popular especially in Prussia.

Arrangements about construction and operation of the railways

The Convention laid down the routes to built, with dates for their completion, and very precise construction standards to be adhered to. The three routes in this concession were to be from Roman to Galatz with a branch to Berlad (288 kilometres), from Galatz via Ploesti (Ploiești) to Bucharest (268 kilometres) and from Bucharest westwards to the border with the Austria on the Danube near Turnu-Severin (369 kilometres).

The line from Galatz to Bucharest had to be finished by February 1872 and the others by August 1872.

In Prussia, everything would have been thoroughly investigated, agreements reached with local interested parties and construction would have proceeded according to detailed plans approved by the *Eisenbahnamt*. Not so in Romania. All that was specified was the names of the places on the route and their exact route was to be proposed by the constructor (i.e. Strousberg) who had to draw up the plans and present them for approval by the government.

When the planning was resolved, transporting the materiel required all the way from Germany presented a further challenge. Strousberg's Hanover works had to deliver 75 locomotives to Romania. One of these was named, of course, *Strousberg*. In June 1869 it was taken from the works to Hanover railway station on a cart drawn by 24 horses (the works did not yet have a direct rail connection) and then by rail to Hamburg docks. As it was being loaded onto the ship, the boiler tore and the locomotive had to be sent back to the works for repair.

This might have been a one-off but it was a reminder of the problems. Romania was an emerging country without developed infrastructure. The worst of the deficiencies was a lack of proper roads: the dirt tracks turned to impassable mud when it rained.

There were only two ways to get things to Romania from Germany: by barge along the Danube, or the long way round by sea from Hamburg around Europe, through the straits of Gibraltar, then the Bosporus and the Danube delta to Galatz or Braila (now Brăila), the only places near the construction works for the railway accessible by ship. Strousberg described it himself:

> "Whole fleets sailed for the Danube, loaded with rails, bridge parts, locomotives, wagons and railway equipment, thousands of ox teams filled the country roads ... to unload larger items from the ships, I first had to install a special crane in Galatz."

On top of this, the flow of the Danube was unregulated, making it prone to frequent flooding, and there were patches of quicksand which made bridge building more difficult. Even common building materials like wood, stone, sand and gravel were scarce; the underdeveloped state of industry in Romania meant that replacements for damaged items could not be obtained locally.

The land on which the railway was to built was a problem too. Any state-owned land was automatically handed over but anything privately owned had to be purchased. Often, Strousberg was unable to agree a price with the landowners and had to resort to using the railway's compulsory purchase powers. Compensation if this happened was fixed on a case by case basis by a court of arbitration and was often set at a very high level.

Indeed it happened so often that costs escalated to a level which could have endangered the whole project. Strousberg found that working in Romania was more challenging than anything which he had previously experienced. Overcoming the problems would take time and lots of money, neither of which the concession holders had.

Use of the proceeds from the bond

The amount of construction capital for each route kilometre was fixed at 270,000 Francs "in Railway Bonds" – an important distinction, as Strousberg did not get anything like 270,000 Francs in cash per kilometre in his hand, but only the amount actually raised by selling bonds with a nominal value of that amount. As subscribers only had to pay 71% of the face value and the placement itself incurred 5 per cent in costs and fees, Strousberg was left with just 66% of the nominal total, that is not 270,000 but 178,200 Francs per kilometre.

As if that was not bad enough, part of this sum had to be reserved to pay the interest on the bond during the construction phase. This was, remember, 7½% of the nominal value of 270,000 Francs per kilometre, that is 20,250 Francs per year. Over the three years of construction about 60,000 Francs would be needed for each route kilometre. In reality it was a bit less as when construction commenced not all of the bonds had been placed, and obviously no interest had to be paid on unsold bonds. Working on a figure of 50,000 Francs per route kilometre in interest to be paid over three years, then just 128,000 Francs per route kilometre were left; not enough by a long way. Strousberg would not have been able to build a line in Prussia, where conditions were less difficult, for that amount.

The interest burden was enormous and the concession holders could only be relieved of it by the government after construction had been completed. This was no good as far as Strousberg was concerned. He needed relieving of the interest payment burden during the construction phase: construction costs would have to be reduced if he was to be able to complete the railway. From the Romanian point of view, however, it was a good deal: if all went well, the government would not even have to pay the interest and even if it did not go so well Romania would still have the economically important railway.

Basically, the amount of capital laid down in the concession was too low, but the terms of the concession forbade increasing it. Yet in his 1876 memoir, Strousberg maintained that he had worked out a price per kilometre which was low, but ought to have sufficed.

As if the money was not scarce enough, strict conditions had been placed on how it was to be used. The whole process was managed by the Bankhaus Jaques in Berlin; the bank administered the bond issue and looked after the proceeds from its sale. Strousberg was under the supervision and examination of the Romanian State commissioner, Otto Victor Ambronn. Since 1860, Ambronn had been the general attorney for Prince Karl Anton of Hohenzollern-Sigmaringen, managing nearly 15,000 hectares of estates in Prussia for the Prince. He was also the Prince's representative on the board of the Märkisch-Posener Eisenbahn (which Strousberg had built), and since 1866 he had been senior privy counsellor for finance in Prussia, a very high official position. In view of the fact that he held these positions of trust with his father and the State of Prussia, it is not surprising that Prince Carol gave him the job of keeping an eye on Strousberg. The auditing procedure was laid down in § 9 of the Convention: Strousberg and his people presented proof of work carried out, materiel delivered and so on and a "Senior Engineer of the Concession Holders" issued (par su parole d'honneur) certificates of completion; the State commissioner checked these and released either money or bonds to sell for that amount to Strousberg.

That was the basic procedure. However, building the lines took years and this could mean that, due to fluctuating market conditions, bonds might only be saleable at a poor rate. To get some degree of protection from this and to ensure that enough capital was raised, Strousberg was expressly allowed by the terms of the contract to sell bonds in advance of work being certified as having been carried out. The revenue from such bond sales had to be held on deposit with the Bankhaus Jaques in Berlin; it was frozen and Strousberg could only draw on it with permission from the State commissioner.

Strousberg made full use of this provision. By the middle of 1870 he had sold bonds totalling 187.5 million Francs in respect of works carried out and 57.5 million Francs "in advance". 66% of the revenue from the advance sale of bonds, some 38 million Francs, was deposited and frozen at the Bankhaus Jaques.

In this way, Strousberg had sold the whole bond issue, but the interest at 7½% on the bonds sold in advance, some 4.3 million francs per year, still had to be paid. The 38 million francs on deposit were only earning 3% on the market, bringing in 1.1 million per year which meant that Strousbergs had to find the difference.

Strousberg needed at least to minimise the financial damage. In April 1870 he came to an arrangement with Ambronn. He was allowed to withdraw 38 million francs in cash from the Bankhaus Jaques but had to replace it with securities to the same value. These securities took the form of shares in his own Prussian railways, paying 5% on their nominal value. The interest problem seemed to be solved, but then the market value of those shares dropped and they no longer covered the 38 million francs. Once again, Strousberg had to find a solution He agreed another swap with the bank: this time the shares were replaced with mortgage charges on Strousberg's properties to the value of 38 million francs. This made the security independent of the stock market's state.

But this meant that the money meant for the construction of railways in Romania was tied up in mortgages. However clever the deal was from Strousberg's point of view the Romanians were unimpressed and Ambronn had to resign; his replacement as state railways commissioner was Ludwig Steege[1].

Construction

Preparatory work actually began in July 1868 although the deal was not signed until December 1868. Strousberg had gathered together 24 key people – civil engineers, surveyors and construction managers – in Galatz from where they began to survey the terrain on the route. Strousberg was a man in a hurry. "Using conventional methods one would have needed two years to draw up the plans," he wrote in his memoirs, "and if you add three years for the construction phase onto that, more than half of the capital would have been used for interest payments."

Strousberg made it clear to his senior staff that he could not afford that. The Prussian vice-consul in Galatz was present when Strousberg, "in best Prussian mode", delivered a fiery speech to inspire them. He gave the go ahead for work to start on the first of October 1868 and by early 1869 ten thousand workers were employed on construction.

Prince Carol's personal interest in the project was obviously a great help. He made repeated visits to inspect progress and took part in opening ceremonies and now and again criticised some things (for example the wagons which Strousberg delivered). This positive attitude was not mirrored by the behaviour of the country's political powers. The Prussian Consul-General in Bucharest reported to the Foreign Office in Berlin that there had been ill feeling towards Strousberg as soon as he was awarded the concession, not

---

[1] Sometimes referred to as Ludovic rather than Ludwig.

just as part of a general hatred of foreigners (which included Prince Carol and his father, Karl Anton von Hohenzollern-Sigmaringen). The political atmosphere was obviously not good. It must have been clear to the Romanians that the railways which Strousberg was engaged on building, would be of great value to the country, but there was no evidence of such thoughts.

14. THE PEAK OF SUCCESS AND THE TURNING POINT

A successful businessman

At the beginning of 1870 Strousberg seemed to be in a very satisfactory position. His railway projects in Prussia were almost complete. In East Prussia, only the short section of the East Prussian Südbahn from Lyck to the Russian border remained unfinished; the concession for the connecting line between Brest and Grajewo had been obtained with work to start later. He was no longer responsible for the few missing sections of the Halle-Sorau-Guben railway. The only project that was behind schedule was the line from Hanover to Altenbeken.

The Dortmund and Neustadt plants were expanding fast and the planned increase in the Hanover locomotive plant's capacity was on schedule. The blast furnaces at Othfresen were still under construction and he had just bought the Altwasser iron ore mine in the Waldenburger Bergland. None of these were giving particular problems.

Abroad, railway construction in Hungary was becoming increasingly fraught as the authorities kept making changes to the plans, which Strousberg had to bear the cost of. In Romania Strousberg had made good progress with construction and thanks to a successful bond placement financing seemed to be secure even if the proceeds were not yet in his hands. Payments for the large projects at Zbirow and Antwerp were up to date. In view of the number of things Strousberg was involved with, things were going alright.

In spite of public criticism, inspired by press articles about his financial system, his industrial achievements made Strousberg popular and even people from the upper echelons of society were not afraid to have direct contact with him.

Strousberg had several private meetings with Bismarck and in 1870 was visited by Crown Prince Carl and his wife to view the gallery in the Palais on the Wilhelmstrasse. He had also become a racehorse stable owner. A confident rider on his country estates and regular race goer, having his own horses running at courses like the Hoppegarten presented an ideal opportunity to mix with other owners and enhance his connections. Strousberg knew what he was doing; he was a master of public and human relations.

Orders and honours

Strousberg's entrepreneurial achievements and increasing social status were recognised by the award of honours. In Prussia he received the *Kronen-Orden (4th class)* on the 27th of February 1864 and the *Kronen-Orden (3rd class*) on the 24th of March 1869; in August 1869 the Duke of Sachsen-Meiningen awarded Strousberg the *Comthurkreuz (1st and 2nd Class)* of the Ernestine Order; The Prince of Hohenzollern-Sigmaringen awarded him the *Ehrenkreuz (2nd Class)* of the Order of the Princely House of Hohenzollern in March 1870.

In March 1869 the King of the Belgians appointed Strousberg an Officer of the Order of Leopold in recognition for his large orders to the Belgian iron and steel industry.

Mary Ann also received a decoration, the *Verdienst-Kreuz für Frauen und Jungfrauen [Service Cross for Women and Young Ladies]*, after the Franco-Prussian war of 1870-1871.

Strousberg never obtained the title of Kommerzienrat [Counsellor for commerce] which his competitor Borsig held, but he never pushed for it. He is reported to have said that the orders and honours meant nothing to him, but he was content to be known as *Doctor* Strousberg. The time frame in which Strousberg was really successful was, in truth, too short to earn honours. On the other hand his induction into the *Corporation der Berliner Kaufmannschaft [Berlin Mercantile Corporation]* in October 1869 can be seen as a recognition of his industrial performance by Berlin's leading bankers and industrialists. In 1870, he was made an honorary member of the Hanover *Arbeiterverein [Workers' Association]* in recognition of his workers' housing projects; recognition from, so to speak, "the other side".

Strousberg was even invited to the official opening ceremony of the Suez Canals in November 1869, but he could not afford the three to four weeks it would have taken him away for.

Personal events

At the end of 1869 and the beginning of 1870, several important personal events occurred for Strousberg and his family: they were able to move into the Palais Strousberg on the Wilhelmstrasse and the Schloss Zbirow and Storousberg and Mary Ann celebrated their silver wedding on the 13th of March 1870.

The interior of the Palais on the Wilhelmstrasse was completed towards the end of 1869 and the family were able to move from their residence in the Bellevuestrasse to their superlative new domicile. Strousberg seems not to have held a particular event to mark the occasion, although the popular writer Friedrich Spielhagen used an imaginary housewarming ball as an excuse to describe the house and its lavish fittings in his novel *Sturmflut*.

In contrast, the moving-in to the Schloss Zbirow was a grand affair. A special train with 20 carriages and wagons conveyed the family and 40 household staff from Berlin, complete with "60 horses and a huge amount of furnishings." Transferring everything in Prague from the main line to the *Westbahn* which ran to Zbirow was rumoured to have cost 2000 Austrian Guilders. The carefully prepared official welcoming ceremony was, admittedly, something of a debacle; Strousberg was not able to accompany his family, as the move was planned for the 15th of July 1870, just four days before France declared war on Prussia and Strousberg could not leave Berlin.

In many ways, his silver wedding celebrations could be regarded as the high point of Bethel Henry Strousberg's life. He had been married to Mary Ann in 1845 at St. Bride's Anglican Church in London when he was 21 and she was not yet 17. Despite their being so young at the time, the marriage was happy. Mary Ann bore eleven children of which four died in infancy. Seven children were with their parents at their silver wedding: the eldest were the two sons, Bethel Henry II and Arthur (21 and 19 respectively) and then the five daughters Agnes, Alice, Hedwig, Edith and Helene (aged between 13 and 5). Strousberg was an exemplary husband and family man whose wife and children meant more than anything else to him. Mary Ann for her part always stood by her husband even when things looked bleak.

A grand reception rounded off the festivities. Carriages thronged the Wilhelmstrasse as their owners delivered cards or alighted to congratulate the couple in person. "Tributes were brought as if he were a king," said one report. It seemed as if all of his estimated 150,000 employees had sent him messages, deputations and gifts. The well-wishers included members of the nobility, well known academics, high ranking military officers and officials.

According to a press report, the gifts filled two rooms in the Palais and included silverware, silver table decorations, a jewellery case covered with gemstones, a silver wash stand, decorated silver and enamel souvenirs and table sculptures, a silver model of St. Bride's church, pearl and opal jewellery, fine porcelain ware, a model oak tree with thousands of silver leaves, and more. Many of the gifts came from the workshops of the Royal Court jewellers, Friedeberg Brothers in Berlin.

Particularly eye-catching was a huge sculpture from the Dortmund Ironworks which had several two foot high figures depicting miners.

Then there were the gifts which could not be displayed indoors. The engineers presented a railway saloon car which had cost 14,000 Thaler, a well appointed steam river launch and finally 16 thoroughbred horses from Romania.

The Berlin *Börsen-Zeitung* (a leading financial daily) viewed the celebrations as the "demonstrative recognition of his importance from the widest circles," and also as the "Evidence of the height to which one can raise oneself in the world of commerce in our time with intelligence and willpower."

The turning point

Only a few months after Strousberg's silver wedding festivities, on July the 19th 1870, France declared war on Prussia.

> "My railway projects and my factories were in top gear, and I myself seemingly prosperous as the war, lucky for the country but not for me, broke out... Looking back on my activities at the moment of catastrophe: there were about 340 Meilen[1] of railway under construction. These were the completion of construction and the associated finance procedures in two directions, with the companies and with my contractors and suppliers amounting to about 140,000,000 Thaler. All in the river, and looking at the disturbances, the interruptions to communications and the cutting out of almost all regulatory and senior management personnel, the loss can hardly be paid."

What Strousberg does not mention here, and which worsened his situation considerably, was the effect on his financing system: all of his work was performed before payment. Strousberg built the lines, his work was checked, accepted by the *Eisenbahnamt*, he received a tranche of shares as payment and only if he sold them did he actually have any cash to pay his suppliers and subcontractors for work they had done or items the had supplied weeks, sometimes months, earlier. Strousberg's notorious cashflow problems often meant that not only the last but also several previous items remained unpaid. If work had to stop because of the war there was no income from the railway companies and Strousberg's due and overdue payments meant that he teetered from day to day on the brink of insolvency.

Rumours circulated that "a very well known industrialist has only been kept afloat by the intervention of several bankers," who had made "Efforts to protect countless small businesses and workers from a double loss." If the subject was Strousberg, and the evidence points to it, it was the first time that he had experienced help from, the banks; but at the end of the day the was the danger of a chain reaction among his business partners.

The outbreak of war had an immediate effect on railway transportin Germany. Mobilisation meant that railway carriages, wagons and of course locomotives were required to take troops to the front, and furthermore they were not returned but used for military purposes inside France. This impacted on civilian requirements. Passenger services all but stopped and the lack of goods trucks had consequences like coal shortages in the Ruhr and in southern Germany.

Between 400 and 500 of the Dortmund Ironworks' 1500 workers were called up. To alleviate the situation of their families, a 'solidarity' scheme was operated: each of the remaining workers had 1 groschen per thaler deducted

---

[1] By "Meile", Strousberg meant, of course, a Prussian Meile of 7532.484 metres (2000 Ruten (Prussian rods)).

from their wages which amounted to 1000 Thaler per month; Strousberg gave the same amount and the total was used to help 180 wives and 280 children. A similar scheme operated at the engine works in Hanover-Linden.

The rumours that Strousberg wanted to close the Dortmund Ironworks proved untrue as Strousberg not only continued operations but completed all the construction work which had started as well as building 50 more workers' houses.

Strousberg wrote in his 1876 memoirs that he had seriously considered suspending his Dortmund Ironworks activities, which he could have done quite easily. With hindsight, a cold commercial decision would have allowed him to conserve his resources and could probably have enabled him to avoid the financial disasters stemming from Romania and later events in Moscow. But he decided not to to this. He claimed to have reached the decision he did because suspending his payments would have affected so many people, even if he did eventually pay up. However, this can not have been the only reason: the annual interest on the Romanian railway bond, 7½% of 245 million Francs amounted to 18,375,000 Francs (14.7 million Marks). True they could be put off, but they would become due later; this would have amounted to a sum which he could not have raised even if he made no further losses during construction of the railways in Romania. Strousberg, unsurprisingly, did not mention this in his memoirs.

The outbreak of the Franco-Prussian war really was the turning point for Strousberg. None of his projects after that seemed to go right.

The Amazing Dr. Strousberg

15. RAILWAYS IN ROMANIA PART II

Strousberg's railway projects and the Franco-Prussian War of 1870/71

At the start of August 1870, an Austrian secret policeman reported to the secret police headquarters in Prague that Strousberg had just sped through the border post from Saxony to Austria in the postal coach from Zittau without stopping, furthermore a second coach had followed, laden with a large and heavy-looking case which the policeman suspected to be full of gold.

Two weeks previously, on the 19th of July 1870, the Franco-Prussian war had broken out, an event which unsettled people and led them to imagine things. Something for which there was a perfectly plausible explanation quickly became suspicious; even secret policemen were not immune.

The economic effects of the war spread far beyond the borders of the belligerent countries, and impacted Strousberg's railway construction activities in Romania hard.

Strousberg employed about ten thousand workers in Romania of whom 1500 or so – mostly supervisors and specialist staff – were German and many of them were called up to the Army. The Prussian military needed almost every passenger carriage and goods wagon to move troops and equipment to the front line and private and industrial requirements had to go by the board. Strousberg found himself unable to move the items which he urgently needed for railway construction purposes in Romania from his factories in Germany.

However, more than 90% of the materiel for the first 550 kilometres of line had been dispatched to Romania by March 1870. This included locomotives, passenger carriages, goods wagons, rails, sleepers, bridge components and much else. Although this did not look too bad, Strousberg's position had become extremely precarious with the outbreak of war. According to the various agreements, he had to completely finish each section of line before it was allowed to open for traffic. A missing sign was enough to mean the line was not "finished", and replacement or substitute items could not be purchased locally as there was no industrial base to supply anything.

This meant that work was only able to proceed in fits and starts. On top of the logistic problems caused by the war, the domestic political climate in Romania was unfavourable too: the Germans had never been a popular choice to hold the concession and now that they had won the war against France Emperor Napoleon III was their prisoner; this was an intolerable thought for the francophile Romanians. This showed itself in the local workforce's day-to-day dealings with Strousberg's team and it showed itself in the Romanian Chamber of Deputies with which Strousberg (not surprisingly, in view of his project's importance) often had to deal.

The state of progress in Autumn 1870

By Autumn 1870 the routes from Roman to Galatz (Galați) and Galatz to Bucharest were almost complete. Two large bridges were still under construction, large sections of track were unballasted and the branch to Berlad (Bârlad) was only partially finished. On the third route, the section from Bucharest to Pitesti (Pitești) was nearly finished but further progress was stalled as Strousberg and the government had not yet agreed the line's route westwards.

Financial trouble

When exactly Strousberg realised that he had to pull out is uncertain. It may have been very soon after the Franco-Prussian war broke out; he cannot have been in any doubt about how badly withdrawal would impact on his businesses.

If Strousberg had already decided to withdraw, then he will not have wanted to invest a single franc more. The first thing he had to avoid was paying the interest coupon which was due on the first of January 1871.

Strousberg undertook certain steps which can only be understood in the light of his decision not to pay the coupon. He had to organise matter so that it would appear as if he was prepared to continue the railway construction in Romania although, in truth, he was no longer interested. His contractual obligation to complete the lines was not only important in respect of Romania, but also to keep up appearances in Prussia.

Strousberg did something spectacular. He founded a new company, the *Allgemeine Eisenbahnbau-Gesellschaft [General Railway Construction Company]* with a capital of 10 million Thaler in ordinary shares and 7 million in priority shares. He proposed to bring the parts of his industrial 'empire' together in this company: the plants, works and factories in Dortmund, Hanover, Neustadt and Othfresen, the mines in the Harz and the Siegerland and the freehold of Unter den Linden 17/18 in Berlin. The value of these objects would cover 14.5 million Thaler of the share capital and the remaining 2.5 million would come from his railway businesses in Prussia. In the press announcements of the new company's formation Strousberg also announced that it was his intention to offer part of the priority shares for sale on the stock market, an intention which the press treated with great scepticism.

His first practical step in Romania was to suspend construction work on the railway lines. That was a sore point, but unavoidable as he did not want to invest any more money in the project. Parallel to this, he opened one of the quasi-finished lines for traffic and even allowed trains to run to a published timetable. These lines were, he claimed, perfectly useable, their opening was justified and therefore the Romanian government would now have to pay the interest coupon due on the first of January 1871.

Contractually, the interest payment could not be offloaded onto the Romanians like this as they had not yet signed off the work and given official permission to commence services.

Next, in September 1870, Strousberg wrote to Bismarck (who was at Versailles in the middle of peace negotiations with the French) appealing for for support in a request to the *Bundes-Darlehnskasse* [a German state-owned bank] for a 2½ million Thaler loan to pay the bond interest coupon due on the first of January 1871. He pointed out that he had carried on construction work on the railways in Romania despite the problems caused by the war and asking for any help and that the war had weakened the financial markets preventing him from liquidating assets to raise cash. Bismarck expressed concern for the holders of Romanian bonds, especially the many small investors he requested the Prussian finance minister, Otto von Camphausen, and the trade minister, Count Heinrich Friedrich von Itzenplitz, to note this and to consider the effects of refusing the application. Itzenplitz rejected this as the Darlehnskasse did not regard the security for the loan which Strousberg was offering as adequate. If the request was turned down then, admittedly the bond holders would lose money, but he would not regard this as a calamity; it was not the Government's job to underwrite an unrealistic rate of return on a private and highly speculative venture. He did not think that Strousberg's industrial enterprises or railways in Prussia would be endangered.

Other steps were taken without a realistic chance of success. There was his request to the Romanians to release 2½ million Francs worth of new bonds to him, for immediate sale. "Bonds," as German diplomat Joseph von Radowitz noted, "for lines which don't even exist on paper yet." Strousberg even had the nerve to advise Prince Carol to order his minister to issue the bond or to replace the ministers. He also put forward this request again, via the Romanian state railways commissioner, Ludwig Steege. Together with the offer to help Romania raise 60 million Francs via a bond issue, if need be buying any unsold bonds himself, which was patently absurd given his financial position.

Finally, on the day before payment was due, he issued a newspaper announcement that the coupon would be redeemed, but on the 31st of March, not the first of January. The reason given was that time was needed to reach agreement with the Romanians about the obligation to redeem the coupon. He persuaded Steege to cosign this announcement, and Steege added a note that his government had never defaulted on any of its obligations and would also honour those in respect of the guaranteed interest on the railway bonds; apart from the delay "the bondholders will not, in any case, suffer any loss whatsoever".

Stousberg received no response to these steps from Romania. The Romanians however were furious at Steege's statement, which totally contradicted Bucharest's very clear intention not to pay the coupon under any circumstances. Steege was immediately removed as railway commissioner and replaced by Theodor Rosetti[1]. On the first of January 1871 the interest coupon was not redeemed, either by Strousberg or the Romanians.

Strousberg acquires himself liquidity

The non-payment of the coupon had forced Strousberg into a very awkward position and he decided that he had to improve his liquidity. The idea of doing this using the *Allgemeine Eisenbahnbau-Gesellschaft* had to be buried very quickly. The press had already been very negative about his intentions when he started the company formation process and now, after the default on the Romanian interest coupon, it would be utterly pointless to offer shares in it to the public. The company therefore decided to wind itself up on the 17th of January 1871.

This meant that those businesses which had been included in the company once again became Strousberg's personal property. He sold the engineering works in Hanover for 3 million Thaler: the new owners renamed it the *Hannoversche Maschinenbau-Aktien-Gesellschaft*, better known as Hanomag. The sale must have been a hard blow for Strousberg as the works had really taken off under his ownership and could be considered as the jewel in his industrial empire.

Strousberg completed another deal to increase his liquidity in January 1871 when he bought back the Neustadt ironworks from the liquidators of the Geneva Credit Bank to whom he had sold them two years previously. Shortly after buying the Neustadt ironworks the bank had, in Autumn 1869, gone into liquidation after a series of deals went wrong. The liquidator was in the process of selling off the assets, whose nominal value totalled 7.3 million Francs. Strousberg did a deal with the liquidator whereby he bought them all for 5 million Francs; to make a profit, he had to resell them for more than that. There was another point which was decisive for Strousberg. He did not have to pay the liquidator until the 1st of September 1871, about half a year later, but the assets which he had bought included a balance of nearly 1.4 million Francs at the Disconto-Gesellschaft bank, which he could draw on straight away. This seemed like a good arrangement to Strousberg and the

---

[1] Theodor Rosetti later became Prime Minister of Romania for a brief period, from April 1888 to April 1889.

idea of getting cash in his hand without worrying about profit or loss fitted his mentality. Whether or not he 'won' is not known, but the deal went through and the Geneva Credit Bank was finally wound up in 1874.

The reaction of Romania

The Romanians had given a guarantee in case an interest coupon was not paid. This was clearly laid out in the contracts and had been further reiterated by high-ranking officials, but now that the situation had actually arisen, they had no intention of actually paying up. Instead of this, finance minister Sturdza issued a statement in which he strongly rejected Strousberg's view that the obligation to redeem the coupon had been triggered and said that other parts of the contract had not been fulfilled: the construction works had not been inspected or signed off, permission to commence operations had not been given and also this could not be allowed as the lines were not yet finished; on the Roman-Galatz line the branch to Berlad had not been built and neither had the bridge over the Sereth on the Galatz-Bucharest line.

An ad hoc commission of enquiry about the coupon redemption issue came to the same conclusion as Sturdza. While the Chamber of Deputies was debating the report, Strousberg's representative (Wächter) delivered a telegram addressed to the Government and the Deputies in the Chamber.

Strousberg's tone was both bellicose and conciliatory: although the government had caused him huge losses and damage he was prepared to show his good will and to pay the coupon if certain conditions were met. These boiled down to the Romanian government immediately making a new bond issue of 4 million Thaler, the revenue from which would be used to pay the coupon and the government regarding the lines from Roman to Galatz (with the Tekutsch to Berlad branch) and Galatz to Bucharest being 'accepted', with Strousberg promising to finish the few outstanding jobs;

Any idea of expropriation amazed him; a proper value should be negotiated on a commercial basis between him and the government.

Strousberg had instructed Wächter to demand an immediate yes or no answer from the ministry. If 'yes' he could come straight to Romania and personally supervise thing. If 'no', he would reject any possible payment of the coupon and "pursue my claim for damages through my government".

The Chamber, partly in response to Strousberg's, provocative behaviour, did several things in quick succession. The lines were inspected by a minister, and then (in accordance with the contract governing the concession) a court of arbitration was appointed. It ruled that the Romanian government was not obliged to accept the lines mentioned in the telegram in their current condition as amongst other things the bridges over the rivers Bistritza and Sereth were missing and work on the branch line to Balatz had not even started.

A second ruling followed: it held that the Romanian government was not obliged to pay the coupon as of the first of January 1871, none of the lines were ready for use, no permission to operate had been given and therefore liability for the interest still lay with the concession holders.

Unrest

At the same time other events led to an increase in general uncertainty.

The status of the deposit held by the Bankhaus Jaques in Berlin became a hot topic again when the new Romanian state railways commissioner, Rosetti, was able to examine the documents deposited at the bank. He found that, contrary to what was previously thought, no actual mortgage deeds were deposited but only notarised guarantees that mortgages on Strousberg's properties would be granted.

This caused a storm of outrage, and there were accusations of embezzlement and fraud, which were untrue as the money on deposit actually did belong to Strousberg. The Romanians brought a civil case in the Berlin district court against all four concession holders, seeking substantial damages, and in April Rosetti even laid criminal charges against Strousberg, Ferdinand Jaques and Ambronn at the Berlin prosecutor's office.

Rosetti repeatedly contacted the prosecutor responsible but he was of the firm opinion that this was a civil matter and a criminal case would only result in the accused bring cleared. Cautiously however he did consult the chancellor's office to ask to what extent he ought to take German interests into account. Bismarck replied that the prosecutor "should not be influenced by such expectations," and that he, the Imperial Chancellor "had no right to interfere in the Crown Prosecutor's decision making process," furthermore he added "even less can a suspicious Wallachian like Rosetti be expected exercise any influence on the decisions of a Crown Prosecutor". There was no criminal trial, which was undoubtedly the correct decision. Withdrawing the money might have breached the contracts, but it was not criminal. However the matter caused a dreadful uproar and the loudest protests came from the Romanians who behaved as if someone had stolen "their" money when in fact they had not yet paid a single penny for their railways.

Against this background, a nasty event occurred in Bucharest. The German community planned a reception on the 22nd of March to mark Kaiser Wilhelm's birthday. Other countries held similar events for their heads of state or national days, but the francophile Romanians, already stirred up by the railway question, viewed it as a triumphalist celebration of the French defeat. There were unpleasant press articles and threatening letters. The consul-general, von Radowitz, consulted the prime minister and chief of police and was assured that the event could go ahead safely.

The reality was different: on the evening of the event a large crowd gathered in front of the venue, the Slatineano Room. Soon stones were flying through the windows and some guests were injured, including the consul general. Eventually the armed mob burst in and the guests had to defend themselves with chairs and bottles. The police watched but did nothing. The prime minister and police chief who had been sent for by von Radowitz, tried to negotiate but had to resort to using the army to disperse the rioters.

That night, von Radowitz went to see the Prince. Because of their inaction he demanded, and got, the dismissal of the police chief and the prime minister. Two days later Ion Ghica's entire cabinet resigned and members of the Chamber of Deputies demanded the prince's removal. The prince talked about abdicating, very possibly the riot instigator's original aim. The Chamber was dissolved and a new government formed with Lascar Catargiu as prime minister.

The toppling of the Romanian government following the intervention of a German diplomat was strong stuff indeed and the mood amongst the population and in the chamber of Deputies could hardly have been more heated.

Romania grabs for the railways

The government remained unemotional, and even considered – with certain conditions – allowing the lines to be completed by the concession holders. A parliamentary commission was set up to explore renegotiating the contract governing the concession.

The majority in the chamber was not prepared to follow this suggestion and there were verbal attacks on Germany, singling out von Radowitz, who was denounced as an agent of Bismarck, taking money from the children of Romania. On July the 17th/29th[1] 1871 the Chamber of Deputies passed, with a small majority, a law on the railways: a court of arbitration would annul the concession held by Strousberg and his consortium; the bondholders would be free to form a joint stock company, which would be obliged to complete the lines; if this did not happen within 30 days after the 'old' concession was annulled, the State would take over, paying the bondholders compensation based on the estimated value of the work completed up to that point. The arbitrator's ruling, including the annulment, happened in October.

The ruling was without doubt unlawful and therefore invalid, but it was the for the world to see. The Romanian government published it in the German press together with the demand to bondholders that they form a new joint stock company within 30 days or face a government takeover with only

---

[1] Romania as a mainly Orthodox country still used the Julian calendar at that time, eleven days ahead of the Gregorian calendar used in western Europe.

limited and uncertain compensation. The Romanian government exerted pressure on the bondholders by revealing that their estimate for the works completed until that point was just 67 million francs; barely one quarter of the bonds' total face value.

It soon became a fait accompli; the authorities seized the railway just a few days later.

Diplomacy?

It was generally accepted that the annulment of the concession and subsequent takeover of the railways was clearly not lawful. Equally, Romania had not fulfilled its guarantee obligations and this was seen as a breach of international legal treaties, but nobody could decide how to proceed against Romania.

Legal proceedings seemed pointless. Even if a German court had jurisdiction, how could its verdict be enforced? Nobody expected a Romanian court to give an unbiased verdict. The idea of using a court in Turkey, Romania's theoretical sovereign, was raised but rejected when Turkey explained that Romania was for legal purposes autonomous. The only option left was to exert political pressure on Romania. However this would require concerted action by the Great Powers, Romania's Guarantors under the Treaty of Paris.

The German side waited until Strousberg said clearly that he would not pay the coupon before demanding that Romania honour its pledge. Radowitz, on Bismarck's authority, sent a note to the Romanian foreign minister on the 16th of March 1871, without success.

At the beginning of January 1871, the Secretary General of the London-based Council of Foreign Bondholders sent a note to the Romanians to remind them that they had not fulfilled their obligations promptly. The Council was highly expert in the field of Bonds and pushed for the matter to be resolved at a conference of the Great Powers, but failed to gain the required support from the British government which took the view that this was business, private speculative agreements between individuals tempted by the high interest promised. The most that could be hoped for was unofficial support. However the Council did manage to persuade the London stock exchange not to allow a new Romanian bond to be listed, and as a result it could only be offered for sale – without much success – in Romania.

Bismarck's attempts to get the great powers to take action against Romania failed. The British government stuck to its opinion and Russia delivered a clear rejection: Strousberg was *persona non grata* in Russia, the Romanian railway routes did not serve Russian interests and furthermore the ruling circles in Romania were thought to be anti-Russian. Austria did remind the Romanian government about its obligations as early as January 1871, straight after the failure to pay the guaranteed coupon, but wanted a negotiated settlement and made it obvious that the matter was not to be allowed to become a political priority.

The only real result of Bismarck's diplomatic efforts was persuading Turkey to warn Romania that their behaviour was unacceptable and eventually to send Prince Carol a strongly worded note threatening "serious consequences" if the railway question was not solved.

The bond holders become active

Romania was obviously not going to honour its guarantee, and some of the bond holders issued proceedings against Strousberg at the *Stadtgericht* (the city's civil court) in Berlin for payment of the overdue coupon. They won, and Strousberg paid up in order to avoid the bailiffs being sent in. Eventually there were so many of these claims that a special court room was set aside to deal with them and both the claim and the response forms were preprinted or duplicated. Strousberg eventually paid out a huge amount in settlements.

With hindsight, Strousberg sowed sympathy from the individual bond holders who took this course, but he complained bitterly about the people who "started the hunt against me, journalists, lawyers and others who mostly did not even have any bonds themselves," but were motivated by bloodlust and *Schadenfreude*.

Some bond holders, notably in Breslau, in Berlin and Vienna, formed themselves into committees.

The new Romanian Railway Company Limited

The committees had basically two choices. They could either challenge the law of July 17th/29th 1871 and the annulment of the concession as unlawful – which would take large-scale political backing – or they could accept both acts as they were including the 30-day limit and form a joint stock company.

They decided on the second alternative, which required rapid action to win over the majority of bond holders and find a strong backer for the new company. The path led to the banker Gerson Bleichröder in Berlin and to the Disconto-Gesellschaft bank.

Completing the Romanian railway needed 66 million Francs. Both banks, and the Vienna Stock Exchange agreed to be involved and so the first hurdle, raising the capital, was cleared.

In October 1871 three committees met in Berlin and with the assistance of the banks drew up draft terms for the contract to be signed with Ronania. The government in Bucharest was informed that a new company was being formed and events in Berlin gathered pace. On the 2nd of November the Disconto-Gesellschaft and Bleichröder published a call to Romanian railway bond holders to join the new joint stock company and declare their agreement with every step that the banks took to ensure its success. Over 80% of the bond holders agreed and on the 16th of November 1871 the banks formed the *Rumänische Eisenbahn-Aktien-Gesellschaft* [Romanian Railway Company Limited]. The government in Bucharest was informed of the new company's formation by telegraph on the same day. The remaining bond holders were asked if they would sign up too and eventually over 99% did so.

The 1872 agreement

The Romanian government was prepared to come to an agreement on the basis of the drafts drawn up in Berlin and on the 22nd of November it published a bill which largely followed those suggestions.

Agreement from the Chamber of Deputies was not a foregone conclusion. The "Red Party" demanded that the railways simply be taken over without compensating the bond holders. Once again the government hesitated, and Bismarck feared that all his diplomatic efforts would have been in vain. Another threat came from a rival group who also bid for the project.

Eventually the Romanian government did decide in favour of the Berlin suggestions and after several days of heated debate the Chamber of Deputies approved the new agreement on December 21st 1871/2nd of January by a majority of 75 votes to 48. The new law confirmed the annulment of the previous concession and laid down the new conditions.

The new company had to do several things: firstly it had to complete the 648 kilometres of route which Strousberg had "nearly finished" by the 1st of September 1872, in just 8 months; secondly it had to build two new short stretches of line in Bucharest and at Galatz and Brada, by the 1st of September and 1st of December 1872 respectively; and finally take over construction of the main line from Pitesti to Virciorova on the western border with construction to be finished in three years.

If any of the deadlines was missed, the Romanian government could re-let the work to a different contractor.

The Bonds were converted 1-for-1 to shares in the new company. This gave a nominal share capital of around 65 million Thaler. Any bond holders who did not exchange their bonds for shares in the new company received only meagre compensation based on the estimated value of work already completed; it is not surprising that only 1% of the bond holders did not take up the offer straight away and by the end of 1873 just 0.2% were not on board.

The company had to raise all the capital required for construction itself with no contribution from the Romanian government. In order to do this without taking on new debt, the company increased its capital by issuing more shares. In principle, Romania still had an obligation to pay a guaranteed dividend – as for the old bonds – of 20,250 Francs per finished route kilometre, but with any payment to the company, not to bond/share holders.

Also covered was the settlement of claims which the Romanian governnent had against the previous concession holders (in effect, against Strousberg). These were the overdue interest coupons from 1871, whose non-payment had sparked the fire, and the claims resulting from the 38 million francs which Strousberg had received from the deposit at the Jaques bank and finally all other monies owed from Strousberg's period in charge of construction (these expressly included claims arising from the expropriation procedures). These claims passed from Romania to the new company. The shareholders accepted these terms at the company's General Meeting on the 26th of January 1872.

In accordance with those terms, a settlement had to be reached between the new railway company and the original concession holders. This was done quickly, by the 10th of February 1872 in fact. Under its terms, Strousberg paid the new company 6 million Thaler in cash, 4 million immediately and 2 million to paid in instalments over 3 to 5 years. The Disconto-Gesellschaft made him a loan for this amount so the new company could have the six million at once.

The settlement included one very important point for Strousberg: the new company agreed to drop all further claims against the original concession holders, which of course included Strousberg.

The consequence: Strousberg has to get more liquidity

Strousberg had to pay 4 million Thaler straight away but he did not have the money. This seemed to confirm what had previously only been speculation: Strousberg had already spent the 38 million Francs from the deposit at Jaques on other things.

So he had to liquidate some of his assets. At that time there was no demand for land in the country, and as a result he had to sell off his remaining industrial empire.

The Disconto-Gesellschaft bank bought the *Dortmunder Hütte* ironworks and the *Glückauf* deep colliery in Dortmund as well as the blast furnaces at Othfresen for a total of 6 million Thaler plus a further 400,000 Thaler for stock at the *Dortmunder Hütte*. Half of this sum had to be used to pay off mortgages and other loans secured on the plant, leaving Strousberg with only 3.2 million Thaler in cash.

The amount paid to Strousberg from the sale of the livestock market in Berlin is not known. The facility had been converted to a joint stock company, the *Berliner Viehmarkt Aktien-Gesellschaft*, in February 1872, and the new company valued its assets [in its own publicity] as being worth "at least

2,000,000 Thaler". It is reasonable to assume that Strousberg did not get quite that much.

Finally, Strousberg had to part with his daily paper, *Die Post*. This raised another 200,000 Thaler; once again the buyer was the Disconto-Gesellschaft.

The total income from these sales was about 8½ million Thaler, less mortgages and other business debts. This concluded Strousberg's involvement with the Romanian railways, but the story is not quite over.

The completion of the Romanian railways

On the 14th of February 1872 the agreements governing the new concession were signed in Bucharest. This meant that the new company had two priorities: finishing construction work and raising the necessary to do so. Strousberg had nearly finished 648 route kilometres, and the 271 kilometres from Pitesti to Virciorova on the western border had yet to be started. The Austrian State Railways were given the job, and they succeeded in completing everything on time, despite the tight deadlines imposed by the Romanians; the final bill in 1877 was 102 million Francs.

It proved very difficult to raise the required capital. Out of the 22.5 million Francs from the settlement with Strousberg, 18.4 million were needed to pay the overdue interest for 1871, leaving only 4 million Francs for the actual work.

Romania: from ox cart to railway

The big winner was undoubtedly Romania. The sheer bravado of taking on such a huge project, using Strousberg as financier for a sum they could not have raised themselves, the cavalier way in which they treated their guarantee obligations – it all paid off in the end. However new capital was required to complete the railways. The Disconto-Gesellschaft bank and Bleichröder offered a tranche of ordinary priority shares with a nominal value of 20.4 million Thaler to be paid for at face value in instalments for sale, but due to the turbulent market conditions of 1873 only 12.8 million Thaler (48 million francs) could be raised.

Further resources were needed. Raising another bond proved impossible as amongst other things the Romanian government refused to pledge the lines as security. Help came, first from the Austrian State Railways and then the Berlin banks, who made loans to a value of 13 million Thaler. Without these loans the money to complete the final sections would not have been available leading to the danger of not finishing on time and therefore not meeting the terms of the concession. The railways could, at last, be completed and enter service although they were at first not profitable due to lack of traffic.

This changed in 1877 with the Russo-Turkish war when Russian troop transports generated a lot of revenue. This made the Romanians keen to take over the railways, and the state made the railway shareholders an attractive offer, which the Railway Company annual general meeting on March 3rd 1880 accepted with a majority of almost 95%. The outline was that shares would be exchanged for Romanian State Bonds paying 6%. The rate of exchange was set at 60% of the face value for ordinary shares and 133 1/3% for priority shares.

Bond holders situation

Contrary to the general view that the bond holders were unlucky victims who lost everything, they still got some return. When the new Romanian Railway Company was formed, the investors received one ordinary share for each bond, but this did not really improve things immediately as the shares traded way below face value: just 13 to 14% in 1876 and 1877. Those investors who sold up then really did lose out, but those who kept their shares until control of the railways passed to the Romanian state, the vast majority of them, had little to complain about.

The purchaser of 100 Thaler face value of Strousberg's bonds in 1868 paid just 71 Thaler. In 1880 he received, in exchange, 60 Thaler in the form of a Romanian government bond. To this must be added interest and dividends of 47.68 Thaler paid between 1868 to 1880. This meant that not only had an investor got all his capital back, but also an effective interest rate of 4.7% per annum: about the same as investing in Prussian government bonds over the same period would have paid. This meant that the Strousberg bonds were not such a bad investment after all.

Certainly some small investors will have sold their share in panic at rock bottom prices during the period of uncertainty so it really was only a good investment for those in it for the long haul.

The positive end result could not have come about without the expert and shrewd negotiations led by Hansemann and Bleichröder with support from the committee of bond holders. However a successful outcome was only possible because they had something that the Romanians really wanted – the railways. Strousberg had actually built, in a very brief time and under trying circumstances, a very solid railway with considerable value.

Strousberg pays the tab

Strousberg had paid the price for his involvement. Incredibly things turned out better for him than if he had tried to complete the railways' construction, which would almost certainly have ruined him. After reaching an agreement with the new railway company he had a total of 6 million Thaler (18 million marks) to pay, but he could keep the 38 million Francs (30 million

Thaler) which were on deposit at the Bank Jaques and there would be no further demands made on him.

The losses which he had to bear were immense. He had to get rid of his industrial empire, precisely those things which promised to deliver a return long term, yet he hung on to his country properties which swallowed up and would continue to swallow up money because they were not fit for sale at that time.

The worst thing undoubtedly was the destruction of his reputation as a 'man who can do anything'.

With hindsight, it has to be asked how Strousberg let himself be drawn in to such a contract. He was after all a successful specialist in the field and was providing both the know how and the money, which the Romanians would never have been able to raise on their own. In other words he was the person giving his all and Romania was just taking, yet it was Romania which was dictating the terms.

There are three main points to be made about the original contract. Firstly, the payment which Strousberg received as general contractor was far too low considering general conditions in Romania. Secondly, the costs of raising capital via the bond issue fell entirely on Strousberg and thirdly the construction deadlines were far too tight, creating artificial time pressure. Why the Romanians were in such a hurry to have things completed never became clear, but if Strousberg had failed to meet the deadlines even by a short time, he could have lost the concession.

Strousberg never acknowledged that the deals he had made were the cause of his failure; admitting mistakes was not part of his personality. If he did make the odd error, it was a consequence of his good nature and desire to help others and never his own fault.

16. ANTWERP

Background

It is an odd tale: a state sells some land to a businessman to develop in accordance with the state's wishes, the purchaser pays a huge sum, and yet within four years the state is not in a position to make the land available to the developer. Eventually the developer pulls out and counts himself lucky to have got away financially more or less intact. The businessman concerned was of course Strousberg, and it is no wonder that he later complained of having been done an injustice and feeling that he had been used.

How and why had Strousberg got involved in the first place? In 1869 Belgium had only been an independent state since 1830. Until then it had been a province of the United Netherlands, from which it split in the September Revolution of 1830: it declared its independence at the end of August 1830, and after some fighting, in which French troops aided the 'rebels', this status was recognised by the five Great Powers at the London Conference and Belgium's neutrality was guaranteed, although it was 1839 before The Netherlands recognised the new state.

Belgium's constitution was quite modern. It was to be a constitutional monarchy; the first King of the Belgians was Leopold I, a member of the German House of Saxe-Coburg. The government was answerable to parliament which had two houses, the *Sénat* and the directly elected *Chambre des Représentants*. Belgian politics was dominated by the opposing Liberal and Catholic Party factions and the French-speaking Walloons had a dominant role (French was the only official language until 1898 and there was no Flemish language version of the constitution until 1967).

In 1869 Leopold II (the son of the first king) had been on the throne since 1865 and the Liberals were in power. At that time the iron ore and coal deposits in Wallonia had allowed an internationally significant iron and steel sector to develop, and other industries such as glass making and agriculture were flourishing as well. Unfortunately this progress had not extended to the country's harbours. Antwerp, Belgium's main port, was out of date but expansion was prevented by the presence on the banks of the Scheldt of the Southern Citadelle, a 300 year old fortress.

The Antwerp city fathers had two ideas: firstly the Southern Citadelle could be demolished and the land sold off, using the proceeds to build more modern fortifications further outside the city; once this was done the now-vacant site on the banks of the Scheldt could be used to lay out a modern harbour with new docks and quays, cranes, warehouses and a railway station with a direct connection to the harbour.

Of course, this proposal would cost a huge amount, far too much for the young Belgian state to bear, and so a partner from the private sector was sought to bring the project to fruition at their own cost and risk. The partner would in effect be modernising Belgium's defence infrastructure, building a new harbour and paying for the privilege as well.

The financial carrot was of course the prospect of a profit from running the harbour at some point in the future, which was by no means certain. It took the government six months to find someone willing and able to take on such a risky project. Eventually, they came to Strousberg, who at that time—thanks to his myriad railway construction contracts all over Europe—was a major customer for the country's steel making and processing industries; in recognition of his services to the Belgian steel industry, in March 1869 King Leopold awarded him the Officer's Cross of the Order of Leopold.

Strousberg had audiences with the king at his official residence, the Royal Castle of Laeken (near Brussels), on the 4th of August and the 14th of October 1869 with finance minister Walthère Frère-Orban leading the negotiations. Strousberg agreed to take the project on.

The Convention of the 14th of October 1869

The Convention on the development of the Antwerp Sud-Citadelle agreed between Strousberg and the Belgian state laid down all kinds of things. The most important of which were that Strousberg would purchase the 98 hectare Sud-Citadelle site from the military administrator. The purchase price was to be 14 million Francs, payable in three unequal instalments: 3,150,000 Francs by the beginning of 1870; a year later 2,583,000 Francs and the remaining 8 million Francs three years after that.

Ownership would be transferred to Strousberg in stages, in proportion to the payments made (22 hectares in the first instance, then 18 hectare and finally the rest of the site, 58 hectares.

In addition Strousberg was obliged to construct, at his own expense, the new harbour and associated installations (which would belong to him).

The costs for the last item were not specified. This meant they could (and did) mushroom; Strousberg must have anticipated very large potential profits. It was agreed that Strousberg could purchase a further 26 hectares of adjoining property which belonged either to private individuals or the City of Antwerp. If no agreement could be reached with the owners on price or if they refused to sell, the land could be confiscated by the courts and given to Strousberg.

In total this meant that 124 hectares were available for development. According to the convention, Strousberg had to use at least 49 hectares to build the harbour and associated facilities; he would be able to do as he thought fit with the other 60 to 70 hectares. Finance minister Walthère Frère-Orban had made that quite clear when the convention was brought before parliament for approval. This was Strousberg's opportunity to make a profit; the juicy carrot to persuade him to build the harbour.

Before there was even a chance of a profit, the project had to be built and of course financed. With his notorious shortage of liquid capital, Strousberg had always planned to have a financial partner but despite this none was to be seen. He did not mention a problem with financing in his 1876 memoirs, although he had to pay the first instalment of over 3 million Francs immediately. Instead, he concentrated on the profits which the venture promised to deliver, ignoring the time before they could be delivered, saying that the amount of shipping passing through Antwerp was evidently growing so fast that the present docks were inadequate and that a new harbour was bound to be profitable as well as which the profit from reselling vacant plots would ore than cover building costs.

Conflicting interests

In the interim, the political situation in Belgium had changed: since the middle of 1870 the Clericals, not the Liberals, had been in power. Replacing Frère-Orban (Finance Minister when the original Convention was negotiated) was Jacobs, quickly followed by Jules Malou. Malou had been up until then and for eight years previously the president of the *Compagnie Immobilière de Belgique*, part of the powerful *Société Générale pour favoriser l'Industrie Nationale*. Malou now had the job of realising his political opponent's pet project, which – according to Strousberg – the Société Générale had wanted itself and only gave up in favour of Strousberg thanks to pressure from Frère-Orban.

There were further complications. According to the terms of the Convention, Strousberg had to put forward detailed construction plans within six months, but the construction office managed to do this in just 65 days. Obviously the plans included details of the private and city owned plots which Strousberg intended to use, and when they became known a storm broke.

The City of Antwerp was generally opposed to the project. Obviously, the central government had not reached an agreement with the City in advance even though the new port south of the city would compete with the existing port to the north, which the city owned. Furthermore, some of the City's own land would be compulsorily purchased for the new project. Strousberg could not have foreseen this clash of interests, as when the matter was decided on in parliament all the members, including those from Antwerp, had voted in favour of the project and awarding it to Strousberg.

The city had several reasons for their rejection of the plan. Their main criticism was that Strousberg's plans required 55 hectare of land, but did not initially use all 49 hectares of the former fort (as laid down in the convention). Instead, only 31 hectares of ex-military land would be used, with the remaining 24 hectares being purchased from the city and private owners.

This began years of argument; but work could not begin until agreement was reached. Eventually the government lost patience. At the end of July 1872 they passed a law which gave Strousberg the go-ahead and also gave him powers of compulsory purchase. Strousberg then requested the City to hand over the plots detailed in the plans, but was met with refusal. He went to court to enforce the purchase, but to his astonishment the *Tribunal de Commerce* in Antwerp ruled, on the 10th of July 1873, that Strousberg did not have the power of compulsory purchase, in other words it refused to apply the law passed in July 1872. Strousberg appealed, but of course things were again held up. It was not until the 16th of February 1874 that the *Cour d'Appel de Bruxelles* das overturned the lower court's judgement and upheld Strousberg's powers of compulsory purchase. Four years had elapsed since Strousberg had presented his plans. Whilst this had prevented Strousberg from starting construction, the Government had also become impatient; the proceeds from the sale of the Citadelle should have provided the money for the new fortifications. On the 5th of November 1872 the government issued a writ against Strousberg demanding that he take over the second parcel of land and for payment of 2,583,000 Francs.

Strousberg had some good arguments on his side against the writ. His Belgian deputies, Hautermann and Bataille-Straatman summarised them in a letter to the editor of the *Précurseur* newspaper on the 8th of November 1872: the letter detailed how Strousberg had fulfilled his contractual obligations, even presenting the plans before they were due and also that the government had taken up to 29 months to issue approvals, thus preventing Strousberg from commencing construction work; to demand that he take over and pay for land which he could not use was clearly an abuse. The government did not reply, despite the scale of the accusations.

Strousberg leaves the project

At the end of 1873, four years after the Convention was signed, nothing had been built and the bickering continued. The legal proceedings against Strousberg had been quietly dropped. Then things began to move. Strousberg sought out the Finance Minister and asked to be released from the contract. The Minister turned this down; he was legally obliged to see the Convention fulfilled and it was completely impossible to release him from the contract. Strousberg could however, if he presented a suitable scheme, give up his rights arising from the Convention. Strousberg took the hint and found a new partner to take over from him, none other than the *Immobilière*.

A contract was signed on the 22nd of December 1873 in which Strousberg agreed to transfer to the *Immobilière* all of his rights and obligations as laid down in the October 1869 Convention. Strousberg was supposed to get back the money which he had actually spent (3,150, 000 Francs paid to the government plus 150,000 Francs for planning costs); however the refund would not be in cash but in shares in a holding company, the *Société Anonyme du Sud d'Anvers*. In addition, very importantly for Strousberg, the *Immobilière* was to make Strousberg a secured loan of 1,500,000 Francs until the 1st of January 1876.

With that, Strousberg's active role in the project ended. Now, the Finance Minister got involved and as if by magic, the conflicts of interest between the central government and the City of Antwerp were settled.

Between January and March 1874 the government signed further contracts with the *Immobilière* and the City of Antwerp. After lengthy and sometimes stormy debates in the parliament, the final result was that the state took up 25 million Francs of capital in the new *Société Anonyme du Sud d'Anvers*.

The *Sud d'Anvers SA* paid the balance of the purchase price for the Sud-Citadelle to the government, about 11 million Francs (14 million Francs, less Strousberg's part payment of 3 million Francs) as well as the purchase prices for the additional land bought from private owners and the City of Antwerp.

The government then took over the building of the harbour on the former Sud-Citadelle site, largely following the plans drawn up by Strousberg and his staff.

The remaining *Sud d'Anvers* shareholders were the *Immobilière* and the City of Antwerp (the corporation) with 31.5% each, Strousberg with 16%, the [Belgian] government with 18%, and various individuals from Antwerp who held 3%.

At this point Strousberg gave up on the enterprise: he sold his shares, at 90% of face value, to the City of Antwerp which then held 47.5% of shares in the *Sud d'Anvers* – the largest single shareholding. Their determined opposition to the original plans had paid off.

This brought Strousberg's Belgian adventure to an end; there would never be a port named Port Strousberg after all.

On the 17th of August 1874, King Leopold struck the first symbolic blow to begin demolition of the Southern Citadelle.

17. THE ATTACK BY LASKER

Lasker's speech in Parliament

On the 14th and 15th of January 1873 the Prussian parliament debated the railway budget for 1873 and funding of 120 million Thaler for expansion of the State railway network. Amongst those due to speak was Eduard Lasker. He belonged to the national-liberal grouping and was one of the most prominent members of the Prussian parliament. He had studied law and been a journalist before being elected in 1865 and had become a lawyer, but did not practise. He had no real professional or administrative experience but felt himself qualified to speak on almost any topic on the order paper. He soon gained a name as an influential parliamentarian and an important voice in the national-liberal grouping. People paid attention to him simply because he was opposed to Bismarck.

Lasker said in the debate that railway construction should be primarily in the hands of the state, with private enterprise only being secondary, helping out when needed. In the long term, the main means of communication should not be in the hands of private individuals, as the "exploitation of routes for individual profit would virtually be a return to the barriers and turnpikes of the middle ages." Lasker then proceeded quickly to his main aim, that is to discrediting the conservative ruling class. His chief target was Privy Counsellor Hermann Wagener; previously editor-in-chief of the conservative newspaper *Die Kreuzzeitung*, Wagener was now one of Prussia's highest ranking officials. Lasker accused him of profiting from his public office—corruption, in other words—by getting involved in the railway business himself and pocketing payments for granting railway concessions.

When Wagener's name was mentioned, all of those present thought immediately of Bismarck, as the two had been close associates since the 1840s. After the debate, Bismarck paid a very public visit to Wagener, who was ill and confined to his apartment. This reinforced the public impression that Lasker's attack on Wagener was really an attack on Bismarck: when Lasker told Bismarck that he had not attacked him, Bismarck retorted "Possibly, but you shot so close to me that a whisker closer and you would have hit me."

Lasker's allegations obviously had something to them, and were calculated. Bismarck would try, ultimately without success, to protect Wagener. This turned out to be correct, as Wagener was forced into reitirement after a disciplinary proceeding in October 1873.

Lasker's other accusations concerned two highly aristocratic members of the Prussian Herrenhaus (House of Lords), the Fürst[1] of Putbus and Prince

---

[1] *Fürst is the hereditary title for the head of the ruling family of a principality, for example the Fürstentum Lichtenstein.*

Biron of Kurland. Again, they were to with railway concessions or their transfer for money, and bore weight purely because of those named.

Lasker then turned to the trade minister, Count Itzenplitz. He was accused of handing out railway construction concessions to those whom he favoured and Strousberg was named as a particularly bad example.

By 1873, there was no ongoing reason for the attack on Strousberg. His railway construction activities in Prussia were almost over, with no new projects in sight. As a parliamentary deputy Strousberg was a political lightweight and provided no threat to Lasker; he had not even spoken once in the house. It was clear that Lasker thought this to be the most effective way of attacking Itzenplitz who had undoubtedly supported Strousberg. Lasker obviously wanted to bring down the trade ministers, and if Strousberg got in the way, too bad.

Lasker's attacks really caused a furore. Lasker called for an investigation into the whole process of granting concessions for railway construction to the private sector, including the financing system devised by Strousberg. In early February 1873 he formally applied for an investigation to be carried out by a seven man parliamentary commission. Lasker did not quite get his wish; instead, on the 14th of February 1873, a Royal Proclamation established a "Special Commission to Investigate the Procedure for Granting Railway Concessions" *[Spezialkommission zur Untersuchung des Eisenbahnkonzessionswesens]*. The parliament appointed the conservative deputy von Koller and Lasker himself to serve on the commission, meaning that the accusers were also the judges.

What did Lasker achieve?

Lasker reached his shot-term political goals very quickly: Bismarck's confidant, Wagener, was forced to resign and retired in November 1873. Count Itzenplitz resigned as Trade Minister. He had indeed taken a huge risk by giving Strousberg a free hand to get round the proscriptive *Eisenbahngesetz* [Law on Railways]. He did this from the best of motives because he believed that this was the most effective way to promote the national interest and was therefore his duty as a minister. When he embarked on this policy Itzenplitz , then aged 62, had the strength to see it through. He was also prepared to face criticism and to take advice; for example in 1869 he sought suggestions for controlling certain irregularities in the railway industry, but got reaction from nowhere except editorial comment in the *Berliner Volkszeitung*. Up until Lasker's attack in 1873 nobody had criticised his policy for encouraging railways in public. At the time of the attack he was 74 and did not have the energy to mount an effective defence (unkindly, people nicknamed him 'Papa Itzenplitz'). His arguments were still valid and his officials presented them just as well, but he could not prevail against the eloquent Lasker. He gave up and asked to be relieved of his office.

The Commission of Enquiry

The commission investigated the process for awarding railway concessions very thoroughly. It also went into the legal and technical issues which arose from the process. In particular the awarding of concessions, financing and construction of 26 lines, including 5 built by Strousberg, were analysed. Leading *Eisenbahnamt* officials, technical experts and other witnesses from the administration, business and the banks were examined. The commission looked at both the theoretical aspects and the practical implementation of Strousberg's finance concept.

The Prussian Parliament published the results of the commission's investigations in November 1873, just 9 months later, as a single volume with 681 printed pages. The greater part, 540 pages, was taken up with transcripts of the submissions. The commission placed its conclusions together under the headings of Shortcomings and Suggestions.

Using the general contractor model for railway construction was not to be abandoned; the practice had repeatedly been legally sanctioned, and the commission agreed with the Trade Ministry continuing to permit this method of construction. Great importance was placed on strict checks by the Railway Construction Office as individual sections of line were completed to ensure that everything had been finished safely and in accordance with the approved plan. Only then would the Office give the go-ahead to open the line for traffic.

There was heavy criticism for Strousberg's method of financing, in which the contractor was paid in shares that could only be turned into cash when sold at less than face value. This resulted in less money being available for construction than was shown in the estimates and could lead to the line being not so well built. The commission did accept the explanation given by representatives of the Railway Construction Office that strict controls ensured solid and safe construction; in addition it was clear to the commission that without this method of financing there would not have been any railway construction. The result of the inquiry was the suggestion that in future the placement of shares for railway construction at less than face value should be allowed, but only if the amount below face value was openly declared in the invitation to subscribe, in the application coupons and on the share certificates themselves: in other words, Strousberg's "System" was sanctioned with minor qualifications. The commission also recognised that the state had itself infringed the law and formally permitted the sale of shares at less than face value in the case of lines which it thought were of importance.

Consequences from the Report

The report was passed to the house of deputies on the 12th of November 1873. One would have expected that Lasker would have been anxious, now that the report was available, to use it to persuade the lawmakers to draw consequences and alter the law to stop people like Strousberg; from further involvement in the railway business, so that they could not cause further damage to national assets. Surely the discredited general contractor model would have to be banned, as would the sale of shares below face value.

But nothing of the sort happened. The commission's report was left to lie for more than 2¼ years. Its examination was finally requested in ebruary 1876, by a conservative member, von Denzin. Lasker's restraint was understandable as the commission had not only not proposed discarding Strousberg's model, but proposed its continued use (with slight modifications).

Had Strousberg's system, as Lasker claimed, really caused so much damage? His railways operated just as well as the other private railways or state-owned railways and they were helping economic development in their regions. But there was one point which nobody mentioned: Strousberg had made too much money, too quickly, from his railways; that was indisputable.

At any rate, it was clear that Lasker was not in a hurry to have the report debated in the assembly. But although it was now obvious that Strousberg was not really the villain he had been painted as, nothing favourable or justifying his actions was said, either in the assembly or in the press.

Concluding observation

What the commission did not have to investigate with regard to Strousberg, and indeed did not go into, was the frequently-expressed accusation that he was a participant in the "Foundation Swindle" *[Gründungsschwindel]*. The pioneers of the industrial revolution in Germany (referred to as the *"Gründer"*) were obviously to earn money from establishing their businesses. Very often, the *Gründer* floated shares in a new joint stock company at an inflated rate on the stock exchange to make a quick profit and then vanished. Strousberg not only had nothing to do with such practices but did almost exactly the opposite: he made payments to those involved in setting up the company, brought shares to the stock market at less than face value and remained loyal to the company until the line was complete. Strousberg made his money not by starting railway companies, but by constructing railway lines.

The "Foundation Swindles" were made possible by an unfortunate loophole in the law passed in June 1870 which allowed railway joint stock companies to be floated without holding a government concession to build a line. By then, Strousberg was not even active in Prussia; his last railway projects in

Prussia had commenced in 1868, long before the law in question was passed. The real speculative fever did not really take hold until much later, after 1871 and 1872, when the country was awash with reparations money, proceeds from the war with France. The bubble did bust, as any kind of economic bubble inevitably does, with the *Gründerkrach* [Founders Crash] on the Vienna Stock Exchange in May 1873.

While Strousberg was constructing his railways, everyone was reasonably happy. He was getting done that which nobody else could, and the economic importance of his railway projects was indisputable. Europe's industrial revolution was in full swing with Germany lagging behind Britain. At that time Strousberg probably made more of a contribution to developing this aspect of Prussia's infrastructure than anyone else.

As far as Strousberg was concerned, the results of Lasker's attacks were pretty bad. It did not matter that the inquiry found he had done nothing wrong, because nobody had the courage to say so. The damage to his reputation would be long-lasting and he was justifiably bitter.

Weishaupt, the Prussian Government's Railway Commissioner, expressed his views to the Prussian Assembly:

> "Strousberg was certainly a man of his times. At a moment when state funds for railway construction were not available, where private industry had withdrawn itself fully from railway construction, where the old companies were resting on their laurels, Strousberg appeared; he raised the hopes of all districts which had until then been waiting in vain and impatiently for railways. Strousberg understood how to arrange things with flair and how to bring new ventures to life: with the help of financial backers like districts and communities it was easy for him to put down deposits and to to form railway companies fulfilling the legal requirements. Was there a moment of doubt for the government to think to not award the concession to these companies?"

18. THE FIEFDOM OF ZBIROW

The Fiefdom of Zbirow

After Strousberg had left the Romanian railway business and withdrawn from the projects in Hungary and Antwerp, Berlin was no longer central to his industrial activities. He had sold most of his industrial ventures in Prussia and all his railway construction in Prussia apart from the last bit of the Hanover-Altenbeken line was finished.

During this period, 1868, he had bought the estates at Zbirow in Bohemia. The iron-ore and coal deposits there gave him the idea of developing the very basic mining and foundry businesses there to become a vast industrial complex, "the Bohemian Manchester".

The project was an utter failure. Questions about the location, infrastructure, quantity and quality of the ore and coal deposits can be set to one side; the main reason why the enterprise failed was, predictably, Strousberg's lack of capital. He could only borrow money short term, at rates of interest that were way above the norm, and only if he could find a bank that was prepared to lend to him.

Strousberg seemed to have forgotten that he had sold all of his revenue sources which would only just have serviced his borrowing anyway. In Prussia his high borrowing costs had been disguised by his even higher profits from railway construction, but this was no longer the case.

Strousberg buys the Zbirow estates

Zbirow was a huge series of estates, totalling over 25,000 hectares including properties at Zbirow itself, Tocnik, Miröschau (now Mirošov) and Wossek (now Osek) as well as various mines and ironworks. It had formerly belonged to the "k.k. Aerar", that is the Austro-Hungarian Crown Estates.

In April 1866 the Austrian government had borrowed 60 million Austrian Guilders from the *Allgemeinen Österreichischen Boden-Credit-Anstalt* [Austrian General Land Credit Institute], secured by mortgages on State properties including the fiefdom of Zbirow.

According to the Peace of Prague, signed on the 3rd of August 1866, Austria was obliged to pay Prussia 30 million Guilders in war reparations, a sum which was raised by a consortium of banks and businesses. In order to repay this sum could only be paid off using the loan from the *Boden-Credit-Anstalt* but half of that was already spoken for. To raise more money, the finance ministry was forced to sell of several properties which included the estates at Zbirow, a large tract of forest in Bohemia and 12 estates in Galicia. The total price was 12.4 million Guilders; Zbirow accounted for 6.5 million. The purchasers were Samuel Simundt, the Russian Imperial Trade Counsellor in

Berlin, and Vinzenz Kirchmayer, banker and President of the Cracow Chamber of Trade. It was purely a business deal for them and later that year the Zbirow estates were sold on to Strousberg for 9.4 million Gilders, a profit of 2.9 million in just a few months. 6.4 million Guilders had to be paid in cash, in instalments, and 3 million was covered by taking over mortgages. To start with Strousberg paid the amounts due promptly, until in 1870/71 he had difficulties due to his involvement with the railways in Romania, although he kept up his payments by taking out a long term loan for 2,650,000 Guilders.

Together with the 50,000 hectares which he already owned elsewhere, the 25,000 hectares of the Zbirow estates meant that Strousberg now owned an area the size of a small German principality, albeit scattered in several countries.

Strousberg's decision to make such an enormous purchase must have been influenced by the fact that, by his standards, he was enjoying good liquidity. He later wrote that in many months the difference between income and expenditure was over a million Thaler in his favour and even it was not all profit he could use it for profit making ventures and then invest the capital in a high value property.

Lulled into a false sense of security, he could not resist the temptation of acquiring such a high status property with neighbours from the Austro-Hungarian nobility. He would gain new duties as a patron of schools and churches and would be mixing on a social level as an equal of people he had only previously met in the course of business — or so he thought.

The renovation and extension of Schloss Zbirow

After acquiring the estate, Strousberg turned his attention to its seat, the Schloss Zbirow [Zbirow Castle]. Most of the medieval castle, apart from the basic structure, the chapel and an adjacent area had been rebuilt; in the 1840s and 1850s the castle had been significantly extended westwards, but under the Austro-Hungarian Crown Estates it had only been used to provide office space and living accommodation for the administrative staff. Strousberg had other plans: the offices would remain, but the castle would be a summer residence for him and his family, their guests and staff. In keeping with the *Palais Strousberg* in Berlin, the castle would be rebuilt in an extravagant style.

The family's apartments were on the upper floor at the western side, with Strousberg's study adjoining, to the south of which were the library and reception rooms, then came a performance room with a small stage (with only a skylight) and a corridor to the main courtyard, which was intended for use as a picture gallery. On the lower floor were the estate offices, billiards, wine and smoking rooms and, underneath the performance room, the kitchens.

An orangery with a walkway at first floor level was built, closing off the main courtyard to the north. A new main door on the west side of the castle was flanked by two sculpted lions. Outside, there was a new park with terraces, fountains and greenhouses and a pavilion from the Paris world's fair. Finally there was the stables with stalls for more than a hundred horses, a mews, a blacksmith's forge and living accommodation for the stable manager and staff.

The water supply for the castle and the stables was pumped by a newly-installed 20 horsepower steam engine from ponds in the valley.

Strousberg's library was particularly noteworthy. It held over 3000 volumes and largely mirrored that of the *Palais* in Berlin. Quite how he ever found time to open a book for pleasure instead of for reference is a mystery.

Agriculture and forestry

The most important of the estate's activities was forestry, which took up some 21,800 of its 25,000 hectares. Strousberg panned to use income from the timber sales to service his loans, but that appeared to be endangered in December 1868, just a few weeks after Strousberg had taken over. Hurricane force winds and heavy snow brought down over a million cubic metres of timber, several year's worth of normal felling. Then, in winter 1870 there was another, even more powerful, storm followed in May 1872 by serious flooding.

Sale of the windfall timber did at least raise money for Strousberg.

In comparison, agriculture was much less important. The landscape was pleasant, but the soil was poor and not well irrigated. Fruit production was disadvantaged by the climate and as a consequence farming concentrated on livestock production. When Strousberg took over, most of the farms were leased; he terminated the leases to take control himself. Altogether there was quite a collection of businesses which included livestock and poultry, a 250 horse stud and extensive fruit orchards with over 22000 trees, market gardens, a brewery and fishponds. However, it was not very profitable. Strousberg complained about the management costs, especially the expense of maintaining 17 parish churches.

Industrial activities and dreams of a "Bohemian Manchester"

In December 1868 Strousberg visited the estates and wrote that Zbirow had cost between ten and eleven million guilders on which interest had to be paid but the storms had transformed the business from a cash cow into a money eater. It had potential, he said, but only someone – such as himself – able to raise funds from other sources could see it through. Having been to Zbirow he was convinced that the area was ripe for industrial exploitation.

A small scale iron industry using the local coal and iron ore had been established for over three centuries. It was centred on Franzensthal (now Františkov in the Czech Republic), very near Zbirow township and on Dobriv, Holoubkau and Straschitz in the southern portion of the estate. Furnaces, mostly wood-fired, produced cast and wrought iron. Strousberg thought that it was primitive and must have been excited at the prospect of introducing modern industrial techniques. At that time, the start of 1869, he still owned a huge revenue generator, that is his industrial empire in Prussia, from which he could service the costs of expansion.

The iron-ore and coal reserves on the estates were only valuable if they could be processed locally which meant that blast furnaces, rolling mills and so on would have to be built. After building the plant, he would be able to make iron and steel in Austria at about the same price as imports from Belgium.

Strousberg set to work immediately, and by the end of 1870 had invested heavily in the iron-ore mines.

What was Strousberg's industrial aim? He planned to expand the ore workings to an area of 600 hectares and the coal mines to 210 hectares, build blast furnaces at Franzensthal, Holoubkau and Dobriv, coking plants in Miröschau and Dobriv, puddle works, rolling mills and forges at Borek and in Dobriv, a Bessemer converter at Borek and a wagon factory at Holoubkau: the chain ran from raw materials to finished product.

However, this could not happen overnight and in the meantime Strousberg's period of good liquidity [during which he had bought Zbirow and decided to expand its industry] was over because of events in Romania. He had to limit his expansion plans and extend the timescale for carrying them out until affairs in Romania were settled at the beginning of 1872. Not for the first time, the newspapers were not particularly impressed with the pans, but that did not bother Strousberg.

Organisation of the management

When Strousberg took over Zbirow at the end of 1868 and drew up his ambitious plans, he already had his hands full with previous projects. In Prussia, the Tilsit-Insterburg line was complete but the other six lines were still under construction. Work was in progress on the railways in Hungary and in Romania, to be followed in 1870 by the Brest-Grajewo line in Russia. His industrial ventures in Dortmund, Hanover, Othfresen and Neustadt were running and being expanded. In addition, there was the project in Antwerp and the "sidelines" in Berlin (the livestock market, the market hall, *Die Post* (the newspaper) and the Geestemünde fisheries) and finally the other estates.

The Fiefdom of Zbirow

Strousberg therefore needed to retain his headquarters and a specialist staff in Berlin. It was therefore imperative to be able to control things from Zbirow and in March 1869 everything was formally restructured to enable this.

A *Generaldirektor* took charge overall and there were directors for each business area, but Strousberg had the final say on important matters especially concerning revenue and finance: pricing for iron and steel products and timber, plans for logging and for personnel decisions. He centralised all income and expenditure at a cashier's office established in Prague and set up a system of reporting for each division, but evebtually this system did not provide Strousberg with enough information. From October 1872 onwards, the directors were required to hold formal meetings every two or three weeks, with a verbatim transcript of all the discussions and opinions going to the *Herr Doktor* in Berlin for his personal comments; these would be written by hand in the margins and could be quite drastic — a clear indication of Strousberg's authoritarian management style and also a sign that he was firmly in control.

The work of the administration in Zbirow

Strousberg had a problem which needed to be taken seriously. The estates at Zbirow had previously belonged to the Austrian Emperor, the highest authority in the land. As a Prussian it was going to be hard work to build up a relationship of trust with the locals.

Timber theft was rife. The locals had become accustomed to helping themselves, and the Crown Estate had tolerated this. In some cases, Strousberg's foresters were forced to return confiscated stolen wood: in one case they were faced by a hundred strong mob. Strousberg behaved badly too: if he needed land for his mines or railway, he just took it, leaving the owner to fight for compensation.

The political situation was important too. Czech nationalism had grow since the 1840s from a cultural to a political movement and it was becoming hard for the Austrian government to keep it down; even members of the Bohemian nobility were beginning to support it.

The liquidity problem gets worse

Events in Romania had forced Strousberg to cut back on his investments in Zbirow, but in February 1872 he had ben able to get out of Romania and the sale of his industrial assets in Prussia gave him some breathing space which enabled him to concentrate on the expansions in Zbirow. However, this meant more expenditure but less income. In 1871 money was already tight and Strousberg resorted to paying his workers partly not in cash but in coupons redeemable for groceries at local stores, although he soon had to stop as the Police intervened to ban the practice.

During 1873 Strousberg was then hit by two events: firstly, the attack in the Prussian parliament by Lasker and secondly the Vienna stock market crash.

The personal defamation and damage to his reputation caused by Lasker's attack prompted Strousberg to leave Berlin and return to London, where had the unused mansion at 5, Grosvenor Place at his disposal as well as a joint firm with Joseph Bray, to whom he was now related by marriage. Strousberg later said that he wanted to keep his business in Berlin but setting up an office in London made it possible for him to use his contacts there; the idea had been to set up a company in London to finance the scheme in Antwerp and also to bid for overseas railway concessions.

Nothing came of these schemes and Strousberg had to hurry back to Berlin to deal with a series of setbacks. The Hanover-Altenbeken Railway was refusing to pay 1.5 million Thaler in construction costs, despite being correctly billed in the normal way, and on the payment of which he had relied. In addition he was being sued for damages in connection with construction work on several railway lines (Halle-Sorau-Guben, Hanover-Altenbeken and Brest-Grajewo) and for unpaid stamp duty on notarised contracts from the short-lived *Allgemeinen Eisenbahn-Bau-Gesellschaft*. Strousberg claimed that all these events were unexpected but in truth they were things which he had been ignoring for years. So it should be no surprise that he lost every case and large damages were awarded against him.

On top of all this came the Vienna stock market crash in May 1873 and the subsequent crisis which meant that one of Strousberg's main sources of finance virtually dried up.

Strousberg was able to raise six or seven hundred thousand Thaler by selling the contents of the Wilhelmstrasse picture gallery, but returning to London to continue his plans there was out of the question.

The expansion of Zbirow stalled, and this became public knowledge. Reports circulated of iron from Belgium and Germany standing waiting to be unloaded at stations, sealed by customs because the estates could not pay the import duty. In March 1873 the Škoda heavy engineering company was prevented from installing previously ordered pit head equipment at the Wejwanow (now Vejvanov) mine because the preparatory earthworks had not been carried out.

The urgent need for cost savings preoccupied the management in Zbirow, especially with regard to wage costs. From 1872 onwards arrears of wages were allowed to build up. Wages were paid in part, and income tax was deducted from salaried staff but not passed on to the tax office. Dodgy practices like these became the norm. Sacking people to save money became almost impossible as they were then entitled to immediate payment of the accumulated arrears.

The workers' situation became critical, and eventually, in November 1873, the workers made a formal complaint to the mining commissioners who ordered the arrears to be settled within three days. Strousberg decided to pay out the workers who had acted as spokesmen and then fire them together at the same time. The rest of the workforce got nothing and the commissioners were informed that the reason was "the Herr Doktor does not recognise any workers' corporation."

Due to the wages arrears situation it is not surprising that the workers were worried about their contributions to the *Bruderladenkasse* (a sort of friendly society, which made small payments to its members in cases of illness or death). The funds belonged to the members, but were administered by Strousberg's management. An audit by the Prague mining commissioners, requested by the workforce, found that the assets of around 113,000 Guilders were untouched but since 1873 over 9000 Guilders had been deducted from wages but not paid in to the fund.

In spite of the large and profitable timber trade, the monetary situation overall was very tight.

19. DEALINGS WITH THE COMMERCIAL LOAN BANK

Strousberg finds a new bank

Strousberg had placed himself in a position of extreme iliquidity. When expanding the new industries at the fiefdom of Zbirow he seemed to have lost sight of the fact that he no longer had any real sources of income. He borrowed more and more money to pump into the "bohemian Manchester", and his debts mounted. More and more of his time was taken up with fending off creditors and he was on the edge of insolvency.

When the Commercial Loan Bank in Moscow offered him a loan—the first time in his career that a bank had approached him—he jumped at the chance. Never mind that the conditions were dreadful, never mind that it all seemed rather convenient as if they were waiting for him, never mind that no reputable bank would touch him with the proverbial barge-pole. All that mattered was to get the money, no matter what.

When the bank collapsed Strousberg would be totally enmeshed. He would be arrested and tried on criminal charges in Moscow and then made bankrupt as a direct result; he would be detained in Moscow for nearly two years and it would be the end of his *Imperium*.

The Commercial Loan Bank in Moscow

The Commercial Loan Bank had only been established since 1870. Its founders and shareholders were respected and influential Moscow businessmen; its customers largely came from the Moscow area too.

The bank's first president, Daniel Schumacher, was a state counsellor and a future mayor of Moscow. The 15-man board radiated solidity, including horary citizens and trade guild officials. Its chairman, Borissovsky, was reputedly one of the richest men in Moscow and the bank was trusted by the public. However, although the bank's management appeared solid, the centre of banking activity in Russia was St. Petersburg, not Moscow, and finding suitable commercial staff proved difficult.

The senior director, Polyansky, had been a highly ranked government official but he admitted himself that he was completely unfamiliar with the business of banking. Another of the directors, Milliotti, was in the same position. Neither of then had enough weight to deal with the Moscow clique on the management board. The manager for foreign business, Prehn, did not make enough profit for the board and was replaced by Gustav Landau, an experienced banker from Warsaw.

Landau became head of the foreign department in early 1873 and quickly developed a huge volume of trading in shares, bonds and currency. Contrary to all normal practice Landau was allowed to sign off on his own, a fact which was circulated to all foreign correspondent banks indicating that it had been approved by the board

The relationship between Landau and his colleagues was strained from the start. Landau earned more than his boss, Polyansky. On top of this, Polyansky and Milliotti only spoke Russian and Landau only spoke German. At that time the preferred language in Russian banking was German and so Landau worked in that language which effectively prevented his co-directors from seeing what he was up to; not a good situation for any company let alone a bank.

By the end of 1873, the Commercial Loan Bank was in trouble because of its trading activities, not least because of the *Gründerkrach* (founders' crash) on the Vienna stock market in May of that year.[1] They had bought large numbers of bonds at a high price before the crash and if following proper accounting practice should have declared a loss then. In March 1874 the bank's board members realised this and were very angry because if it became public knowledge, as major shareholders they stood to lose large amounts. In addition the figures showed that the bank had bought more bonds than its articles allowed, and that would be obvious when the accounts were published.

What did they do? They falsified the accounts. Using retrospective posting dates, they made it look as if 930,000 roubles in securities had in fact already been sold to other banks at the (higher) pre-crash rate.

This meant that declaring a loss was avoided and at the same time the securities were "hidden" and fell off the balance sheet, their place being taken by money owed by the banks who had 'purchased' the securities. In reality the securities, although no longer on the books, remained the bank's property along with the rate risk; some of the certificates were even still on bank premises.

The board did the same thing for the ongoing – 1874 – business year, to the tune of 286,000 roubles and so by the end of 1874 over 1.2 million roubles in securities had been hidden.

Before the board took these measures they sent the directors out of the meeting and gave the job of making the alterations to the head book keeper, Loshetshnikov (who later claimed to have 'discovered' the deception).

The accounts still had to be passed by the bank's shareholders at their annual general meeting. To ensure a majority, shares with voting rights held in trust

---

[1] Germany and Austria had seen an economic boom during the Gründerjahre (founders' years) from German unification in 1870-71 to the crash in 1873. The boom was fuelled by a new incorporation law which made it easier to incorporate new enterprises and reincorporate old ones. Euphoria over victory in the Franco-Prussian war in 1871, and an influx of French war reparations led to massive stock market speculation especially in railways, industry and shipping. Like all booms it proved unsustainable and on the 9th of May 1873, the Vienna Stock Exchange crashed. Several Vienna banks failed leading to a reduction in the amount of money available for business lending. French payment war reparations to Germany ended in September 1873 which added to the effects of the crash there.

were distributed to friends and relatives of board members and then reregistered to the correct owners later without their knowledge. The ballot papers were discretely marked in order to keep an eye on voting. This shows that the board knew exactly what it was doing.

Landau, whose mistakes had caused the problems in the first place, had his authority to sign on his own withdrawn by the board and now needed Polyansky to countersign agreements but the damage had been done.

Strousberg's dealings with the Commercial Loan Bank begin

In 1874 Strousberg was about to start doing business, although he did not know it, with a bank whose board was without scruples, a management team who neither trusted one another nor cooperated with one another and published falsified balance sheets.

The relationship began in a rather strange way. Strousberg had a long-standing arrangement with the firm of Manczyk & Schlesinger, a fairly minor private bank in Berlin, which he used for small jobs. One of the partners, Manczyk, had just come back from one such job in Russia and reported that he had met an old acquaintance, Gustav Landau, in St. Petersburg: Landau was now a director of the Commercial Loan Bank in Moscow; they had come to speak with Strousberg, and Landau (who had followed and admired Strousberg's career for years, he said) was prepared to do business. In short, Landau offered Strousberg advance, payable via Manczyk & Schlesinger, on condition that Strousberg took part of the loan in 'effects'[1] which the bank was stuck with at the price which the bank had paid, which was higher than their market value.

Obviously this meant the stocks and bonds which Landau had bought before the crash and which were the reason for the accounts being falsified. As an example, if Strousberg was due to receive a loan of 500,000 Thaler he would get 100,000 Thaler in 'effects', which he could sell for 40,000 Thaler, a loss of 60,000 Thaler; effectively a fee of 12% on the whole sum in addition to the interest on the main amount. And that is just a simple example. The proportion of 'effects' might be higher and their market value lower, so the conditions were really usurious.

The whole thing was most odd. Strousberg was being offered loans which he had never asked for, by a bank he had never heard of, at horrendous rates of interest. The question has to be asked, was Strousberg's reputation already so bad or had Manczyk told Landau that things were so bad that he thought it was worth a try?

Landau thought that the high risk was acceptable as he saw the chance of getting the bank out of the hole he had dug with his disastrous effect trading.

There was indeed interest on both sides and soon there was a considerable amount of business being done on the basis of payments made partly in cash

---

[1] Toxic assets, in current terms.

and partly in effects; of course, by acting as middlemen Manczyk & Schlesinger were able to pocket plenty of commission.

Loans made to Strousberg probably came to over seven million roubles. More than two million roubles vanished by accepting payments in 'effects', commissions for Manczyk & Schlesinger and 'gifts' for the bank's directors (it is thought that Landau alone pocketed over a million).

Details of the loans

The first two loans were advanced to Strousberg by Manczyk & Schlesinger acting on behalf of the Commercial Loan Bank. Strousberg did not have a direct relationship with the Russian bank himself at that time.

In March 1874 Strousberg was in the process of withdrawing from the project in Antwerp. He had already given the Belgian finance minister, Malou, notice of his intention to withdraw and that he wanted his initial payment of 3,150,000 Francs to be returned by the Belgian state: however he was still waiting for his money, and so he obtained "a substantial sum" as an advance on the expected repayment from Belgium. The payment arrived more quickly than expected, during that same month in fact, and Strousberg paid back the advance.

As a replacement he received a second loan of 1 million Thaler, also via Manczyk. This was secured by a mortgage on the industrial premises at Zbirow in favour of the Commercial Loan Bank; because of this Strousberg viewed the loan as long-term and planned to use the money partly to invest in the expansion of the industrial activities at Zbirow and also to realise a long held ambition. The fiefdom as a whole was heavily mortgaged and Strousberg planned a division, with the mortgages being registered against the agricultural and forested land, the Schloss Zbirow and the administrative buildings. The industrial sites and the workers' housing would be made debt-free. This would separate them from Strousberg's agricultural land and forests in Zbirow in order to make them available as security for a new loan.

The existing mortgage creditors were prepared to cooperate in this, but they required 600,000 Thaler to release Strousberg from his mortgages. He proposed to take this amount from the loan made by the Commercial Loan Bank.

Strousberg and Gustav Landau met in person for the first time in May 1874. At this meeting Landau explained that the bank did not regard the loan as long-term because they were not in the mortgage business and would want to be repaid by the beginning of 1875 at the latest. Strousberg explained that he could not do so as he had used the money for long-term projects; he suggested to Landau that his bank extend the loan period, as he could then use the resources in Zbirow "to support construction enlarge the property and at a suitable time place the mortgage elsewhere". Landau, at least according to Strousberg, was in favour. At any rate it is clear that both Strousberg and Landau wanted to carry on doing business.

The next deal was the first one not brokered by Manczyk & Schlesinger but negotiated directly with Landau: the bank was to finance delivery by Strousberg of an order of railway wagons for Russia. Strousberg wanted this order for the railway wagon works which he was building in Holoubkau. He had agreed with the Russian railway magnate S. S. Polyakov to supply 2000 wagons for the Kursk-Charkow-Asow railway.

For every wagon which he dispatched to Poljakow—certified by producing a waybill to the bank— Strousberg would receive an advance of 600 roubles (later revised to 1200 roubles. This was all to be paid in cash, so there was no troublesome payment in "Effects" to deal with.

Strousberg had great difficulty in actually fulfilling the order at all. When he made the agreement with Polyakov and fixed the delivery dates ((1000 wagons by the end of 1874 and a further 1000 by the middle of 1875), the wagon works in Holoubkau were almost finished but not quite ready to start production. Strousberg had to find a way out and solved the problem by leasing a wagon works at Bubna, a suburb of Prague.

The Bubna works had hardly any orders at that time due to the economic situation which meant that Strousberg was able to make a good deal with the company which owned them. He leased the factory for a period of seven years for an annual payment of 54,000 Austrian Guilders. There was an option to purchase the factory for 910,000 Austrian Guilders after this period had elapsed and he paid 30,000 Austrian Guilders per year, which would be deducted from the total if he exercised the option to purchase, leaving 700,000 Austrian Guilders to pay. If he did not take up the option then the money would be lost. Strousberg had complete control over the factory and made his son *Prokurist* for the firm.

Acquiring the factory cost 84,000 Austrian Guilders per annum which Strousberg, in his typically over-optimistic manner expected to cover easily. But it was not so easy. Despite long hours and seven day working at both Bubna and Holoubkau Strousberg could only manage to deliver 1700 wagons on time; he did build the remaining 300 but they were so late that Polyakov refused to take delivery.

Strousberg obviously wanted to keep both hid own works at Holoubkau and the leased Bubna factory busy. He saw the deal with Polyakov, who was prominent in Russian railway circles, as a way in to the trade in railway wagons for Russia. He agreed the financing by the Commercial Loan Bank of a second batch of wagons. This would also be of 2000 trucks, but they had not been ordered by Polyakov or anyone else for that matter: they were what the building trade calls a 'speculative build', a very risky proposition especially during an economic downturn.

The Commercial Loan Bank was prepared to finance the plan, despite the risk, and was even ready to help sell the wagons on the Russian railway market as they saw the chance of "disposing of more foreign effects."

The 2000 wagons in this second batch were supposed to be ready for delivery three months after completing the batch for Polyakov, but the bank's financing was meant to start immediately—even though there were not yet any wagons to deliver. It was really financing of work in progress, and a special kind of document had to be invented to back it: the provisional waybill ("Frachtbrief-Promesse"). This document looked very similar an actual waybill except that it had the word "Promesse" (promise) after its heading and the remark "to be delivered after completion" (*"Nach Fertigstellung zu liefern"*.) It it quite clear that these bits of paper did not document finished railway wagons. In effect they were glorified IOUs. In spite of this, the same insurance policies were attached to them as were associated with proper waybills, although no actual goods were shipped and there was no insurable risk.

Strousberg presented the provisional waybills to the Commercial Loan Bank from April or May 1875 and on their strength received advances: 600 roubles per promised wagon to start with, shortly thereafter raised to 900 roubles. Incredible, because as Strousberg conceded, when the amount was increased, he had not yet delivered a single wagon.

If they were ever delivered, the 2000 railway wagons would require around 15 kilometres of sidings to store them on: the bank therefore rented enough track on the Smolensk Railway. As it turned out a much shorter length would have been enough because only 105 wagons from the second batch were delivered. The sidings were also used to store the 300 wagons which Polyakov had refused to take delivery of.

These 405 wagons were still without a buyer as the economy was still sluggish. Any wagons that Strousberg had actually sent to Russia had been sent 'on spec.' And it was widely rumoured that he had empowered the Commercial Loan Bank to sell them at any price.

The Commercial Loan Bank's advances in respect of the second batch of wagons eventually came to 1.9 million roubles, but the only 'security' which the bank had were the 405 wagons mentioned. There were very few possible buyers, and by summer 1875 Strousberg had only managed to deliver 119 wagons to the Waagtal-Bahn, which was his own project. In Holoubkau there were enough parts in stock to a build another 200 trucks: it was only possible to complete and sell them to Russia later, by which time Strousberg had already gone bankrupt. In 1881 there were 60 of the trucks made by Strousberg in use on the Charkov Railway which nobody wanted because their accumulated storage costs were more than their value.

Although Strousberg's wagon production capacity by now far exceeded the number that could be sold, after leasing the works at Bubna he had bought yet another wagon works, the *Elbinger Aktien-Gesellschaft für Fabrikation von Eisenbahnmaterial [Elbing Railway Materials Production Company]* in Elbing (now Elblag in Poland). This factory, which had produced over 2000 wagons per year at the beginning of the 1870s, was now out of use. Even under Strousberg it did not reopen; the purchase was a failed venture.

Strousberg returns to railway construction

Strousberg was initially not successful in his attempts to find new sources of income. During the winter of 1874 he spent several months in St. Petersburg looking for new projects. There was talk that the city of Petersburg required a horse tramway, but according to Strousberg you would only have a chance if you used the 'golden key' on the councillors (that is to say bribed them) which he could not do. He did however buy the closed down Babushkin Rail Fastening Factory, which was already bankrupt: this acquired him property in St. Petersburg cheaply, and he was required to own local property before he could register in St. Petersburg as a "First Grade Merchant". He duly registered; having that status might be useful for any future business in Russia.

In the meantime he returned to the area which had earned him more than any other: railway construction. The first project which he was offered was to complete the Mehltheuer-Weida Railway; the Waagtal-Bahn and the Paris-Narbonne line would follow.

The **Mehltheuer-Weida Railway** had been started with high hopes at the beginning of 1872. Just 36 kilometres long, it was meant to link Mehltheuer, not far from Plauen in Saxony, to Weida in Thuringia in order to provide the southern commercial areas around Hof and Plauen with the shortest route to the north, including Gera, Erfurt and Magdeburg. Despite its short length the line passed through four states, all of which had to be involved in the concession-awarding procedure. The company wanted to finance construction of the line with 3.5 million Thaler, raised by issuing shares and bonds. However it was the usual story: the bonds could not be placed with the public even via the appointed general contractor, Grambow, who was forced to suspend work in November 1874 because the money had run out.

Strousberg jumped in at the end of 1874 and took on the task of finishing construction by autumn 1875. However, the line was not ready by that date, despite strenuous efforts by Strousberg. He invested 1.5 million Marks but had only recouped 1.25 million in bonds. At the end of October he was arrested in Moscow, so a second suspension of work was unavoidable. In mid-1876 the company went bankrupt. In 1878 the Saxony government took over the job of finishing the line and it was finally opened on November 14th 1883.

The **Waagtal-Bahn** was also a project to finish and extend a line on which work had been interrupted. Initially the plan had been to convert the horse-drawn railway from Pressburg (now Bratislava, capital of Slovakia) to Tyrnau (now Trnava in Slovakia) for steam locomotives, but the plans were then revised to extend the line along the Waag valley towards Trentschin and over the Vlara pass to make a connection between Troppau and Mährisch-Ostrau and the border with Upper Silesia possible.

The project was backed by the Breslau *Discontobank* and the Vienna *Wechslerbank*, but it did not have a state guarantee. In the wake of the Vienna stock market crash in May 1873 the *Wechslerbank* collapsed and an attempt to rescue the project by getting the Bankhaus Bleichröder in Berlin to take over the *Wechslerbank*'s share failed when Bleichröder's partners rejected the idea or participation categorically. The railway company's board wanted construction to continue and eventually succeeded in interesting Strousberg. Obviously there were doubts about his taking charge because of his attitude and (lack of) commitment to other schemes in Hungary, notably the Neutratalbahn and the Nordostbahn.

But despite the concerns Strousberg was given the job in February 1875. The route from Tyrnau to the Vlara pass, some 97 kilometres was to be built, at a cost of 6.5 million Austrian Guilders. The costs were to be borne by the *Eisenbahn-Gesellschaft Waagtal-Bahn* (*Vágvölgyi Vasut* in Hungarian) and the holders of the State concession were three Counts, Breuer, Zichy and Erdödy.

Strousberg was to receive his payments according to monthly invoices for work carried out, not in cash but in the form of bond certificates issued by the railway company. It was then up to Strousberg to sell them to the public and raise the money for building materials and wages.

The bond certificates were 'good' paper, backed by entry in the railway land register, but they were missing one vital thing: a guarantee from the Hungarian state. Without this, and this is why the Bankhaus Bleichröder had refused to get involved, the Vienna Stock Exchange would not allow the bonds to be listed; this meant that they could not be traded in Vienna, an almost insurmountable obstacle to their public sale. They were listed on the Budapest Stock Exchange, but that was little use as the major money market was in Vienna. Strousberg blamed hostility from the Austrian State Railways for the Vienna Stock Exchange's decision but it was too late: he had signed the contracts without a guarantee.

Work began in the 13th of April 1875 and as usual with Strousberg made good progress. It even seemed possible that the first 52 kilometres from Tyrnau to Waagneustadtl (Vagujhely) would be completed before the agreed date, the 1st of May 1876. But this turned out not to be possible because of Strousberg's arrest in Moscow and the subsequent insolvency of the business. How things then proceeded would be up to the insolvency administrator in Prague.

The **Paris-Narbonne Railway** was different: in the cases of the two railways mentioned above Strousberg was actually working on a real construction project, at least until his arrest in Moscow. However, the Paris-Narbonne railway remained a scheme on paper only.

In February 1875 Strousberg had been granted a concession for a line from Paris to Narbonne. This would be over 800 kilometres in length and construction costs were estimated at 500 to 600 million Francs.

Strousberg wrote later that he had become involved because of a group of British financiers which approached his London office to offer him the construction work for the line. This group had already registered a company, which had bought up legal rights and construction plans and had begun preparatory work using its own technical staff. Payment would be made in shares in this company, and some had already been reserved for him. Later, some of them would turn up as evidence at Strousberg's trial in Moscow: certificates for 3,717,300 Francs of shares in the Paris-Narbonne Railway Company which had been pledged as loan security, together with contracts with Strousberg, a map of the projected route and, finally, a demand to Strousberg to make a further payment on his shares.

This confirmed what Strousberg had said, but nobody believed: the Paris-Narbonne Railway Company had existed and Strousberg was involved. True, he had not actually built anything but he had never claimed that he had; but he had been chosen as the contractor for two sections of the route. These were the 154 kilometres from Bourges to Gien and from Argent to Beaune-la-Rolande in the Departements Cher und Loiret, east of Orléans and under concession to the Compagnie des Chemins de Fer de Bourges à Gien et d'Argent à Beaune-la-Rolande.

On the 23rd of Marh 1873 Strousberg had agreed with this company to prepare plans, carry out certain earthworks and structural works and to pay a deposit. But he did not fulfil his obligations. After his arrest in Moscow, the company brought a civil case against Strousberg at the Tribunal de Commerce de la Seine in Paris and requested the court to annul the March 1875 and make Strousberg liable to pay damages set provisionally at 100 Francs. Judgement was passed in Strousberg's absence, on the 11th of December 1875. This was the third venture to be ended by Strousberg's arrest in Moscow.

The situation in Zbirow

Despite his financial plight Strousberg continued to operate his factories and even ordered more equipment.

The main source of income at Zbirow continued to be from sale of timber but the revenue from these was not even enough to pay the fiefdom's wages bill in full. This meant that Strousberg could only make part payments on at best on the new equipment and his suppliers eventually had to make claims to the administrator when insolvency proceedings against Strousberg began. The works had ongoing requirements for new materials and the amounts which Strousberg eventually owed, especially for pig iron and steel products from the Rhine and Ruhr were considerable.

Strousberg's expectation of further help from the Commercial Loan Bank in Moscow must have played a part in the decision to carry on.

Purchase of the Schatzlar collieries

In August 1875 it became known, to general incredulity, that Strousberg had purchased the collieries at Schatzlar in Bohemia (now Žacléř in the Hradec Králové Region of the Czech Republic). The puzzle of how, with his well-known money problems, he could afford such a purchase was soon solved: the acquisition required almost no resources. The previous owner, a Baron Silberstein, was so heavily in debt that the collieries had already been sequestrated by his creditors. Included in the 2 million Austrian Guilders sale price were the assumption by Strousberg of 1.7 million Austrian Guilders of Silberstein's debt related to Schatzlar. He gave the Baron bills of exchange for 100,000 Austrian Guilders and a promissory note (basically an IOU) redeemable five years later for the remaining 200,000 Austrian Guilders.

Why Strousberg wanted the collieries is not clear. It is possible that he could have used the coking grade coal from Schatzlar to supply the planned blast furnaces at Zbirow. However, the first effect was that Silberstein's former creditors had now become Strousberg's creditors, and Schaffner – his lawyer in Prague – had to fend them off.

This purchase did not make much impact, either industrially or financially. When Strousberg went bankrupt, the receiver sold off the Schatzlar collieries for 2 million Austrian Guilders to a consortium of mortgage lenders whose interest at that value was entered in the Land Register.

But first of all, he had to use all means possible to stay afloat. One device that he used was to issue bills of exchange to raise cash. 285,000 Marks came from no less than 20 small lenders like this. On top of this 221,000 Marks came from Mendelssohn & Co in Berlin, 141,000 Marks from Manczyk & Schlesinger and even 250,000 Marks from old business ties to Romania: over 900,000 Marks in all. Admittedly, Strousberg had to accept dreadful discount rates for this paper; the talk was of rates up to 50% per annum.

Expensive as it was, this method did at least allow Strousberg to raise money. However, after the usual three month lifetime, the bills came back to Strousberg for redemption at face value. On top of this, other commitments were constantly falling due. Monitoring what was due and when it was due, reminding Strousberg, making sure money was available to redeem the bills or agree postponement of due dates became such a financial juggling act that it took a clever man to do it: this man was Strousberg's lawyer in Prague, Dr. Cornelius Schaffner.

Schaffner kept a meticulous diary of all business transactions and from the beginning of 1875 up until u Strousberg's arrest in October of that ear it takes up 220 pages. This remarkable document shows Strousberg heading uncontrollably towards insolvency and records each event, from the efforts to make cash available, to appeals to creditors for patience, their reactions and, in some cases, their harsh countermeasures.

Some creditors were fairly aggressive in their attitudes. Henri Marchot from Brussels, Strousberg's long term iron supplier sent the bailiffs in on the 27th of October 1875, when Strousberg had already left Zbirow for Moscow, to secure walking possession on various items: machinery, cattle and horses, the famous carriage amid four, and a phaeton. Carl Beringer from Stuttgart was owed 'only' 1230 Austrian Guilders but he got his money by threatening to start insolvency proceedings at the bankruptcy court, and this was as early as the first quarter of 1875.

Schaffner was constantly occupied negotiating about the payments which Strousberg still owed on the Tereschau estate and the mines at Wejwanow which he had taken over in 1872 and not yet paid for. Other creditors who had allowed credit secured against assets, like the transport company Schenker (security of five railway wagons at Bubna) or the Vienna *Creditanstalt* bank (loans secured on stocks of metal) clamoured constantly for payment and he had to keep them at bay: the *Creditanstalt* charged 15-19% interest, rates which showed what sort of cuustomer this well regarded bank thought Strousberg was.

The entries in Schaffner's diary show clearly that, way before his arrest in Moscow, Strousberg was in such a calamitous financial position that he was virtually insolvent.

The Commercial Loan Bank – the last resort?

In this situation Strousberg had to turn again and again to the Commercial Loan Bank for money as he could not take anything out of his recent railway undertakings. At what rate he made his demands is not known but his debts to the ban eventually came to over seven million roubles.

Strousberg's debt mountain was growing by the month and Landau und Poliansky allowed this to happen. Strousberg kept on making unexpected withdrawals by presenting bills of exchange which the bank felt obliged to honour. Strousberg knew that the bank could hardly do otherwise, as it had to avoid showing anything which might cause doubts about its creditworthiness. The bank's directors were well aware of what was going on, shown by the fact that for months on end the bills presented by Strousberg were not shown in the bank's internal monthly summary accounts.

Strousberg had put up several items as security for the loans, all from his latest railway ventures: 1,184,000 Austrian Guilders in Waagtalbahn bonds and 3,717300 Francs in Paris-Narbonne Railway shares; the original certificates were deposited with the bank.

The stated values were realistic in as much as that Strousberg had either made payments to or done work to those values for both companies. Converted to

Russian currency they came together to almost 1.5 million roubles. In reality they were hardly credible as security for a loan: the Waagtalbahn bonds were not listed by the Vienna Stock Exchange and therefore virtually impossible to trade, and it was not possible to demand back. In effect, he now owed the bank so much against such inadequate security that if called in the securities then the bank itself would be endangered. Keeping Strousberg going was therefore the bank's main concern and for his part Strousberg was looking for a way to support this position of mutual interest with a new consolidated form of security.

The Deutsch-Böhmische Actien-Gesellschaft

Strousberg planned to consolidate all of his industrial interests into a new company, limited by shares. He could then offer shares in this company to creditors as security for loans. The new *Actiengesellschaft für deutsche und böhmische Eisen- und Stahl-Fabrikate* [German and Bohemian Iron and Steel Products Company] was registered in Berlin in summer 1875. It had a nominal share capital of 25.5 million Reichsmark of which 10.5 million Reichsmark were ordinary shares and 15 million Reichsmark were priority shares.

The new company included all of Strousberg's remaining industrial interests. In Germany these were the Neustädter Hütte ironworks, the Siegerland and northern Harz iron ore mines, the Marienhütte ironworks in Danzig, and in Bohemia the industrial enterprises on the Zbirow fiefdom (the blast furnaces at Franzensthal, Strasic and Holoubkau, the rolling mills and forges at Am Borek and in Dobriv, the Am Borek bessemer converter and housing complex, the Holoubkau wagon works and its housing complex, plus 73 ironstone quarries and 13 collieries). All specified in Article 33 of the Company's Articles of Association. All of these were Bethel Henry Strousberg's own property. He received the above-mentioned 23.5 million Reichsmarks in shares from the company in payment, thus becoming its sole shareholder.

According to the comany's articles, Strousberg was obliged to finish building all the works by the 1st of July 1877 and also to construct another six blast furnaces and lay another 60 kilometres of line for the works railway.

Although Strousberg had decided to consolidate everything into a joint stock company, he wanted to run it himself as before. For this reason, article 35 allowed Strousberg to run things exclusively until the 1st of July 1877.

Strousberg expected his "Bohemian Manchester" to be complete by mid-1877.

Things were structured in such a way that although legally the company owned the plant, Strousberg owned all of the shares and ran everything. From a practical point of view nothing had changed. This was Strousberg's intention: he wanted to use the assets, which had now been incorporated as a company, as security for loans from the Commercial Loan Bank. Technically, all he now had to do was to pledge the shares as. security, far easier than obtaining a mortgage on each property separately.

12 million Mark in priority shares were pledged to the Commercial Loan Bank. The share certificates, together with other securities (bonds from the *Waagtalbahn* and Paris-Narbonne Railway shares) were deposited in the bank's vaults.

The works and plants were not yet complete. Their book value could be reduced, but the problem remained of providing their full value as security in the future. Strousberg brought something else into play. In March 1875 his son, Bethel Henry jun., visited the Commercial Loan Bank in Moscow, accompanied by Wartenberg, attorney for a Vienna bank, H. v. Goldschmidt & Co. Wartenberg explained that his bank intended to lend Strousberg about 9 million Austrian Guilders in July or August, secured on the works at Zbirow. This money would be used to finish the works off and then the management of the works would come under the bank's trusteeship.

Goldschmidt & Co. had already ordered an independent valuation of the Zbirow works to be carried out by an expert engineer. The estimate of 24 million Marks was in line with the 23 million Marks in the company's articles.

During his trial in Moscow Strousberg's defence lawyer, Spiro, observed that the values in this estimate had to be viewed as realistic and could not have been overstated, because they were not simply made up by Strousberg, but obtained by Goldschmidt & Co to use as the basis for assessing a loan to Strousberg.

Goldschmidt & Co were not able to make good on their promise as such a loan would have been too much for them. They had lent Strousberg 1.5 million Austrian Guilders, but this was not enough to save him.

The last days in Zbirow

On the 15th of October, Strousberg received a telegram from the Commercial Loan Bank in Moscow saying that in order to put his affairs in order and reach a settlement with his creditors, he was requested to travel to Moscow.

For Strousberg, this could mean only one thing: the bank in Moscow was prepared to negotiate and help him reach a settlement, and to do this they were going to grant him a bridging loan; after all, if they were going to say 'no' then why would they ask him to go in person? In optimistic anticipation of fresh funds, he even had his staff make out the receipts and mortgage redemption certificates to be signed by his major creditors when they were paid off.

On the other hand, Strousberg knew how urgent the discussions in Moscow were: on the same day that the telegram from Moscow arrived, the press reported on a meeting of his creditors and commented that his situation was now so bad "that a catastrophe must be expected daily". Before departing for Russia, Strousberg did his best to put his open affairs in order. The most important thing was the granting of a general power of attorney to his son Bethel Henry. Stopping in Berlin on the way, to sort things out there, he departed for Russia, arriving in St. Petersburg on the 24th/12th of October.

20. ARREST AND TRIAL IN MOSCOW

Crisis at the Commercial Loan Bank

At the end of September 1875 the bank's books were audited. The bank's third director, Milliotti, deputising in his absence for Polyansky, was presented with a bond for 67,000 roubles which the bank had accepted (agreed to pay). He asked to look at the transaction book and was horrified to find that—against all the regulations—the bond's acceptance had not been entered. He informed the board of management, who in turn had the books checked by the bookkeeper. The checks revealed further irregularities, and a full audit was ordered. The audit revealed that Strousberg was indebted to the bank to the tune of about 7,000,000 roubles. The board was told and on the 5th of October it was clear to everyone in the bank that the level of Strousberg's indebtedness placed the bank in a perilous position.

What was to be done? Should the bank close down straight away, or inform the Finance Minister first in the hope of a government rescue? The board was split: Landau favoured waiting and negotiating with Strousberg, whose arrival was expected imminently but Milliotti was for informing the Finance Minister immediately; he was supported by the board members who feared the consequences of rumours about Strousberg's fate. Polyansky was called back to Moscow from his holiday in the Crimea.

The bank's leadership were all agreed that the true situation should not become public. On the first of October, the monthly account summary was published as usual, making no mention of the irregularities and therefore knowingly deceiving the public.

Over the next few days, until the board members and directors travelled to St. Petersburg to meet the Finance Minister on the 9th of October, there was a lively trade in Commercial Loan Bank stock as members of the board, their families and close friends and Landau unloaded most or all of their shares. What was more, they withdrew their deposits from the bank, while ordinary people who knew nothing of the crisis continued to pay money in. In total, about 2.5 million roubles were paid out, virtually emptying the bank's vaults.

On the 9th of October, by which time Polyansky had arrived, there was a further meeting of the board and directors. A deputation of them set off for St. Petersburg the same evening. Their meeting with the Finance Minister on the 11th of October was inconclusive: the idea of a bailout for the bank was rejected, but the Minister did not definitively express an opinion as to whether or not the bank should shut.

On the same day a prominent Moscow citizen, Alexeiev, went to the bank to present some of his company's cheques for payment. On hearing that all of the directors and some of the board members had gone to Petersburg, he was alarmed enough to inform the state prosecutor's office as the bank had, effectively, nobody in charge and everything might simply be removed. The prosecutor's office immediately had the bank sealed to prevent this from happening.

Strousberg is lured to Moscow

Back to Strousberg. At the end of September, negotiations concerning the promised loan from Goldschmidt were not yet concluded, but Strousberg nonetheless still needed money to finish the industrial plants at Zbirow and he hoped, once more, for help from the Commercial Loan Bank. He wanted a large amount and sent one of his friends and advisors, Dr. Stern, to Moscow to fix things; one of his arguments would be that the bank's interests were now so tied to Strousberg that they had to help. Effectively "If you do not lend me the money, I'm finished and I'll take you down with me." But still, Landau kept Stern waiting for over three weeks.

On the 3rd of October, by which time the bank's management was well aware of how bad the situation was, they sent the telegram which persuaded Strousberg to travel to Moscow. It was so worded that he thought Dr. Stern's negotiations were at last going to be concluded successfully and his personal presence was more or less a formality. Together with his secretary, Max Flatow, Strousberg set off for Russia and arrived in St. Petersburg on the 12th of October (Dr. Stern was already there).

In Petersburg Strousberg found the bank's delegation of directors and board members which had already held meetings with the Finance Minister. However, they did not mention this to Strousberg, but talked instead about his wishes. Dr. Stern was quite forthright and said that the bank had to let Strousberg have even m,ore money. Borissowski, the Chairman of the management board, invited Strousberg to Moscow, and he went, in the belief that further negotiations would take place there. On arrival he renewed his demand for more money and estimated his requirement at two million roubles.

But there were to be no negotiations, as while the delegation was still in St. Petersburg the State Prosecutor had ordered the bank sealed and the Examining Magistrate had begun his investigations.

On the 13th of October the bank officially ceased trading and the directors were arrested. On the same evening the Examining Magistrate took statements from Strousberg at the Hotel Dusseaux in Moscow "as a witness in the bank affair"; Strousberg's secretary, Flatow later stated at the trial that Strousberg had asked the magistrate when they had finished the interview "whether he was free" and got an affirmative response. The very same day Strousberg obtained a visa to leave Moscow and on the 14th of October he departed by train for Petersburg.

There followed a dramatic series of events. The Commercial Loan Bank had in its possession nine bills of exchange issued by Strousberg, totalling 165,000 roubles, issued on the 14th of April 1875 and payable (by Strousberg) after six months; that is, on the 14th of October. However, the bills were disputed on the

13th, a day before they were due, and on the 15th the bank went to the Moscow police and asked them to enforce payment by Strousberg of 165,000 roubles in silver. When the police discovered that Strousberg had already left for St. Petersburg, they telegraphed their colleagues there to arrest him. Strousberg's train had not yet arrived and so the head of the St. Petersburg detective department and three officers commandeered a locomotive and raced to meet the approaching train. Strousberg was detained on the 14th on arrival in Petersburg and on the following day was sent back to Moscow. On the 16th the Moscow police locked him up in the "Debt tower". He was imprisoned, not for punishment or on remanded in custody, but as part of the then normal process of making a debtor pay up.

Protesting the bills on the 13th of October was of course unlawful; they were due on the 14th and therefore it would only have been possible to protest them on the 15th (the day after the due date), as before then Strousberg would mot have been in default and could not be liable to arrest for debt. However, by the 15th, Strousberg, with a valid exit visa, would have already crossed the border into Germany.

After Strousberg's departure both Flatow and Dr. Stern were briefly detained and their papers confiscated on shaky grounds: "One, because he did not know where Strousberg had gone, and the other because he did know." After his release, Flatow went straight to the German consul in Moscow, Lanbereau, to get him to do something about Strousberg's unlawful arrest, Lanbereau declined to get involved as it was not his job, he was a diplomat; but he did then give the real reason:

"Yes, the *Herr Doktor* is coming to me to ask for help now, but in Romania he ignored me and did not return my greetings even though I had been introduced to him."

A second approach to Lanbereau shortly afterwards, made by Strousberg's lawyer, Spiro and one of Strousberg's old colleagues, Eduard Blaß[1] (who had travelled to Moscow), also failed.

Since the 11th of October, when he had closed the bank, the Examining Magistrate had been holding a preliminary enquiry into the directors of the Commercial Loan Bank. Strousberg, under debtors' arrest, was interviewed under caution as part of this process.

His last interview as a witness was on the 29th of October (the 10th of November). A week later, on the 5th of November (17th of November) the Examining Magistrate issued a judgement which made "Dr. Bethel Henry Strousberg" a co-defendant in the case against the bank's directors. Strousberg was accused of persuading Polyansky and Landau to give him loans of more than seven million roubles against completely inadequate security.

---

[1] *Previously the technical director of the Dortmund Ironworks.*

What had happened? The Examining Magistrate in a criminal trial had interviewed a man against whom no charges had been laid as a witness under caution. The man had then been joined as a co-defendant in the same case, using his own witness statements as evidence. An obvious abuse of process, even in Russia: Strousberg's lawyer quoted the relevant regulations, meant to protect the accused from just this; even in Russia it was a principle that one could appear in court as either a witness or the accused in the same case, not both.

Shortly after Strousberg's arrest, bankruptcy proceedings opened both in Prague (on the 28th/16th of October) and Berlin (on the 4th of November/23rd of October 1875. Strousberg, sitting in prison in Moscow, could not stave it off any longer.

The almost universal opinion was that keeping Strousberg in Moscow was against the interests of his creditors and he had to be released to sort out his tangled affairs. Representations were made to the Trade Ministers in Berlin and Vienna by both creditors and his workers to exert pressure in that direction, but without success.

As well as this there were attempts at intervention on a personal level such as that from Count Lehndorff who asked Herbert von Bismark for help in getting Strousberg freed. His four youngest daughters even wrote to Kaiser Wilhelm on their father's behalf, but they were politely turned down.

The circumstances surrounding Strousberg's arrest were so peculiar that they must have been at least not opposed by 'those at the top'. A bank failure was involved and obviously the authorities did not want the whole of the Russian banking sector to come under close scrutiny. The failure of the Commercial Loan Bank had to be presented as a one-off and not a reflection on Russian banks in general.

Strousberg was the ideal scapegoat to be the main defendant in a show trial. The prosecutor would mention Lasker's attack in the Prussian assembly saying that it was generally known that Strousberg had paid railway construction contractors and suppliers in dodgy shares for substandard work; further there was talk of Strousberg having used the *"goldenen Schlüssel"* [*"golden key"*] i.e. bribery.

A special court room with space for 2000 onlookers was constructed at an expense which was not really justified for the matter in hand, that is the insolvency of a fairly unimportant bank. [Most of the bank's debts would soon be paid off anyway. At the end of January 1876 the Royal Commission for the Liquidation of the Moscow Commercial Loan Bank (appointed on the 30th October/11th November 1875 8 to take the place of a normal liquidator) began to pay out 50% of registered claims against the bank, with a further 20% following at the beginning of June; small creditors, with claims of 1000 roubles or less even received the final 30% in July 1876, although admittedly paid from the bank board members' own pockets.

Strousberg in custody

The debtors' prison in Moscow was part of a dilapidated building, opposite the Kremlin walls. As a better-off debtor, Strousberg's lot was not too bad compared with the poor debtors whose accommodation was underground. He shared a room with three other inmates; the room was partitioned into two bedrooms and a day room. The wallpaper was torn, the floor was dirty and the furniture shabby, but on the plus side Strousberg could receive visitors including his secretary, Flatow, and his valet brought his meals over from the Hotel Dusseaux. He could receive and send post and packages, and from time to time went to be questioned—still as a witness— by the Examining Magistrate. One of his first visitors from Germany was the engineer Eduard Blaß who observed that Strousberg was bearing up well and had lost weight but otherwise was in good health.

Things changed when Strousberg became a defendant rather than a witness. He was moved to the "Casemate" prison in the Bassmannaya district where he was placed in a barred cell and nobody could gain access to him. Landau, the former director of the Commercial Loan Bank, had also been incarcerated here until he became so ill that he was 'released' to house arrest. Spiro, Strousberg's defence counsel, applied unsuccessfully to have Strousberg moved back to the debtors' prison for the sake of his health, but he did manage to have Strousberg permitted to see visitors from the 21st of December 1875 (the 2nd of January 1876). However the situation remained hard and Moscow was experiencing winter cold, with temperatures as low as -30 degrees.

A few days later, on the 26th of December 1875 (the 7th of January 1876), Strousberg was released from custody after all. He moved into an apartment at the Hotel Krüger and was not allowed to leave Moscow: house arrest really, although he was allowed to go out for walks if escorted by policemen. He could see anyone and his post was not censored. He was even allowed a visit by his wife.

The charges and the first session

The Examining Magistrate's report ran to 14 printed volumes, with a further four listing civil claims and finally a file of criminal charges brought by the procurator. These were made public in April 1876. There were three groups of accused:

The bank's directors, Landau and Polyansky were accused of lending, having accepted a bribe from Strousberg, seven million roubles without sufficient security and of attempting to hide the lack of security by publishing falsified accounts on the 1st of October 1875; Strousberg was accused of bribing the directors to obtain the loans; and the board members were accused of false accounting, in that they published or allowed to be published, falsified account summaries in order to preserve their dividends and maintain the share price; neglecting their supervisory obligations, thereby making the unlawful loans to

Strousberg possible; allowing the bank to continue trading although aware of its financial position and by doing so concealing the true position from public knowledge; further they had sold their own shares and withdrawn their own deposits before the matter became public.

After several postponements, the first hearing took place on the 29th of May (the 10th of June) 1876, but the hearing lasted just two hours. Several witnesses had not turned up including (from Berlin) the bankers Jaques, Manczyk and Schlesinger, Strousberg's deputy Breitsprecher and the insurance director Hartmann. Most of the defence counsels except Spiro, Strousberg's, lawyer, wanted an adjournment. The presiding judge declared that the court could not do without statements from the missing witnesses and adjourned proceedings indefinitely, which was a bitter disappointment for Strousberg. He had hoped to be able to attend the bankruptcy hearings in Prague and Berlin, but now he would have to remain in Moscow and he did not know for how long.

Strousberg's memoirs

Whilst waiting for the trial to resume Strousberg remained under house arrest in the Hotel Krüger. Since his release from prison he had been busy writing his business memoirs, *"Dr. Strousberg und sein Wirken"* ["Dr. Strousberg and his deeds"], a 486 page book written entirely from his formidable memory, without reference to his business records or use of a library.

It was not an autobiography in the usual sense, as it is confined to depicting Strousberg's business career. Apart from a few details of his origins, there is hardly anything personal and hardly anything about his wife and children; no details either of his adventures in England and certainly no mention of his conviction for embezzlement.

It really is a book in which he justifies and defends himself. Strousberg defends the foundation of joint stock companies as necessary to initiate large projects and says that by matching capital and intelligence serious investors could act as middle men. On the other hand he sharply criticises those whose only motive is to make a profit from forming companies. Another point which he criticises is the way in which the banks were uncooperative towards his railway businesses in general and the "Strousberg System" for financing railway construction in particular: the shares could only be sold to the public after the work had begun, but large sums of money were required to finance the work during its progress. He had been prepared to take out personal loans for this purpose, but the banks thought it too risky, and he had to resort to paying subcontractors and suppliers with bonds. Those bonds were treated with suspicion by the Prussian banking establishment and this had a negative effect on Strousberg's creditworthiness outside Germany as well.

Strousberg's real complaint was about the lack of a commercial relationship with the banks, albeit that they did not want him as a client, and he did not want them meddling in his business.

He also tackled the criticisms that he had acted dishonestly by artificially ramping up his share prices, pointing out that he had invested huge sums of money amongst other things buying over 300,000 Morgen of land. He justified his land purchases, citing a wish to leave an estate to each of his seven children and also saying that by making the purchases he had saved the previous owners from ruin, to say nothing of the workers.

This supposedly altruistic motivation is a recurring theme and includes the cattle market in Berlin and other projects. Obviously the book gave a one-sided view of Strousberg's works, but when it was published in Berlin it sold out in just a few days and there were soon second and third editions. The book awakened great public interest, not just because of the impending trial, but also as a work of literature: sparkling prose and a gripping tale, it linked with Strousberg's London pamphlets and self-penned magazine articles except that now he was writing in German and on his own behalf.

The trial and the court

The trial finally got under way on the 12th/14th of October 1876, with the verdict being delivered on the 2nd/14th of November after 25 days in session.

A special court room had been set up in a large building dating from the reign of Katharine II. The large circular room in the centre of the building, 25 metres high and 20 metres across was divided into two. Including those in the galleries, about 2000 members of the public could be accommodated.

The larger half of the room was reserved for those involved in the trial. The court itself was in the middle. Armchairs were placed in an amphitheatre-like arrangement for the jurors, lawyers and accused parties. Opposite the jury were the accused and their defence lawyers, whilst the numerous witnesses faced the tribune. Representatives of the press had desks behind the tribune.

The court room had its own telegraph office—open until midnight—and a special courier collected mail at seven in the evening to be sent on the overnight mail train to St. Petersburg.

The presiding judge, Peter Antonovich Deyer, was a high-flyer in the Russian legal system and had proved his competence in several difficult criminal cases. He enjoyed trust from all sides.

Guilt or innocence were purely a matter for the jury to decide. The three judges (the presiding judge and to others) only decided on the punishment if the accused were found guilty. As in many other countries, the jury was selected at random from a list of eligible persons. The correspondent from *The Times* was a bit unfair when he described it a being made up entirely of illiterate peasants. In reality there were twelve full and two reserve jurors, including seven businessmen, two civil servants, two farmers, two tradesmen and an ordinary worker.

The prosecution was lead by Obinsky and Ssimonow, from the Procurator's Office.

The trial proceedings

The spectators watched the proceedings and saw witnesses come and go and listened to the lawyers and their clients. Eventually the trial drew to a close.

The jury delivered its verdict on Sunday the 24th of October 1876. Strousberg was found guilty of damaging the Commercial Loan Bank by obtaining loans totalling seven million roubles with insufficient security and by offering bribes (two of the directors, Landau und Polyansky were found guilty of taking bribes).

The next day, the prosecutors called for the three main defendants—Strousberg, Landau and Polyansky—to be "Banished to Siberia for Resettlement", that is without a set time limit.

On the 2nd of November 1876 the court confirmed this punishment in respect of Landau and Polyansky but they decreed that "The Prussian subject and St. Petersburg merchant B. H. Strousberg, 52 years old, after removal of all of the rights and privileges he enjoys in Russia shall be expelled to abroad and banned from returning to the territory of the Russian Empire", with the proviso that if Prussia did not accept him then he would be banished for four years to a remote region (but not Siberia).

The court's reasons for these decisions were given verbally and not reported by the press or officially recorded. The possible reasons can however be guessed at based on a questionnaire which the presiding judge gave out to help the jurors reach their decisions.

The questions concerned either an individual defendants or groups of defendants. They raised several points to consider.

With regard to the board members: were they guilty of falsifying the accounts and failing in their supervisory role; and further whether they sold their bank shares and withdrew their deposits when they, but not the public, knew of the bank's vulnerability? [Insider trading, although the term had not been coined.]

Had the directors made loans of more than seven million roubles to Strousberg without insufficient security and had they been lead to do so by bribery? Further, had they been involved in false accounting?

Had Strousberg, to the detriment of the bank, received over seven million roubles in loans without providing adequate security, and had he used bribery to obtain the loans?

The verdict on the board members

The jury agreed that the year-end accounts for 1873 and 1874 as well as the interim figures published on the 1st of October 1875 had been falsified but nonetheless they only found the directors, and Polyansky guilty, not the board members.

That is truly amazing, as Polyansky had admitted and the third director, Milliotti, had confirmed that the board had discussed the problems posed by the bank's holdings of worthless bonds and how to hide them from public gaze; *a meeting which was recorded in the signed minutes.*

Despite this, the board members denied any involvement. You can understand why reports spoke of them embracing each other in congratulation when they heard the verdict.

Only two board members were found guilty of anything: one—Schumacher—because he had withdrawn his money from the bank, and the other—Borissovsky—for selling his shares when the bank's plight was not yet public knowledge. Schumacher escaped with a month in prison and Borrisovsky was banished to a remote region for a year.

The verdict on the Directors and on Strousberg

While the verdicts and sentences on the board members did not directly affect Strousberg the jury's verdict on Landau and Polyansky certainly did: Strousberg was found guilty of obtaining loans without adequate security by bribing the directors and Landau and Polyansky were found guilty of making the loans and taking bribes for so doing.

The procurators demanded that both the directors and Strousberg be banished to Siberia but although Landau and Polyansky were banished, Strousberg was merely deported to Germany; his 'sentence' was hardly a punishment at all.

Why was the severity of the sentences so different? Nobody forced the bank to lend Strousberg the money without adequate security; it was their decision. Anything criminal must have been either deception on the part of Strousberg, or bribery.

Deception, fraud or swindle were not charges laid against Strousberg. The prosecution did not raise it, nor was it one of the things listed for the jury to consider in the presiding judge's questionnaire.

When Strousberg was given the loans everyone, including Landau, knew just how precarious Strousberg's financial situation was, and precisely because of this wanted to do business with him. Landau believed (correctly) that he had found someone onto whom he could offload his worthless financial instruments.

Strousberg's defence counsel, Spiro, argued almost reassuringly that at the time Strousberg had assets of nine million Thaler and must have been creditworthy; how else could he have run up debts of 149 million Marks? But that was not the point. Strousberg's virtually hopeless illiquidity was an open secret and should have sounded the alarm to any lender. The bank could not have been deceived about Strousberg's "situation".

The same was true for the securities. The papers and certificates did exist and were available in the bank; the directors could examine them to see whether or not they were usable as securities. They were indeed on the table in the court room.

In the case of the second batch of wagons the bank could see that the waybills were only "promissory" and the finance did not relate to completed wagons, but to wagons yet to be built (and most of them were built, until Strousberg's arrest and trial prevented further work).

The Waagtal-Bahn bonds were secured by being entered in the land register and also by the deposits paid to the government as a condition of being granted the railway concession, but they could not be traded on the Vienna Stock Exchange and so Strousberg deposited them with a bank as he could not sell them.

The certificates from the Paris-Narbonne Railway showed that Strousberg had put more than three million francs into the project, but as the money could not be clawed back they were of no use as security.

The German-Bohemian Company priority shares were shares in a company whose factories were still under construction; even a trainee banker is taught that these are worthless as in the event of liquidation all one has is a pile of scrap.

There can not have been any attempt at deception, because it should have been quite clear, if the bank had examined them properly, that the stocks and papers were of no value as security for the loans. Whether or not Strousberg himself acted in good faith regarding the 'insufficient' securities is not really important when deciding on his guilt, as it was purely up to the bank whether or not to advance the loan.

It probably was not terribly important in Strousberg's calculations that the securities might one day actually be worth their value, if the industrial plants at Zbirow and the Paris-Narbonne Railway were completed and if the Waagtal-Bahn bonds became tradable His mentality and his great optimism made him think of planned works as being already finished. He certainly had no doubt that the industrial plants at Zbirow would be completed and in his mind's eye he could already see their smoking chimneys even if in truth only the first foundations had been laid. Because of this optimism, he could not see why the bank would not let him have a further two million roubles to finish the job.

What then of the bribery allegations? It is easy to say that it was generally known that doing business in the Balkans or in Russia required "fees", "commissions" and "gifts", but in this case there could be a grain of truth in it. Although there was evidence of payments from Strousberg to the directors and he himself admitted making the payments, the court chose not to punish him. Certainly, during the trial Strousberg was able to say that the respected contractor Meck had 'obtained' a railway concession at a cost of 1½ million roubles and no one seems to have objected to what was a pretty blatant hint of bribery at high levels.

Another indication of a relaxed attitude to bribery comes from an article published at the beginning of the trial by the Prague newspaper *Bohemia*. They made a point of saying that the presiding judge, Deyer, had distinguished himself by "being unbribable, despite having to manage on his poor official salary." By contrast the paper reminded its readers of the Romanian judges who awarded farmers a hundred times the true value of the land compulsorily purchased by Strousberg for railway construction, and then split the profits. In these countries, the odour of bribery seemed to go practically unnoticed and this could be why Strousberg was virtually acquittal.

The court might also have doubted whether the alleged "bribery" was the main reason for the loans being granted. The bank was just as eager to make Strousberg the loan, getting rid of useless bonds in the process, as he was to take it. Why should Strousberg have resorted to bribery, when the bank wanted to lend him the money?

Strousberg's "punishment" showed that the court could not find that he had actually done anything criminal, so he had not committed bribery. So how could the directors then be banished to Siberia for taking the money?

This was not really a contradiction, as unlike Strousberg the directors had broken both legal and moral obligations to the bank. They knew quite well that making loans of that size to Strousberg was irresponsible, and by accepting "gifts" from Strousberg they were in a hopeless conflict of interests.

The press was critical of the different verdicts on the defendants. The *Frankfurter Aktionär* said that it looked as if the Russian judges were determined to consign Strousberg to Siberia. A paper which had long been critical of Strousberg, the *Allgemeine Zeitung Augsburg* said that the verdict was practically a pardon. This view was shared by the Berlin *Börsen-Zeitung* which found it laughable that the strict Russian court system had handed down a punishment which gave Strousberg exactly what the Russian police had denied him: return home.

Bitter ending

The court had ordered that Strousberg be deported, and nothing would have pleased him more than for this order to be carried out straight away. But this did not happen; instead Strousberg was detained for a long time in Russia and it took over ten months before he was allowed to leave for Germany. Strousberg was not kept in prison but he was allowed to live in an hotel, under strict police supervision, until the Prussian government agreed formally to his return. This took until the end of November.

However, there was yet another spanner in the works. Due to the wording of the judgement attempts could be made to enforce civil claims against Strousberg and as, obviously, he had no means of paying it looked as if he might be imprisoned for debt. The authorities were only allowed, it was said, to imprison Strousberg for debt (a civil matter) after the criminal punishment had been carried out. That punishment was deportation which would of course put him out of reach, a dilemma which had a comic side.

Strousberg can not have seen the humour in the situation; neither could his creditors in Germany and Austria who hoped for Strousberg's early return to help salvage some of their money.

Strousberg's continued detention in Moscow was explained by the authorities as being because he might be needed as a witness in possible proceedings concerning the Commercial Loan Bank. At the end of December 1876 rumours even surfaced that he was again under debtors' arrest.

The authorities took steps to legalise Strousberg's continued unlawful detention: the liquidation commission applied to have Strousberg declared insolvent and open bankruptcy proceedings against him. Strousberg did not actually have any assets in Russia which could be divided amongst creditors, but under Russian bankruptcy regulations imprisonment for debt, for several years, could be ordered. Maybe this would squeeze something out of him after all, and perhaps his friends would buy him free.

On the 1st of June 1877, Strousberg was declared insolvent and actually placed under debtors' arrest, but only briefly: after the German ambassador intervened, the Czar ordered the declaration lifted and Strousberg was set free, but he was not home yet. It required Bismarck to intervene again, via the ambassador, before the justice ministry eventually gave up. The decision had to approved by a committee which took several hours.

This—finally—cleared the way for Strousberg's "deportation": on the 10th of September 1877 he was able to set off accompanied by a Gendarmerie officer, and on the 12th of September 1877 crossed the border at Eydtkuhnen (now Chernyshevskoye in the Kaliningrad region of Russia). The Russian official handed Strousberg over to the custody of the Prussian Border Commissioner, who promptly released him. Strousberg then travelled via Königsberg, where he met his wife at last, on to Berlin where was greeted by a large number of friends.

Strousberg was back in Germany. The day after his return he wrote to Bismarck expressing his thanks for the chancellor's help in securing his freedom. He did not send the letter direct though; Mary Ann had it sent via Herbert von Bismarck.

Strousberg, now aged 54, had been stuck in Russia for nearly two years during which time he had been made bankrupt in Berlin and in Prague which ended his entrepreneurial career.

21. BANKRUPTCY PROCEEDINGS IN BERLIN AND IN PRAGUE

Bankruptcy is an unpleasant business. Everyone involved loses out, and the administrators and the person about to be made bankrupt will do their utmost to avoid it, but sometimes it is unavoidable. Bethel Henry Strousberg owed unsecured creditors some 74 million Marks, an enormous amount, and the sale of assets was expected to enable a dividend of just 1%. It was an extreme case which seemed to seal Strousberg's fate as an entrepreneur.

Strousberg had literally nothing to do during the liquidation process. Still detained in Moscow, he had to look on powerlessly as everything he had achieved went under the hammer. Other people were making the decisions now.

The opening of the bankruptcy proceedings

Strousberg had been taken into custody in Moscow on the 15th/27th of October 1875, and on the very next day, the 28th of October, bankruptcy proceedings for Strousberg's assets in Austria opened at the Commercial Courts in Prague: Strousberg himself had given instructions by telegram from Moscow to start the process. Bankruptcy proceedings for his assets in Germany opened a week later, on the 4th of November, at the County Court in Berlin.

Parallel proceedings in Prague and in Berlin were unavoidable. Strousberg had assets and liabilities in both Germany and Austria, but bankruptcy stopped at national boundaries. Nevertheless, the two administrators (Dr. Josef Tragy in Prague and Dielitz in Berlin) worked together closely throughout to prevent claims being registered at both courts.

The Berlin court officially fixed the day on which Strousberg ceased trading as the 19th of October 1875, a week before his arrest.

The situation in Berlin and in Bohemia

While the bankruptcy proceedings in Prague began quickly, the court in Berlin waited until the question of who would cover the costs for the proceedings could be definitively answered. When proceedings did get under way, it put paid to wide;y circulating calls for attempting to get Strousberg released from arrest in Moscow: he was the only person who knew how his businesses worked and it was thought that his presence could help to get a better price for the assets.

There were more pressing considerations regarding operations in Bohemia. Strousberg's factories were still working and construction activity was ongoing employing thousands of workers, which meant that cessation of trading would have immediate and widespread consequences.

The *Neue Freie Presse* reported that "News of the bankruptcy caused an indescribable agitation in Zbirow, and the workers took such a threatening stance that the General Command immediately sent two battalions of infantry from Rokytzan [the nearest garrison] (now known as Rokycany) to the threatened places. The workers had already started to take actions. There was a danger that the factories and the castle would be destroyed. The military intervened and restored calm without the use of weapons. The workers were informed that the factories would be operating normally for the time being and only those workers employed on the construction projects (about 2000 men) were going to be dismissed."

The army occupied a local hotel as headquarters, blocked access to the castle and carried out nightly patrols; it took weeks before they were able to leave.

No more wages were paid at the Bubna railway wagon works and the 500 or so workers were promised that they would be paid next week. Work resumed and wages were paid on the 20th of October. Shortly afterward though, negotiations for state aid for Bubna and Holoubkau came to nothing and most of the fiefdom's workshops closed down without paying anyone.

On the 19th of December, 300 workers from Bubna marched on the Prague house of insolvency administrator Tragy demanding, without success to be paid. A smaller group of 80 to 90 proceeded to the *Statthalterei* (Governor's Residence); the Governor only received a three-man deputation and the result was the same – none of the workers got anything.

The bewildered workers pinned their last hopes on Strousberg, who seemed to them to be the only person from whom help might be expected, if diplomatic interventions in Moscow secured his release and return to Bohemia. A delegation of workers from Zbirow went to Vienna to see the Austrian finance minister and a petition was sent to the Austrian trade minister. In Moscow, both the Austrian and Prussian consuls were given instructions to make representations for Strousberg's release.

None of these representations were successful, as neither in Moscow nor St. Petersburg was it thought of letting Strousberg go; he was virtually a pawn in a game.

The bankrupt assets

Dielitz, the insolvency administrator in Berlin, delivered a comprehensive report on Strousberg's business activities and assets to the creditors' meeting on the 16th of November 1875.

In Bohemia, there was industrial, forestry and agricultural complex at and in Prussia the (much reduced) industrial holdings comprising the Neustädter Hütte ironworks, the iron ore mines at Siegen and the Marienhütte ironworks at Danzig. There was also property in Berlin and in Neidenburg, and the estates mentioned in Chapter 11 (excluding Krasnosielc in Poland, Lniannek in Schwetz district and Tarnowo in Posen district, which had already been sold beforehand).

Before things stated, there was the question of what actually belonged to Strousberg, especially in Bohemia. Strousberg had put most of these industrial undertakings into the new *Deutsch-Böhmische Aktiengesellschaft*. If this transfer had been carried out correctly from a legal point of view it might mean that those assets were protected from seizure by the creditors. However, the transaction had not succeeded in a legal sense: the new limited company was domiciled in Prussia and could only obtain rights and property in Austria if it gained an Austrian state concession. Schaffner, Strousberg's lawyer, had tried in vain to get this. He had spent several days in Vienna with Strousberg in the Finance and Interior Ministries, but the ministries would not grant a concession and by then bankruptcy proceedings had opened.

Because on this the Austrian insolvency administrator, Tragy, lodged a legal challenge against the transfer of ownership of Strousberg's industrial properties and mines to the *Deutsch-Böhmische Aktiengesellschaft*. The matter was raised in the *Oberlandesgericht* (Higher Regional Court) in Prague and then brought before the *Obersten Gerichtshof* (Supreme Court) in Vienna; both courts rejected the transfers. This meant that the industrial sites remained Strousberg's personal property and became part of the bankruptcy.

The debts

No list of all creditors survives but those records that do survive show just how much of a crunch Strousberg was in. Both large and small invoices remained unpaid, from tailor's bill to investments on his country estates The list of unpaid debts also shows that right up to the point when he ceased trading Strousberg was still active as an industrialist; new plant for the *Marienhütte* ironworks at Danzig and purchase of adjoining land, for example.

The single largest claim registered in the bankruptcy came, bizarrely, from the *Aktiengesellschaft für deutsche und böhmische Eisen-und Stahlfabrikate*, owned by the subject of the bankruptcy, that is by Strousberg: they had issued all of their shares—25.5 million Marks— to one shareholder, Bethel Henry Strousberg, but had not received the 'payment' because the transfer of assets to the company had failed for legal reasons. In addition, Strousberg had not fulfilled his obligation, laid down in the company's articles, to complete construction works. The company registered a claim for over 36 million Marks, which was obviously not recognised.

Measures taken in the Prague proceedings

The Supreme Court in Vienna had decided that the industrial works still belonged to Strousberg personally and formed part of the bankrupt assets and so Tragy, the administrator, could take charge of them.

However, they were only partially complete, and there were not enough funds in the estate for Tragy to have the work completed. He did decide to keep some of the operational factories going as long as their products could produce immediate income. The Holoubkau wagon works still had materials for wagon building in store and Tragy was able to have another 250 wagons manufactured and sold to customers in Russia. Pig iron production was only possible at the works in Straschitz which had charcoal fired blast furnaces. Tragy had just enough pig iron produced there for the requirements of the foundry in Dobriv, which was making articles with a guaranteed market — cast-iron grave crosses.

Tragy's decision to keep some facilities going was largely meant for the welfare of the workers, whose situation was desperate. The works employed some 3 — 4000 workers who had not received any wages for weeks or even months. Although there was no cash available when the bankruptcy proceedings opened, Tragy justified his decision in his final report to the Bankruptcy Commissioner, saying "I had to have the courage to keep the works going partially and just let the workers go gradually" as if the workers had all been fired at one go, "The possibility of danger for the property despite their exemplary behaviour could not be altogether excluded." Strousberg, looking on from Moscow, criticised Tragy's behaviour but he could obviously not have known that in order to keep the workers in employment Tragy had advanced 20,000 Austrian Guilders from his own pocket.

Tragy also had to make a decision about the Bubna wagon factory. Buying out the lease was out of the question as this would cost another 300,000 Guilders; therefore it was returned to its original owners, the *Erste Prag-Wiener Actiengesellschaft für Fabrikation von Waggons und Eisenbahnbedarf*. In accordance with the earlier contracts, all of Strousberg's annual payments were lost; the factory was legally returned on the 14th of December 1875.

Strousberg's contract for construction of the Waagtal-Bahn became long drawn out and troublesome. The railway company took legal action and managed to force through a major change in payment terms and conditions: instead of monthly payment for work completed—as specified in the original contract—payment was to be made on the basis of an expert valuation of the railway facilities which Strousberg had constructed. As a result, the previously-calculated 1 million Guilders owed to Strousberg by the Waagtal-Bahn company magically turned into a claim against the bankruptcy estate for the same amount. In 1878, this claim was recognised by the courts as being legally valid.

Disposal of the properties

Disposal of the estates at Zbirow, Miröschau, Tocnik and Wossek, that is the former Fiefdom of Zbirow without the industrial sites, took several years to complete.

Initially, the *Wiener Hypothekenkassa* (Vienna Mortgage Institute) auctioned off the fiefdom for 3.9 million Guilders, but the Supreme Court in Vienna blocked the sale as Karl Count Lehndorff had applied for review in view of Strousberg's imminent return from Moscow. A further auction was held on the 27th of February 1879, and the estates were finally sold to Prince Josef zu Colloredo-Mannsfeld for 3,350,000 Guilders.

This sum was enough to almost completely pay off one of the primary registered creditors, the Vienna-based *Allgemeine österreichische Bodenkreditanstalt*: they lost 'only' 350,000 Guilders. But other registered creditors, further down the list were not so lucky and between them lost some 8.6 million Guilders. These included the *Wiener Hypothekenkassa* (2.5 million Guilders); the *österreichische. Hypothekar-Kredit und Vorschussbank*, Vienna (1.3 million Guilders); the *Rumänische Eisenbahn-Aktien-Gesellschaft* (1.75 million Thaler); the *Dortmunder Bergbau-AG* (250,000 Thaler); Moritz Simon, Königsberg 300,000 Thaler; Hugo Fuchs, Berlin 417000 Thaler; the Dukes of Ratibor (50,000), Ujest (50,000) and Lehndorff (25,000) together 125,000 Thaler; and the bankers Manczyk & Schlesinger, Berlin 120,000 Thaler.

These figures show the loss for each creditor after this auction, but they are not a final amount as the larger creditors had sums secured on several properties.

The estate at Tereschau was sold back to its former owner, Frl. Srnka, for 85,250 Guilders, half the 177,000 Guilders which she had sold it to Strousberg for in 1870. The Wejwanow now (Vejvanov) coal mine estimated at 138,000 Guilders, went for only 10,500 Guilders.

The auction dates for several industrial plants were put back after Strousberg's return, until September/October 1877. These were the ironworks at Holoubkau, Straschitz, Franzensthal and Dobriv, which were then sold by the *Wiener Hypothekenkassa*, as well as the wagon works at Holoubkau, the Borek rolling mills and Bessemer converter with the workers' village and hotel as well as the coking plant in Dobriv. The latter group of plant was bought by a Belgian-led consortium which included Marchot plus

161

Manczyk & Schlesinger from Berlin. These auctions brought in another 940,000 Guilders although the estimated value was 2.7 million Francs, quite a difference.

The reason why Strousberg had wanted these dates put back soon became obvious: he leased this large industrial complex back from the new owners, although as he was still not discharged from bankruptcy the contracts were in the name of his eldest daughter Agnes, who was 21. Strousberg, who had just returned from Moscow, was in business again, although nothing of consequence seemed to come of it.

In respect of the bankruptcy proceedings in Berlin, nothing is known about the fates of the iron ore mines in the Siegerland and Harz areas. The *Marienhütte* at Danzig fetched 142,000 Marks at auction in June 1876. The *Neustädter Hütte* was not auctioned off until the 3rd of February 1879; in 1880 it became Bethel Henry Strousberg's property again (this is discussed in the next chapter).

Strousberg's Berlin and Neidenburg properties were also disposed of, although the properties which he actually occupied kept changing. For example, he had to give up the showpiece building at Unter den Linden 17/18 as early as spring 1871 and move his main management offices to Jägerstrasse 22 but he had sold both this property and the nearby Jägerstrasse 61a before bankruptcy proceedings opened. On the other hand, he had acquired the villa at Tiergartenstrasse 29 from his business friend Rauschning.

What happened to the *Palais Strousberg*, the prestigious and flamboyant house at Wilhelmstrasse 70, became a matter of great public interest and speculation. There were all sorts of rumours, even the Prussian royal family were named as potential buyers. The British ambassador in Berlin, Lord Odo Russell, was seriously interested in turning the building into the British Embassy, but he was only interested in renting, not in purchasing. This eventually happened, in a deal brokered by the banker Bleichröder: the *Palais* was auctioned via the lawyer Holthoff for 900,000 Marks (considerably over the 600,000 estimate) on the 2nd of March 1876. The actual purchasers were the Dukes of Ujest and of Ratibor—who had been Strousberg's partners in the Romanian railway construction saga. The 1877 edition of the *Berliner Adreß-Buch [Berlin Address Directory]* shows the British Embassy as tenant.

Strousberg's enormous land holdings which had at one time totalled over 75,000 hectares, had already diminished before the bankruptcy proceedings began. The vast *Herrschaft* of Krasnosielc in Poland (27,000 hectares on its own) and another 4,500 hectares split between Lniannek in West Prussia, Tarnowo in the Province of Posen and Dahlewitz in Brandenburg had already gone. When he went bankrupt, Strousberg "only" owned 19,000 hectares, excluding Zbirow.

All of the remaining country estates were mortgaged to the Disconto-Gesellschaft bank as security for the 2,000,000 Thaler (6,000,000 Mark), loan which they had made in 1872 to settle the Romanian railway affairs, which Strousberg's backers (the Dukes of Ujest and of Ratibor and Count Karl Lehndorff) had also made guarantees totalling 500,000 Thaler (1,500,000 Marks). Repayments had already reduced the amount outstanding to 4 million Marks before the liquidation began and this sum was reduced by a further 3,400,000 Marks by auctioning off the estates.

The Disconto-Gesellschaft had to write off the remaining 600,000 Marks, but it is worth noting that the Alt-Laube estate went to Adolph von Hansemann, the Disconto-Gesellschaft's owner and the *Herrschaft* of Lissa went to a member of his family; the Priebisch and Garthe estates were bought by the Duke of Ujest.

Other disposals

The administrators disposed of the stored items and fittings at the various plants and works fairly quickly, right down to the plants in the greenhouses and wine in the cellars at the Schloss Zbirow. This raised some 2.5 million Guilders, 400,000 Guilders of which went on salaries and wages during the period of administration and the rest paid off some 5,000 smaller creditors.

There were some other notable auctions, such as the sale of Strousberg's famed mares in November 1875; over 1000 people came to the auction in the yard of the *Palais* at the Wilhelmstrasse in Berlin including the cream of the aristocracy and the financial world.

In February 1876 the equipment from Strousberg's factories went under the hammer. A ring of industry people worked together to keep the non-specialists out. They bid the prices up and up.

At Zbirow too the carriages from the mews and horses from the stud were sold off. The estimate, which was just about reached, was 45,000 Guilders.

The sale of art works and books, both in Berlin and in Zbirow aroused considerable interest. Strousberg had already been obliged to sell his famous collection of paintings in 1873, as a consequence of the turbulence following the Vienna stock exchange crash, raising between 600,000 and 800,000 Thaler (1.8 to 2.4 million Marks). The collection had contained nearly 200 items and was renowned as being one of the best private galleries in Berlin with an excellent selection of contemporary German, French and Belgian paintings. It was bought by the Berlin art dealer and auctioneer Rudolph Lepke, who was able to resell most of the paintings straight away; the remainder were sold for 467,000 Francs in Paris on the 31st of March 1874.

The libraries in Berlin and in Zbirow, which each held more than 3,000 titles, were sold at auction by Lepke in June 1876 and May 1882 respectively.

Discharge from bankruptcy

Both sets of bankruptcy proceedings came to an end in 1878. The decisions were reached by the creditors meetings held in Prague on the 23rd of August and in Berlin on the 17th of December.

The conclusion of bankruptcy proceedings also meant that a criminal investigation against Strousberg was in effect over as well: a number of witnesses had been interviewed on the question of whether Strousberg bore any criminal responsibility for his activities. Most of the witnesses thought not, and those that did tended to argue that if a person lives in luxury but does not pay his workers their wages then he must be guilty of something. Morally, probably. Criminally, no. In November 1876 criminal proceedings against Strousberg were dropped.

One of the people interviewed was Tragy, the Prague insolvency administrator. He was extremely critical of Strousberg's book-keeping: the last set of balanced accounts had been done in 1872, book-keeping at the individual plants in Zbirow had been for the most part "totally insufficient and disorganised", "so that one gains the impression that drawing up a complete balance sheet was not a consideration for Dr. Strousberg." Even more astonishing was bankruptcy commissioner Siegert's statement that in none of Strousberg's company books could be found errors so bad as not to be able to see the state of the assets and liabilities reliably.

A settlement could now be approved. In summary, after fully paying off the Class I and Class II preferential creditors Strousberg promised to pay the other creditors a 'dividend' of 3% (in three instalments: one third immediately, one third in two years, and one third in four years time).

In spite of the tiny dividend, the creditors meetings approved the arrangements by large majorities (87% in Prague and 90% in Berlin). One of the reasons for this acceptance was probably that Strousberg had handed over everything—including assets in his wife's name— to the creditors. It was also acknowledged that his problems began in earnest with the outbreak of the Franco-Prussian War for which he was not responsible: this was in fact explicitly stated in a session of the Berlin *Stadtgericht* [City Court] on the 2nd of January 1879.

Taken together, the debts registered in the bankruptcies came to 150 million Marks, of which 74 million were recognised as valid by the courts. Strousberg's promised immediate payment of 1% meant that he had to find 740,000 Marks. He did not in fact ever earn or raise the almost 1.5 million marks which he would have needed for the two further instalments.

22. BACK IN BERLIN AND IN LONDON

Family and friends

Whatever had happened, Bethel Henry's family and friends stuck by him. Mary Ann was the loving wife and mother who was at his side in good and bad times; her loyalty never wavered. She did everything possible to obtain his release from detention in Moscow including appealing to the Kaiser, to Bismarck and to Bleichröder. She enjoyed universal respect and admiration.

Four of Strousberg's eleven children had died in infancy. The two oldest, his sons Bethel Henry II and Arthur, both married daughters of Strousberg's railway construction business partners George Barclay Bruce and Joseph Bray respectively; his youngest daughter Helene married an Englishman, John William Louth whose father had been an engineer building railways in the German province of Schleswig.

Out of the other four daughters, Hedwig died at the age of sixteen (the same age as her mother had been when she married). Alice and Edith remained unmarried. In 1879 Agnes married Hans von Kleist, son of a German Count. Agnes, as the daughter of a bankrupt, did not have the right status for the noble Count Ewald von Kleist and he made his son give up managing one of the family estates. Hans returned to the army as an officer, eventually becoming a General.

The Strousbergs had a large number of descendants on both the English and German sides. Their oldest son Bethel Henry II had one son, also named Bethel Henry, who remained unmarried and so the Strousberg name died with him. Their daughter Helen Norah married a clergyman, the Reverend Rupert Strong, and their son Rupert, a poet and writer, died in Dublin in the early 1980s. Arthur, who died at the age of 23, only had one daughter who married "English".

On the German side, Agnes had five children who mostly married within the Prussian nobility. In total, there were probably about 50 to 55 grandchildren and great-grandchildren on the English side and about 35 on the German side.

The family held together, even during the difficult times following Bethel Henry's return from Moscow. He was able to become an industrialist again, on a small scale, thanks to their generosity. George Barclay Bruce and Joseph Bray (both of whom he was related to by marriage), his son Bethel Henry and Alexander Littlejohn, an old friend from his early years in London, pooled their resources and purchased from Strousberg's bankrupt assets the disused Neustadt Ironworks (*Neustädter Hütte*), its associated plant and buildings and more than 23 hectares of land. They paid the administrator 100,000 Marks, and about a year later sold it on to Strousberg himself for

450,000 Marks. Any feelings of horror or outrage at making a 'profit' from a poor bankrupt can be laid aside: the money for the purchase was an "irrevocable loan" to Strousberg for ten years (until the 1st of April 1890) and became the first new mortgage registered against the properties.

Strousberg therefore became, without paying for it himself, the owner of the Neustädter Hütte again. The large mortgage also served to protect him from the attentions of creditors who would have to raise 450,000 Marks to pay off the mortgage before they could get at the Neustadt properties.

The whole transaction was little more than a disguised gift to Strousberg. Bruce and Littlejohn passed on their shares of the repayments, Littlejohn in favour of the Berlin lawyer Lorenz Karsten, and Bruce in favour of a pensioner named Meares in Bournemouth. Karsten had been Strousberg's lawyer for years, and this was obviously way of compensating him for unpaid fees; a similar thing could have applied to Meares.

Strousberg was soon busy. He demanded that the local authorities in Neustadt evicted the "unemployed work-shy elements" who were squatting in the works housing. His demand for the council to pay all of the back rents was, unsurprisingly, turned down. Was this the old Strousberg again?

Strousberg was also helped by the people who had been his partners in railway construction in Romania. At the end of 1872 the Prussian tax authorities demanded 90,000 Thaler stamp duty[1] from Strousberg on the contracts setting up the *Allgemeinen Deutschen Eisenbahn-Bau-Gesellschaft* — although the company had never actually existed. The Duke of Ratibor intervened with the King on Strousberg's behalf, but the Finance Minister kept to his hard line and even the King eventually gave up. The tax authorities could not even be persuaded to accept payment in instalments.

The Dukes of Ujest and Ratibor and Karl Count Lehndorff, all helped generously when Strousberg was detained in Moscow for two years from the end of 1875. Mary Ann and her five daughters were only allowed to draw 20 Marks a day subsistence from the bankrupt estate, and the three of them jointly donated 1,000 Thaler a month, despite having been left out of pocket to the tune of 500,000 Thaler by the settlement in respect of the Romanian railways.

This did not mean that Strousberg and the aristocrats enjoyed what might be called a proper friendship; the social gap was simply too large. Strousberg himself made this obvious when he wrote "I never never took them to my family, as they never brought their wives."

Strousberg's personal friends seem to have been few in number, but a few names are worth mentioning such as the Egyptologist and writer Georg Ebers, who took Strousberg's younger son Arthur—suffering from

---

[1] *Payable on notarised contracts*

tuberculosis—with him to the dry heat of Egypt shortly before his death at the age of 23. His father ordered a memorial from the sculptor Reinhold Begas which showed the dying young man bending over his wife. Unfortunately by the time it was finished Strousberg was not able to pay for it. In 1930 the city of Berlin purchased it and, rededicated as a war memorial, it still stands in the Reinickendorf cemetery.

"Das Kleine Journal" and Emma Vely

Around the end of 1878 or beginning of 1879, Bethel Henry established *Das Kleine Journal* [The Little Journal], a popular magazine. Strousberg was the publisher and, as he had with his London magazines, also wrote many of the articles himself. It was sold by street vendors—something new—for 5 Pfennigs. Strousberg initially set up the editorial office in Dorotheenstrasse 78—79 but a year later it moved to Jägerstrasse 69.

The format, focusing on topical affairs and original articles was quite successful and *Das Kleine Journal* became well known.

In October 1879 Strousberg wrote to Emma Vely, a well-known author of society novels, to ask if she wished to be a contributor to *Das Kleine Journal*. She sent something in immediately, but did not actually meet Strousberg until January 1880 in Strousbergs editorial offices. She raised the question of fees, he remarked on her decisiveness and the ice was broken. It began a close but platonic relationship which lasted until Strousberg's death. It was recorded in Emma Vely's extensive diary and in about 150 letters which Strousberg sent to her. They give a glimpse into his personal side which can not be found elsewhere, and give a commentary on events in the later years of his life.

From their first meeting Strousberg often spoke frankly about himself, "about his crash, his struggle, his detention, most beautifully about his wife and children." Emma was impressed by his winning manner and how Strousberg "could see straight through people like glass." A few days later, Emma brought Strousberg the manuscript of a novel and agreed to go with him to a theatre performance. Emma was most impressed by the way in which Strousberg behaved and by the respectful manner in which other theatregoers, including members of the nobility, greeted him.

Emma also accompanied Strousberg to one of the grand Berlin social events, the Opera Ball, and before returning to her home in Herzberg in the Harz, visited Strousberg's villa in the Tiergartenstrasse. For this visit Emma was accompanied by her sister Bertha.

After Emma returned home the two exchanged letters frequently. Strousberg's language was extravagant and gushing, altogether not the kind of thing one would expect from a hardened businessman.

Perhaps one can explain Strousberg's behaviour quite easily. He had become isolated, and with his beloved Mary Ann's worsening health he had simply found somebody to confide in.

Working on *Das Kleine Journal* placed a lot of strain on Strousberg. He wrote that he worked "Out of necessity and duty, not out of love, from 9 in the morning until 2 at night." He constantly complained of being tired out by the work and that he would love to recuperate in Herzberg. On top of this his constant money problems meant that paying salaries and fees was always a worry. From time to time, probably to save money on printing, even had *Das Kleine Journal* printed on his own press.

Strousberg only held onto *Das Kleine Journal* for a brief period, probably only until autumn 1881, when he became increasingly aware of the difficulty of rebuilding his career in Germany and decided to move his residence and his family back to London. At any rate it no longer belonged to him when he died in May 1883.

Das Kleine Journal existed, under various owners, until the early 1930s. It was even, for a short period after the Kaiser's abdication in 1918, controlled by the Communist Party. They had published the first two editions of *Die Rote Fahne (The Red Flag)* from the *Berliner Lokal-Anzeiger* works, which they had occupied, but had to vacate the premise. They succeeded in buying *Das Kleine Journal* and on the 18th of November 1918 the first copies of the *Berliner Mittagszeitung (Das Kleine Journal)* appeared, together with the third edition of *Die Rote Fahne* (editors Karl Liebknecht and Rosa Luxemburg—the publishing house of a failed capitalist, owned by communists.

Strousberg's final entrepreneurial ventures

The Neustadt Ironworks, which had come into Strousberg's possession again in 1880 with help from the family was soon up and running. It is not known how much it produced or whether it made a profit: however, there do not seem to have been any great financial problems like inability to pay the wages. Strousberg visited the works regularly, sometimes accompanied by Emma Vely. He retained ownership until his death, although in 1883/84 a holding company, the *Aktiengesellschaft Strousberg zu Berlin*, was named as the owner for property tax purposes. The situation regarding those mines which he still owned in the Harz region was similar. Strousberg often visited Emma Vely in Herzberg and her husband Carl F. Simon (a small-scale publisher) in Lauterberg.

Strousberg also continued to travel to Prague and operated the works in Holoubkau, am Borek and in Dobriv on the former fiefdom of Zbirow (which he had leased from its new owners after it was sold during the bankruptcy proceedings). However "the losses there were even higher than I had thought." He intended to incorporate them into a new company, but this plan was never realised.

Then there were projects which turned out not to be feasible, mostly at an early stage.

He wanted to start a publishing house where he did not have to bother with all the details (as he had been forced to with *Das Kleine Journal*). Emma Vely would be the creative force and her husband Carl Simon would take care of the business side, but the idea never got of the ground due to a lack of capital and Simon's poor management skills. Strousberg's vague hope that Simon could issue the novels printed as serials in *Das Kleine Journal* in book form or even print his unpublished manuscript for *Fragen der Zeit, Teil II* proved illusory.

There were plans for new publishing ventures in London: a magazine called *Truth* (again using Emma Vely's talents), and another called *National Economy*. They never happened.

Strousberg had another possible project on the go during this period. An (unnamed) group of financiers from Paris was supposed to be providing him with the resources to construct a railway in Westphalia, for which he supposedly already had a concession. This was apparently going to involve his "Danzig interests", his mines in Saalfeld and the Neustadt Ironworks. He produced memoranda on the project, travelled to Paris where had lengthy discussions and talked about it in his correspondence with Emma Vely but like the possible magazines in London it came to nothing.

Further difficulties in Berlin

On the 22nd of February 1881 Bethel Henry had a very bad day when he was maliciously, in his view, accused of causing someone great financial damage. On the 9th of March he had to appear in court for the whole day, but he did not report what for. It must have been very stressful and a few days later Emma Vely received a note from Bethel Henry: "I am lying in bed, right arm is at the moment completely paralysed, no danger, but great pain, have had myself bled in order to travel but without success." It was probably a slight stroke.

Some time later, at the end of July, Strousberg's home was visited by the bailiffs. They left him the furniture but took "thousands of small items with sentimental value," although he added "I'm actually very relieved that the things have been collected, as that danger has been unsettling me for months."

Strousberg had kept his composure over this blow, but worse was to come. At the end of October he returned to Berlin from a stay in he was arrested and spent three hours in a gaol cell. Allegations had been made to the state prosecutor that he had concealed assets from them. They opened an investigation and questioned Strousberg's former staff employees and servants. Strousberg thought that the accusation had come from one of his creditors, a banker named Fuchs, based on allegations made by one Herr Uhlmann. However when Uhlmann was questioned under caution he could not substantiate the allegations. After the inquiry, Strousberg's former employee Wild, who had worked for him for 27 years and whom Strousberg thought was involved in the intrigue, took his own life.

The matter never came to court and Strousberg did not even have to formally give evidence. Strousberg felt that the bad publicity resulting from the affair was enough to totally ruin his reputation and to wreck any plans he might have for the future.

Return to London – Mary Ann dies

Strousberg saw more and more that he would never be able to improve his situation in Germany. He therefore looked to his old contacts in London. In July 1881 he was able to pick things there up and decided to return there with his wife and three daughters. He rented a furnished flat in Craven Street off the Strand.

The family's return to London was overshadowed by a deterioration in Mary Ann's health, which had already begun to decline in Berlin. Now, after returning to London her mental state soon got so bad that she had to be "sent to the country accompanied by an attendant."

During all this Bethel Henry had continued to further his business contacts in London. He seemed to be doing "a deal in the oil business" and by the end of 1881 Strousberg thought that everything was going satisfactorily and, three months later, that he might have to travel imminently to Constantinople. Once again his optimism was premature and the deal fell through.

In May 1882, he did really seem to be on to something: he travelled to Madrid in connection with a railway construction scheme. At the end of August he wrote from Pamplona that he was at the already-commenced construction works. But the project was halted and Strousberg returned to London.

While he was on the way back Mary Ann's illness worsened, and she suffered a severe stroke, dying on the 11th of September 1882, aged only 55. Bethel Henry's brother, Ferdinand, had to meet him at the railway station and break the news. Ferdinand's wife had been with Mary Ann at the end.

Mary Ann's death was obviously a hard blow for Bethel Henry. He wrote to Emma Vely:

> "Today I am quite exhausted, I've seen the dear various and am fulfilling my obligations. If I should describe my feelings to you, analyse my situation, I can not do it; to know that one is completely separated from somebody

one has been an item for with for 38 years is the tearing of the ties which one's own life hangs from. I am completely confused, can not think about the future and seek to forget by being busy."

Soon though he had to attend to another duty: Mary Ann's coffin was dispatched to Berlin for interment in the family mausoleum alongside Hedwig and Arthur.

After Mary Ann's death, the Strousbergs, father and unmarried daughters, were soon to leave London. Because of a lack of money the flat there was given up. The daughters went to join their married sister on the Kleist family property in Zolondowo (now Żołędowo) near Bromberg in Silesia (now Bydgoszcz in Poland). Bethel Henry himself returned to Berlin, where he went to live in a residential hotel at Taubenstrasse 40.

Back in Berlin at last

Strousberg now went back completely to writing and journalism.

Already, in 1879, he had had his first major work *Über Parlamentarismus [About Parliamentarianism]* printed and published under the title of *Fragen der Zeit, Teil I [Questions of the Age, Part I]*. In this book Strousberg compared the German constitutional arrangements with those in Britain and the United States of America, whose constitutional arrangements he considered to be the most solidly based. He felt that he was speaking as a slf-appointed *Praeceptor Germania* a position which he felt able to fulfil as he had "been dedicated to these affairs all my life."

He singled out the strong—far too powerful, in his opinion— position of officialdom and the bureaucracy in Germany for particular criticism. In favour of the officials was their honourable and correct behaviour, but they tended to act in the interests of the State, i.e. the government, rather than the interests of the Nation which were often seen as separate or even opposing. In Britain however there was more of a public Service ethos. Strousberg took the view that parliament ought to have more control over officialdom and not a single official belonged in parliament or should be allowed to speak there.

He also criticised the nobility and their tendency to regard industry and trade as being second class occupations. In the Prussian system, titles were passed down to all male descendants and not just to the oldest son. In Britain on the other hand, only the oldest son (or other male heir) inherited a title with the younger sons returning to 'commoner' status. On the other hand it was possible for ordinary people to become, though hard work and land ownership, elevation to the nobility. It is quite obvious that this refers to Strousberg's disappointment at never having the chance, despite his massive land holdings and unlike the landed gentry in England, to climb the social ladder.

Strousberg considered various other topics in his 160 page work. The political parties, the workers, the military and even the monarchy were all discussed at length although not in a very structured way.

The subsequent work *Fragen der Zeit, Teil II [Questions of the Age, Part II]* was more systematic. At the time of his death Strousberg had completed the the text, but not published it: the State Archive in Merseburg (Saxony-Anhalt) holds a copy of the 328 page long handwritten manuscript with the author's own corrections.

This second part deals with parliamentary life, the military, the crown and officialdom. It does not contain much new when compared to the first part, apart from the last of the five chapters on economic reform. He makes a sharp attack on the brutal methods of "Manchester capitalism", a particularly hard variant of industrialism. Strousberg warned that the workers could "make themselves familiar with the military resources of Manchester capitalism and use the principles to make the best weapons against the middle class". He was all in favour of free trade but opposed to dogmatism.

Other major themes covered in Part II included protectionist customs policies—which he rejected— as well as the competitiveness of German industry, which Strousberg thought to be acceptable. He did however criticise the mentality of the mentality of German manufacturers who paid too little attention to the differing requirements and tastes of foreign consumers. His rejection of socialism, which he described as a "plague" has already been mentioned. Strousberg clearly saw his activities in the field of workers' welfare as a kind of anti-Socialism.

Strousberg had announced that he would shortly be bringing out a second part of *Fragen der Zeit* in a short publication entitled *Zwei Fragen, die nicht brennen [Two questions which are not burning]*. In it he had written about customs tariff and railway questions saying that the time was not ripe for legislative measures as the questions were not understood and peoples feelings got in the way.

Another study concerned itself with the field of shares, redolent of essays about the idea of the Limited Company which Strousberg had written in his young days in England. Strousberg was about to publish it when he died; his son, Bethel Henry II, had it published posthumously.

Strousberg's essay called *Berlin, ein Stapelplatz des Welthandels durch den Nord-Ostsee-Kanal [Berlin, a hub of world trade because of a North Sea to Baltic canal]* on the subject of a ship canal from the North Sea to the Baltic was somewhat unusual. He suggested a route using the river Elbe as far as Wittenberge, a canal from there to Berlin, and from Berlin to Oderberg or

Schwedt an der Oder and then using the river Oder to reach Stettin and the Baltic. The route eventually chosen and actually built between 1887 and 1895 runs in a straight line across what is now Schleswig-Holstein from Holtenau to Brunsbüttel. He had worked out a whole load of technical details and financial projections for the project, so one can see that his interests had no limits especially when it came to things which really caught his imagination.

Manuscripts of a few studies remain in existence, their subjects varying from "The measurement of popular prosperity" to "The defeat of liberalism", "Parliamentary relationships", "Count Andrassy and Austrian politics" and "Nihilism in Russia". These were journalistic works which showed Strousberg's broad range of interests.

During this period Bethel Henry lived frugally from his writing in a residential hotel in the Taubenstrasse, looked after by his former manservant Schwartz's wife: she was now married to the hotel's owner, Otto Mischel. Strousberg still had his old servant Albert Lehmann and the services of two secretaries as he dictated, rather than wrote, most of his work. His daughter Helene recorded that he did not live in poverty or misery as he was helped out [financially] by 'old friends from Königsberg'.

But was there a final glimmer of hope? In July 1883, once more in London, he wrote to the private banker Arthur Gwinner in Madrid, who had just liquidated his bank there and asked whether he was planning to open another bank or whether he could refer him to another bank "who would transact the business with me." Wishful thinking surely: reality was quite different and he told Emma Vely that he had been forced to give up smoking to save money.

Sudden death

Bethel Henry died in Berlin on the 31st of May 1884. He had been planning to visit his daughter and her husband at Zolondowo for Whitsuntide; his other daughters were there as well. His bag was packed ready for the night train but when he returned from having dinner in the cafe at the Kaiser he suffered a heart attack, and despite medical attention, died at 10.30 p.m.

He was interred in the family mausoleum at the Matthiaskirche in Berlin-Schöneberg on the 4th of June 1884, joining his children Arthur and Hedwig and his wife Mary Ann. His family followed the black coffin, preceded by his grandson bearing his orders and decorations. There were not many mourners, apart from family there were a few friends: Major Dunker, Colonel von Falkenstein, the African explorer von Schoeler, the architect August Orth, Hermann Geber but only two journalists, George Davidsohn from the *Berliner Börsen-Courier* and Paul Lindau.

More significant were those who did not come: no representatives from industry, commerce, the railways, officialdom or from the towns and communities which grew and increased their importance because of Strousberg's railway construction schemes.

Although only a few people attended the funeral, obituaries appeared in many leading newspapers. They did not shy away from mentioning some of Strousberg's less attractive characteristics: the Vienna *National-Zeitung* spoke of "his ambition to be a Great Man, his belief in being able to make everything from nothing, which turned the point of a pyramid into its base" and the Berlin *Börsen-Zeitung* spoke of his "catastrophic optimism" and his method "of always having to plan new ventures in order to hang on to and complete the old ones." There were some more positive pronouncements too, even in papers which had previously had nothing good to say. The *Aktionär* recognised that the railways which Strousberg had built "today form an important part of the Prussian state railway network." The *New York Times* saw in him a creator, whose works carried the mark of foresight. The *Kleine Journal* even dared to remind people that those who had bought Strousberg's bonds and shares had made profits, not just losses.

BIBLIOGRAPHY

- *Der europäische Eisenbahnkönig Bethel Henry Strousberg*
  Joachim Borchart, C.H. Beck, Munich 1991, ISBN 3-406-35297-9
- *Der Eisenbahnkönig Bethel Henry Strousberg*
  Manfred Ohlsen , Verlag der Nation, Berlin 1987, ISBN 3-373-00003-3
- *Der Eisenbahnkönig, oder, Rumänien lag in Linden : Materialien zur Sozialgeschichte des Arbeiterwohnungsbaus*
  Wolfgang Voigt, AG SPAK, München SPAK, 1982, ISBN 3-92312615-8
- *Dr.Strousberg und sein Wirken, von ihm selbst geschildert*
  Bethel Henry Strousberg, J. Guttentag, Berlin 1876; paperback facsimile edition, Adamant Media Corporation 2006 ISBN 0-543-82530-2
- *Hanomag Lokomotiven*
  Lothar Spielhoff, Podszun Motorbücher, Berlin 2004, ISBN 3-86133-352-X
- *Iron Kingdom: The Rise and Downfall of Prussia, 1600-1947*
  Christopher Clark, Allen Lane, London, ISBN-10: 0713994665
- *Aufstieg und Fall des „Eisenbahnkönigs" Bethel Henry Strousberg*
  (№ 5 in the series *Miniaturen zur Geschichte, Kultur und Denkmalpflege Berlins*)
  Horst Mauter, Interessengemeinschaft für Denkmalpflege, Kultur und Geschichte der Hauptstadt Berlin, Kulturbund der DDR, Berlin 1981

ABOUT THE AUTHOR

Richard Hunt was born in 1964 in Leeds and attended Queen Elizabeth's School in Crediton, Devon and Tadcaster Grammar School in North Yorkshire.

He holds a B.A. Degree in European Business Studies from Humberside College in Hull and the German degree of Diplom-Betriebswirt from the Fachhochschule Münster in Germany.

He works as a freelance translator, writer and desktop publishing consultant.

For more information, visit **www.calcaria.co.uk**

Index

Allgemeine Eisenbahnbau-Gesellschaft......... 102
Ambronn, Otto Victor................ 86, 91, 92, 106
America
   1849-1850 visit... 11
Antwerp
   City of Antwerp (the corporation).......... 119
   opposition to development of Sud-Citadelle 117
   proposal for new harbour........................ 116
   Southern Citadelle..................................... 115
   Southern Citadelle, agreement on development.. 116
   Strousberg leaves the Sud-Citadelle project 118
Austrian banks
   Allgemeine österreichische Bodenkreditanstalt, Vienna.. 161
   Creditanstalt, Vienna................................ 142
   Goldschmidt & Co, Vienna....................... 144
   Hypothekar-Kredit und Vorschussbank, Vienna... 161
   Union-Bank, Vienna........................... 82, 83
   Wechslerbank, Vienna.............................. 139
   Wiener Hypothekenkassa (Vienna Mortgage Institute).. 161
Austrian newspapers
   Bohemia, Prague.. 154
   National-Zeitung....................................... 174
   Neue Freie Presse...................................... 158
Austro-Hungarian Ausgleich (Compromise). 79
Bankruptcy
   amount owed to unsecured creditors..... 157
   date of final creditors meeting in Berlin. 164
   date of final creditors meeting in Prague 164
   date proceedings opened in Berlin.......... 157
   date proceedings opened in Prague........ 157
   sale of art works and books...................... 163
   sale of equipment from Strousberg's factories... 163
   sale of stored items and fittings............... 163
   sale of Strousberg's famed mares............ 163
   terms of final settlement.......................... 164
   unrest at Zbirow.. 158
Begas, Reinhold.. 167
Belgian newspaper
   Précurseur.. 118
Belgium
   constitution.. 115
   independence from United Netherlands. 115
Bellson, Reverend Robert.................................. 23
Berlin Livestock Market.................................... 68
Berlin Market Hall.. 70
Berlin: commercial property
   Jägerstrasse 22... 162
   Jägerstrasse 61a... 162

Unter den Linden 17/18........................... 162
Berlin: commercial property:
   Akkerstrasse/Brunnenstrasse................... 67
   Behrenstrasse.. 67
   Heydtstrasse, "Moritzhof"......................... 67
   Jägerstrasse 22.. 67
   Jägerstrasse 61a.. 67
   Unter den Linden 17/18..................... 67, 102
Berlin: magazines and publications
   Fragen der Zeit, Teil I [Questions of the Age, Part I]... 171
   Fragen der Zeit, Teil II [Questions of the Age, Part II]... 172
   Literarisches Leseblatt (Literary Paper)... 23
   Zwei Fragen, die nicht brennen [Two questions which are not burning].................. 172
Berlin: residential addresses
   Bellevuestrasse 9........................... 23, 67, 74
   Dorotheenstrasse 55................................... 23
   Lenneéstrasse 8.................................... 23, 67
   Tiergartenstrasse 29......................... 67, 162
   Wilhelmstrasse 70............................... 67, 74
Bismarck, Otto von
   intervention in Romania......................... 108
   Prussian politician and first German Chancellor.. 103, 107, 120
Blaß, Eduard.. 147
Bleichröder, Gerson............................ 109, 112, 113
Borsig, August.. 48
Bray, Joseph
   construction contractor.................... 59, 165
   general contractor for East Prussian Südbahn.. 33
   general contractor for Tilsit-Insterburg line 31
   general contractor, Berlin-Görlitz line..... 37
   resignation as general contractor for East Prussian Südbahn... 33
   resignation as general contractor, Berlin-Görlitz line... 37
British newspapers
   Morning Chronicle..................................... 15
   The Times................................... 17, 18, 25, 151
Bruce, George Barclay
   Bethel Henry junior's father-in-law.......... 62
   consulting engineer............................ 59, 165
   engineering consultant for East Prussian Südbahn.. 33
   engineering consultant for Tilsit-Insterburg line... 31
   engineering consultant, Berlin-Görlitz line 37
Building Societies
   description of.. 9
   legal regulation... 10
   The Fifty Pound Building Society.............. 9

The Times Building Society............................ 9
Camphausen, Otto von
   Prussian finance minister........................ 103
Carol, Prince of Romania............ 85, 86, 87, 91, 93
Catargiu, Lascar: prime minister of Romania 107
Christie, Robert... 14
Commercial Loan Bank (Moscow)............ 132, 135
   Background... 132
   falsification of accounts.......................... 133
Compagnie Immobilière de Belgique
   Belgian company.............................. 117, 119
Das Kleine Journal... 167
   disposal by Strousberg........................... 168
   establishment... 167
   format... 167
Date of marriage to Mary Ann Swan................. 8
Dickens, Charles.. 8
Die Post, Strousberg's newspaper..................... 73
   first issue... 73
   nominal publisher................................... 73
   sale and disposal.............................. 74, 112
East Prussian Südbahn..................................... 32
Ebers, Georg
   Egyptologist.. 166
Egestorff's Machine Factory, Hanover............. 51
Engels, Friedrich... 12
Estates owned by Strousberg
   Alt-Laube, Posen Province................. 61, 163
   Dahlewitz, Brandenburg..................... 62, 162
   Diepensee, Brandenburg........................... 62
   Garthe, Posen Province........................... 163
   Gross Peisten, East Prussia....................... 61
   Hohenfier, West Prussia........................... 61
   Jaszkowo, Posen Province........................ 62
   Klein-Antonin, Posen Province................ 62
   Krasnosielc, Poland................................. 162
   Krasnosielce, Poland................................. 62
   Krumfliess, West Prussia.......................... 61
   Lissa, Posen Province......................... 61, 163
   Lniannek, West Prussia...................... 61, 162
   Miruczin, Posen Province......................... 62
   Miröschau, Fiefdom of Zbirow............... 125
   Moholz, Silesia.. 62
   Mszanno, West Prussia............................. 61
   Neu Garthe, Posen Province..................... 62
   Priebisch, Posen Province.................. 61, 163
   Schwadtken, East Prussia......................... 61
   Sienken, East Prussia............................... 61
   Strassforthr, West Prussia........................ 61
   Tarnowo, Posen Province................... 61, 162
   Tocnik, Fiefdom of Zbirow..................... 125
   Wiecherts, East Prussia............................ 61
   Womwellno, Posen Province.................... 62
   Worienen, East Prussia............................. 61
   Wossek, Fiefdom of Zbirow.................... 125
Fiefdom of Zbirow.. 125
   Agriculture and forestry......................... 127

Dobriv.. 128
Franzensthal.. 128
Holoubkau... 128
Industrial activities.. 127
Schloss Zbirow [Zbirow Castle].............. 126
Straschitz... 128
Franco-Prussian War
   declaration of... 98
   effect on Dortmund Ironworks............... 98
   effect on railway transport...................... 98
   effect on Strousberg's financing system... 98
   Strousberg's activits at outbreak............. 98
Freikonservativen
   political party, Prussia............................ 73
Frère-Orban, Walthère
   Belgian politician............................ 116, 117
Geestemünde fisheries................................... 71
German banks
   Bankhaus Bleichröder........................... 139
   Bankhaus Jaques, Berlin............. 91, 92, 106
   Bundes-Darlehnskasse, Berlin.............. 103
   Disconto-Gesellschaft........................ 40, 74
   Disconto-Gesellschaft, Berlin 109, 111, 112, 163
   Discontobank, Breslau.......................... 139
   Manczyk & Schlesinger, Berlin 134, 135, 141, 161, 162
   Mendelssohn & Co, Berlin..................... 141
German newspapers
   Allgemeine Zeitung, Augsburg.............. 155
   Berliner Börsen-Courier......................... 173
   Berliner Lokal-Anzeiger......................... 168
   Berliner Mittagszeitung......................... 168
   Berliner Volkszeitung, Berlin................. 121
   Börsen-Zeitung, Berlin.................... 155, 174
   Der Aktionär.. 174
   Die Kreuzzeitung, Berlin....................... 120
   Die Rote Fahne (The Red Flag), Berlin... 168
   Frankfurter Aktionär, Frankfurt............ 155
Gesetz über die Eisenbahn-Unterhnehmungen 27
Ghica, Ion: prime minister of Romania.......... 107
Gottheimer brothers... 7
   Berton Gottheimer............................... 7, 8
   Lesser Gottheimer.................................... 7
   Peter Gottheimer................................. 7, 8
Görlitzer Bahnhof.. 39
Hansemann, Adolph von
   owner of Disconto-Gesellschaft........ 113, 163
Henley, Joseph W.. 14
Hinckeldey, Karl Ludwig Friedrich von
   Chief of Berlin Police and Prussian Secret Police.. 22
Hitzig, Friedrich (Architect)
   designer of Berlin Market Halle............. 70
Hodgkin, Thomas.. 17

Index

Hohenzollern-Sigmaringen, Prince Karl Anton of
    father of Price Carol of Romania......... 85, 91
Hudson, George.. 13
Inowrazlaw
    place in East Prussia...................................... 3
Itzenplitz, Count Heinrich Friedrich von
    Prussian trade minister............... 25, 103, 121
Jaques, Ferdinand
    owner of the Bankhaus Jaques................. 106
Jena, University of....................................... 5, 23
Joint Stock Companies Act............................ 14
Keyserling, Count Heinrich............................ 87
Kleist, Hans von
    husband of Strousbeg's daughter Agnes. 165
Kulmiz, Paul von... 58
Königsberg
    description of... 5
    main city in East Prussia........................... 3, 7
Landau, Gustav
    director of Commercial Loan Bank, Moscow.. 134, 135
Lasker, Eduard
    Prussian national liberal politician.......... 120
Lehndorff, Count Karl................................... 163
Lehndorff-Steinon,
    Count Karl... 87
Liebknecht, Karl
    editor of Die Rote Fahne......................... 168
London
    date of Strousberg's arrival......................... 7
London & Birmingham Railway..................... 16
London & Southampton Railway..................... 9
London: magazines and publications
    Conspiracy Detected (pamphlet)......... 15, 23
    Judgement before Trial (pamphlet) 15, 18, 23
    Lawson's Merchant's Magazine............ 12, 21
    Sharpe's London Magazine................... 13, 21
    The Assurance Record............................ 11, 12
    The British Journal....................................... 12
    The Chess Player... 12
    The Trademan's Journal............................. 12
London: magazines planned but never published
    National Economy..................................... 169
    Truth... 169
London: residential addresses
    Bartholomew Close..................................... 11
    Craven Street... 170
    Grosvenor Place.. 64
    Mornington Road.. 16
    Newgate Street... 7
    Sydney Place, Brompton............................ 17
London: trial for embezzlement...................... 10
Louth, John William
    husband of Strousberg's daughter Helene 165

Luxemburg, Rosa
    editor of Die Rote Fahne......................... 168
Malou, Jules
    Belgian politician...................................... 117
Marchot, Henri... 142
Marx, Karl... 12
Mary Ann Strousberg.................................. 165
    death of... 170
Matthews, John.. 17
Moscow
    criminal charges regarding Commercial Loan Bank... 149
    Strousberg imprisoned in Casemate....... 149
    Strousberg in debtors' prison.................. 149
    Strousberg under house arrest......... 149, 150
    trial proceedings...................................... 151
    trial verdicts... 152
Neidenburg
    place in East Prussia................................ 3, 4
Neustadt Ironworks (Neustädter Hütte)
    1869 purchase and expansion................... 55
    purchase from bankrupt assets................ 165
    use of peat-gas... 55
Northern Harz iron ore workings................... 56
Oak Mutual Life Assurance and Loan Company 16
obituaries... 174
Orders and honours
    Belgian Order of Leopold.......................... 96
    Order of the Princely House of Hohenzollern.. 96
    Prussian Kronen-Orden............................. 95
    Saxon Comthurkreuz of Ernestine Order 96
Orth, August (Architect)
    design of Görlitzer Bahnhof...................... 39
    design of Palais Strousberg....................... 62
    design of renovations, Schloss Zbirow..... 64
Othfresen Blast Furnaces............................... 56
Palais Rohan, Vienna-Jägerzeile.................... 64
Palais Strousberg
    construction costs...................................... 63
    description of interior................................ 62
    design and construction............................ 62
    sale and use as British Embassy............... 162
Pillau
    port in East Prussia...................................... 7
Prussian Railway Authority (Eisenbahnamt) 28, 29, 30, 31
Radowitz, Joseph
    German diplomat..................................... 103
Railway Concession Investigation
    establishment... 121
    publication of report................................ 122
Railway route (Russia)
    Brest-Grajewo............................ 35, 36, 128
Railway routes (Germany)
    Berlin-Görlitz............................... 37, 47, 48

179

East Prussian Südbahn.................. 25, 36, 95
Görlitz-Zittau-Reichenberg...................... 40
Halle-Sorau-Guben.................. 41, 42, 95, 130
Hanover-Altenbeken......... 41, 43, 95, 125, 130
Lübbenau-Camenz-Dresden.................... 40
Mehltheuer-Weida................................. 138
Märkisch-Posener Bahn....................... 41, 42
Märkisch-Posener Eisenbahn............... 86, 91
Rechte Oder-Ufer-Bahn............................ 41
Tilsit-Insterburg.......... 25, 27, 31, 32, 86, 128
Tilsit-Insterburg line................................ 36
Weisswasser-Muskau................................ 40
Railway routes (Hungary)
    Neutratalbahn... 83
    Nord-Ost-Bahn........................... 80, 82, 83
    Waagtalbahn... 83
Railway routes (Romania)
    Bucharest-Turnu Severin-Austria............ 89
    Galatz-Ploesti-Bucharest......................... 89
    Roman- Galatz... 89
    Roman- Galatz (Barlad branch)............... 89
Ratibor, Duke Victor of.......... 41, 87, 161, 162, 163
Reichstag of North German Confederation
    Strousberg as member of........................... 75
Reinickendorf cemetery............................ 167
Romania
    1868 convention on railway concession 87, 92
    1872 agreement with the new railway company.. 110
    constitution.. 85
    emergence as nation state........................ 85
    government takeover of Strousberg's railways... 107
    logistical problems.................................... 89
    railway bond issue.................................... 88
    railway concession.................................... 88
    railway construction arrangements.......... 89
Rosetti, Theodor
    Romanian state railways commissioner 104, 106
Royal Astronomical Society........................ 16
Royal Geographical Society................... 16, 21
Royal Geological Society............................ 16
Royal Society of Arts.................................. 16
Saull, Devonshire....................................... 16
Schatzlar
    purchase of collieries at......................... 141
Segen Gottes-Grube coal mine................... 58
Seydewitz, Otto Theodor von..................... 75
Siegerland iron-ore workings...................... 57
Silver wedding celebrations....................... 97
    gifts and tributes..................................... 97
Simon, Carl
    publisher, husband of Emma Vely........... 169
Société Anonyme du Sud d'Anvers
    Belgiam company................................... 119

Belgian company.................................... 119
Société Générale pour favoriser l'Industrie Nationale
    Belgian company.................................... 117
Spielhagen, Friedrich von........................... 96
SS Washington... 9
Steege, Ludwig
    Romanian state railways commissioner 92, 103, 104
Strausberg, Abraham.................................... 3
Strausberg, Baruch Hirsch........................... 4
Strausberg, Nehemias.................................. 5
Strausberg, Philipp Ferdinand...................... 4
Strousberg's daughters............................. 165
    Alice... 165
    Edith.. 165
    Hedwig.. 165
    Helene... 165
Strousberg's death
    date of... 173
    interrment... 173
Strousberg's descendants......................... 165
Strousberg's sons..................................... 165
    Arthur.. 11, 165
    Bethel Henry II................................ 10, 165
Strousberg, Ferdinand................................ 11
Strousberg's doctorate............................... 23
Strousberg's system of financing railway construction... 29
    Risk for the general contractor................ 30
Swan, George... 8
Swan, Mary Ann... 8
Swiss banks
    Geneva Credit Bank............................... 104
Sykes, Colonel William Henry..................... 17
Ujest, Duke Hugo of... 41, 42, 86, 87, 161, 162, 163
US newspaper
    New York Times..................................... 174
Vely, Emma
    as companion to Strousberg.................. 167
    diary and correspondence with Strousberg 167
    first contact with Strousberg................. 167
Vistula Lagoon... 7
Wagener, Hermann
    Prussian Privy Counsellor..................... 120
Waterloo Life Insurance Society................. 23
Wuthenow, General von
    Prussian General....................................... 4
Zollparlament (first German parliament)
    foundation of.. 74
    Strousberg as member of......................... 74

www.ingramcontent.com/pod-product-compliance
Ingram Content Group UK Ltd.
Pitfield, Milton Keynes, MK11 3LW, UK
UKHW041437180426
11947UKWH00007B/497